Chicken Soup for the Soul.

BILLY GRAHAM & ME

Chicken Soup for the Soul: Billy Graham & Me
101 Inspiring Personal Stories from Presidents, Pastors, Performers, and Other People Who Know Him Well
Steve Posner and Amy Newmark. Foreword by A. Larry Ross. Afterword by Billy Graham.

Published by Chicken Soup for the Soul Publishing, LLC www.chickensoup.com
Copyright © 2013 by Chicken Soup for the Soul Publishing, LLC. All Rights Reserved.

Cover and Interior Design & Layout by Brian Taylor, Pneuma Books, LLC

Distributed to the booktrade by Simon & Schuster. SAN: 200-2442

Publisher's Cataloging-in-Publication Data
(Prepared by The Donohue Group)

Chicken soup for the soul : Billy Graham & me : 101 inspiring personal stories
  from presidents, pastors, performers, and other people who know him well /
  [compiled by] Steve Posner, Amy Newmark ; foreword by A. Larry Ross ;
  afterword by Billy Graham.

  p. : ill. ; cm.

ISBN: 978-1-61159-905-3

    1. Graham, Billy, 1918---influence--Literary collections.   2. Graham, Billy,
1918---Influence--Anecdotes.   3. Evangelists--United States--Literary collections.   4.
Evangelists--United States--Anecdotes. 5. Anecdotes. I. Posner, Steve, 1953- II. Newmark,
Amy. III. Ross, A. Larry, 1953- IV. Graham, Billy, 1918- V. Title: Billy Graham & me VI. Title:
Billy Graham and me

BV3785.G69 C45 2013
269/.2/092   2012954878

PRINTED IN THE UNITED STATES OF AMERICA
on acid∞free paper

22 21 20 19 18 17 16 15 14 13   01 02 03 04 05 06 07 08 09 10

Chicken Soup for the Soul.

BILLY GRAHAM & ME

101 Inspiring Personal Stories from Presidents,
Pastors, Performers, and Other People
Who Know Him Well

Steve Posner & Amy Newmark
Foreword by A. Larry Ross
Afterword by Billy Graham

Chicken Soup for the Soul Publishing, LLC
Cos Cob, CT

·CONTENTS·

·FOREWORD·

A. LARRY ROSS

*President of A. Larry Ross Communications, founded in 1994,
has more than thirty-seven years' experience in mainstream
and Christian public relations, including serving as
director of media / public relations and principal
spokesperson for evangelist Billy Graham since 1981*

OVERVIEW

Since 1993, Chicken Soup for the Soul—one of the world's most iconic, recognizable and trusted brands, renowned for sharing uplifting stories—has inspired readers all over the world with more than 500 million copies of its 250 or so titles, translated into more than forty languages.

But the book you hold in your hand is unique and unprecedented, marking the only time in its twenty-year history that the *Chicken Soup for the Soul* series has focused on a single individual—evangelist Billy Graham. Regardless of your familiarity with Mr. Graham or your identification with his message, more important than the person are the transferable principles by which he lives his life.

This original anthology contains 101 personal and anecdotal stories by some of the most significant world changers and influential leaders in government, business, sports, entertainment and religion, as well as friends and relatives of Mr. Graham who know him best.

Just as Billy Graham's influence and impact transcend religious, racial and political boundaries, so does the list of contributors to this volume as they reveal and confirm his place in history. Prominent Christian pastors, leaders from other faiths, celebrities, heroes, regular citizens—and remarkably, every living U.S. President—collectively document the effects of Mr. Graham's worldwide ministry over more than six decades.

Contributors include a sheer diversity of leadership representing myriad professions, geographical locations, political persuasions and faith traditions, all of whom coalesce around the common denominator of utmost respect for one individual—including those who do not share his perspective or worldview.

Considering the current polarization and politicization of our nation, it is extraordinary to have voices from all walks of life, representing a full spectrum of ideology and methodology, joined in praise for an inclusive Christian leader known for unwavering conviction in a biblical worldview. During this arguably unparalleled period of divisiveness in America and our world, there is, perhaps, no other individual who has been able to unite diverse people like Billy Graham has.

Because Mr. Graham never compromised his integrity nor watered down his message to achieve consensus or reach critical mass, it is his character and integrity that have engendered such an unprecedented tribute. In a sense, this celebration of friendship and influence is a first look at the evangelist's legacy—while he is still alive.

This volume reflects Mr. Graham's counter-intuitive, inclusive approach to public ministry, electing to have his story chronicled not by an official biographer, but rather through the lens of others sharing how his message influenced or impacted their lives.

Billy Graham faithfully preached a timeless message in a timely way at the intersection of faith and culture. He put the green grass of the Gospel down low where "even the goats could get it," showing how the Bible speaks to personal and societal problems, and always providing an opportunity for audiences to respond by making a personal faith commitment.

Early in his ministry he helped define and give credibility to Evangelical Christianity. His crusades brought unity, visibility and credibility to the local church. He was a catalytic unifier of the Church around shared priorities rather than differences, cultivating mainline churches and prompting Protestant/Catholic cooperation in evangelism.

In the absence of an official spokesperson, for years Billy Graham was perceived as a senior statesman and the perennial "go to" authoritative resource for the media on issues related to the Christian faith and a biblical worldview. While his emphasis was evangelism, not ecumenism, during his travels Mr. Graham also met with and gained the respect of leaders of other faiths.

Though primarily an evangelist, Mr. Graham worked tirelessly as a man of conscience, compassion and peace, often facilitating rapprochement between disparate groups. He provided leadership influence by example in racial/denominational reconciliation, civil rights, social justice and de facto international diplomacy by pioneering early ministry efforts behind the Iron Curtain. As a spiritual entrepreneur, his vision had a seminal influence to found or encourage others to seize a timely opportunity to initiate more than thirty separate ministry organizations.

But the remarkable thing about him is that there is no

difference between the public and private Billy Graham. He is the same individual one-on-one over a meal or in a meeting back at the hotel as he is behind the pulpit. Though he is a spiritual confidant to some of the world's foremost leaders in government, entertainment, sport and business, he made anyone in his presence feel like the most important person in the world at that moment.

A LIFE WELL-LIVED AND A LORD WELL-SERVED

I am honored by the invitation to pen the foreword to this anthology tribute to a man whose prophetic voice has not only influenced three generations as "God's Ambassador," "Evangelist to the World," and "Pastor to Presidents," but has had a profound impact on my life as a colleague, friend and significant spiritual mentor.

But first I must reframe the underlying premise, "Billy Graham & Me," into the lexicon of the man himself, who would be more deferential and self-effacing, identifying the source of his strength and success as "Billy Graham & God." I have merely been privileged to have a front-row seat at the game to observe that spiritual partnership firsthand and watch Mr. Graham's agenda-less servant leadership unfold over more than three decades of his public ministry.

FIRST IMPRESSION

I was raised in Wheaton, Illinois, a suburb twenty-five miles west of Chicago, where Mr. Graham received his education and where my father was a Bible professor in the graduate school that is now located in the building on campus that bears the evangelist's name.

I will never forget the first time I heard Billy Graham preach, when I was just nine years old—though it is not a happy memory. One hot, muggy Sunday afternoon in June 1962, with a temperature of 94 degrees and 97 percent humidity, my parents dragged my brothers and me to the final meeting of his Greater Chicago Crusade at Soldier Field, adjacent to the lake downtown.

I was sitting in the next to last row in the corner of the stadium—one of 116,000 people in an overflow crowd under the blistering sun—and Mr. Graham was just a speck on a small platform at the other end of the field. All I can remember is how thirsty I felt, though I must admit it was purely physical, not spiritual, like the craving of so many others who attended his meetings.

Little did I know in my youth, however, that the providence of God would so closely intertwine our lives—Billy Graham's and mine—as the faculty house that was my boyhood home would have to be moved in order to build The Billy Graham Center; I would myself graduate from Wheaton College thirty-three years after him; and later I would transition from a mainstream corporate and agency public relations career to serve as his personal spokesperson for, at this writing, thirty-two years.

FIRST INTRODUCTION

The first time I was introduced to Mr. Graham was in fall 1976, shortly after graduating from college, while working for a meeting planning firm that organized convention logistics for large corporations. I was an intern, assigned to help with the Holiday Inn Franchise Holders convention in Memphis. As a reward for working hard, the president of our company asked me which of the many celebrities and marquee speakers I wanted to meet personally.

Without hesitation, I asked to meet Billy Graham, who had spoken at a prayer breakfast for attendees that morning. The president told me that at that very moment he was having his picture taken with the client's board of directors across the hall. The next thing I knew, we barged through the door, interrupting the photo shoot, and my colleague said presumptuously, "Billy Graham, this young man went to your alma mater and would like to meet you."

I was mortified, as the evangelist was seated in the middle, surrounded by at least twenty-four directors standing in two rows. He smiled, stood up, shook my hand and we spoke privately for several minutes. He then turned to the group and for another ten minutes shared about our common heritage, values and biblical worldview, using my interruption as an opportunity to share his own personal testimony of faith.

I would later observe that this was Mr. Graham's constant priority, practice and platform, to boldly — yet sensitively — share the transformative power of the Gospel message as any occasion would allow. And God has honored his faithfulness.

POWERFUL PREACHER

The universality and accessibility of Mr. Graham's message was powerfully impressed upon me one Friday evening in 1984 when he preached to the upper echelons of British society, including the Queen of England, several members of the Royal Family and the Lords and Ladies of London at a black-tie dinner.

The following Sunday afternoon, I accompanied the evangelist to an outdoor park in London's East End, where he was scheduled to address a crowd of 5,000 low-income immigrants. As our vehicle approached the venue, I asked Mr. Graham what message he planned to preach, to which he replied, "The same sermon I gave to the Royal family two nights ago."

A LIFE MARKED BY HUMILITY, INTEGRITY, AUTHENTICITY AND LOVE

My longtime pastor in Dallas defines success as "when those who know you best, love you the most," and that certainly holds true for Billy Graham. In an era where confidence in institutions is crumbling, and even religious organizations are being scrutinized or Christian leaders criticized for behavior inconsistent with their beliefs, he has long modeled courage, character and conviction and stood as an example of how to finish well.

Associate evangelist Ralph Bell once referred to Mr. Graham as a leader "who walked with the Lord daily." That is the measure of the man—who he really is—and the source of his spiritual strength and power.

Through the years, many reporters have asked me to sum up Billy Graham's life and legacy in one word. But in response, I have to use four: humility, integrity, authenticity and love—each of which I have observed consistently in my travels with him.

HUMILITY

In July 1999 I accompanied Mr. Graham to the local NBC affiliate in Jacksonville, where he did a remote interview with Katie Couric on *Today*. While waiting in the green room, the floor producer asked me if he would be willing to sign her copy of his recently published memoirs, *Just As I Am.*

Despite symptoms of Parkinson's that made writing difficult, he was happy to oblige, which so touched the young woman that she asked Mr. Graham if she could pray for him. That moved me deeply, as it was the first time in my quarter century of traveling with him that someone took such an initiative, rather than asking him to offer a prayer on his or her behalf.

After the producer left the room, Mr. Graham turned to me and said genuinely, "I have never understood why in the world anyone would want my autograph." At first I thought he was joking, but then realized his puzzled sincerity was reflective of his self-identification as "a country boy called to preach," who could not fathom why the Lord chose him to be blessed with such spiritual responsibility and global opportunity.

As best I could, I tried to clarify for Mr. Graham what his inscription in her book meant to that young woman and others who made similar requests through the years, explaining his obvious influence and the significant impact of his ministry on her, since she had made a faith commitment at one of his crusades as a teenager. To my surprise, he responded, somewhat matter-of-factly, "I have only asked for one autograph in my whole life."

Now it was I who was flummoxed, as I sat in stunned silence trying to determine who that individual would have been, going over in my mind myriad celebrities, influencers and world changers Mr. Graham had met during his travels.

At first I thought it was Babe Ruth, whom I knew he greeted after a ballgame when he was twelve years old. My second candidate was President Truman, whom he met on his first visit to the White House in the early 1950s. Or possibly it was Winston Churchill, who summoned the young evangelist to his chambers after his successful mission at Wembley Stadium in 1954 to ask him the secret of gathering such huge crowds (which

Billy Graham explained was due to the Holy Spirit, not anything he had done).

When I sheepishly turned to Mr. Graham and asked if any of these individuals had been worthy of such a request, he said, "No." Acknowledging I would probably never be able to guess, he explained, "It was John Glenn. He and I sat next to each other at the March 1998 *TIME* magazine 75th anniversary gala at Radio City Music Hall honoring all living cover subjects.

"As we got up to leave, John asked me for my autograph," Mr. Graham continued. "I replied, 'I've never asked anyone in my whole life to sign something. Could I have yours?' And so we swapped autographs!"

INTEGRITY

Among the many examples of Mr. Graham's personal, spiritual and financial integrity, I remember when he kicked off the twelve-week, six-city Mission England tour the summer of 1984 in Bristol, west of London. In their coverage of the opening service, local papers appealed to their readers' British reserve through articles criticizing the "emotionalism" of the American evangelist's meeting. Their evidence was the fact that the choir sang softly during his invitation for people to come forward to make a faith commitment.

So for only the second time in the history of their ministry, before the start of the meeting the next evening, Mr. Graham told program director Cliff Barrows to refrain from having the choir sing during the invitation. But the next day, the headlines in the paper read, "The emotionalism was in the silence," and Mr. Graham decided that if he was going to get criticized, they should at least do it right, and they went back to the choir accompaniment for the rest of the mission — and ever since.

AUTHENTICITY

In August 2005, just two months after he had preached his final crusade in New York City, I went to visit Mr. Graham at his log cabin home in western North Carolina. On the flight to Asheville, I reflected on an observation shared by a pastor friend that every individual needs three things in order to find fulfillment in life: someone to love, something to do and something to anticipate.

As I drove up the mountain to call on Mr. Graham, I realized that for the first time in more than six decades the evangelist had only two out of three of those elements. He still had Ruth, his marriage and ministry partner of then sixty-one years; he was working on a new book and remained regularly engaged with the ministry he founded; but he could not look forward to another crusade planned for the near future.

I knew that Billy Graham always believed and lived what he preached, but I wondered how that applied to his current life stage. What mindset would I encounter in the forward-thinking evangelist, who had always focused on the next thing and who had been a part of current events on the world stage since the Truman Administration?

While sitting together on his back porch for several hours, eventually watching the sun start to set over his beloved Blue Ridge Mountains, I asked Mr. Graham how he felt. He replied, "I have never been more at peace in my life. My wife Ruth has been there for me as I traveled the world in itinerant ministry. But with her recent medical needs, it is now time for me to take care of her. God has enabled me to do that, and I am looking forward to spending more time together." Ruth passed in 2007.

During my most recent visit to Mr. Graham's home, despite physical limitations of his own, I found him once again filled with passion and purpose. As he sat in his favorite chair in the den, he told me how he felt called to deliver one more sermon about the need for renewal in the Church and revival across America.

It was obvious that, though his body might be physically weakened, the heart of the evangelist continued to beat. He had already selected his text, Galatians 6:14, which he had posted in big letters on the wall beside him and recited to me, "'May I never boast, except in the Cross of our Lord Jesus Christ...'" In his characteristic authenticity and transparency, he then stressed that when he gets to heaven he is going to lay any awards and rewards received in this life at the feet of Jesus.

LEADERSHIP WITH LOVE

Several years ago I had the opportunity to share the story about Mr. Graham and John Glenn at the *TIME* gala with a former bureau chief of the magazine. He smiled, acknowledging that he was at that event, and told me I needed to know "the rest of the story."

He then informed me that the black-tie dinner in question was held in March 1998, during the period following President Bill Clinton's impeachment by the House of Representatives. Minutes before the event was scheduled to begin, organizers were in crisis mode, as iconic sports figure Joe DiMaggio had refused to sit next to the President at the head table.

Further, no other celebrity or marquee figure in attendance would accept that offer and they seemed reluctant to be photographed with him in the midst of the political kerfuffle. When Billy Graham was approached about the situation, he declared, "I'll sit next to the President. He's my friend!"

What mattered most to Mr. Graham was to faithfully lift up the name of Jesus with authenticity and integrity to the great and the low, the high and the humble. Though he never compromised the Gospel or the dimension of the reality of God's judgment, unlike some other Christian leaders whose messages come across as condemning, in my experience Mr. Graham always functioned as a "paramedic," rather than a "policeman," for the Kingdom of God.

Billy Graham represents a balance of grace and truth. He is a man of humility, integrity, authenticity and an agent of God's love, who despite his many gifts and ability, the Lord used more for his availability. He had an audience of One, and would consistently "suit up and show up," leaving the results to the Lord he served, and giving all the glory and honor to God, knowing that he was operating with faith in His strength and power from above.

December 3, 2012

·INTRODUCTION·

STEVE POSNER

Instructor at the University of Southern California and author of
Spiritual Delights and Delusions *and* Israel Undercover, *among others*

When I met Billy Graham in 1979, he was the most influential evangelical preacher in the world. Today, more than three decades later, he remains a powerful presence. His enduring stature is not only the result of his captivating sermons. It is the man, not just the preacher, who millions of people honor and admire.

The personal stories in this book show us why so many individuals from differing faiths, nationalities, and political beliefs regard Billy Graham as a touchstone of goodness. They come from people who have been inspired by his lifelong determination to live by the words of Jesus, rather than to just speak about them.

The first Billy Graham Crusade was held in 1947 at the Civic Auditorium in Grand Rapids, Michigan, but it was his 1949 appearance in Los Angeles that catapulted him to fame. Standing inside a gigantic tent dubbed the "Canvas Cathedral With the Steeple of Light," Billy Graham delivered a series of sermons that reached 350,000 people. "Held Over By Popular Demand" read a local flyer, and indeed he was: the revival kept going and going, far past the original three-week schedule, stretching on for nearly two months. The impact was huge, even for Hollywood. The popularity of the young preacher, just thirty years old, was unprecedented.

Billy Graham went on to hold more than 400 crusades in 185 countries. He never ceased to remind us that his popularity came from God, and that he was merely a vehicle to spread His message of forgiveness, redemption, and service.

With characteristic humility, he often said that throughout his six decades of ministry, there was always a risk that he might one day succumb to the temptations of fame. He was aware that, like many others, he could fall victim to the allure of wealth, pride, and passion that come with celebrity. Such disarming honesty connected him to the average person, because many of us know that we too might be led astray if we had such global fame and power.

He refused to pretend that he was the best or wisest among us. That honor, he insisted, belonged to God. However often the headlines blared about Billy Graham the evangelical superstar, he would guide us back to the real news that he lived to tell: No one is hopeless, for God's love can redeem us.

I once asked him about the fate of those who do not share his faith. "I don't try to play God, saying you're lost and you're saved. That's between the person and God," he said. "I think we are told to proclaim Jesus Christ as the way, the truth, and the light, but God will decide who is saved and who is lost."

When I asked if he was able to distinguish between the word of God and the word of Billy Graham, his answer was simple: I try to stay faithful to Scripture. "Being an Evangelist simply means that I am to declare the Gospel, and the word 'Gospel' means the good news," he said. "And the good news is that God loves you and He loves everybody."

Many authors have thoughtfully written about Billy Graham's charisma and his oratory, yet the stories in this book reveal something different. They give us an inside glimpse of the ways in which the everyday Billy Graham has lived as a loving father, brother, grandfather, uncle, mentor, pastor, statesman, and friend.

I am deeply grateful for the generosity of all the contributors. They took the time to graciously share their experiences so we could draw inspiration from them.

My wife, Mona, was instrumental in the writing of this book. Personally working with the contributors, she was deeply moved by their reflections about Billy Graham. As a result of her inspired insight, she was able to bring together a diverse group of people to create a combination of stories that carry a universally uplifting message. The book's value is directly attributable to her participation and wisdom. She represents the spiritual heart of this project.

I want to thank Amy Newmark, the talented and tireless publisher at Chicken Soup for the Soul, who worked with me on this project. My appreciation also goes to the company's CEO, Bill Rouhana, who believed in this effort from the beginning.

This book could not have written without the support of Billy Graham's personal spokesman, Larry Ross. His cheerful assistance and steadfast dedication to Mr. Graham was inspirational and invaluable. Mr. Graham's representative, Michael Crisp, helped guide this project to its completion. Billy Graham's chief-of-staff, David Bruce, gave us the opportunity to coordinate our work with the Billy Graham Evangelistic Association. I am grateful to them all.

Bryan Aubrey deserves great praise for his astute editorial skills. My gratitude goes to Bob Jacobs, Annette Norris, Cynthia Lane, Susan Heim, Mary Lou Lohr, Mia Maturen, and Jesse Posner whose valuable participation was essential. My assistant, Marilyn Muerth, demonstrated her usual excellence when assembling all the complex pieces needed to complete this book. D'ette Corona, assistant publisher of Chicken Soup for the Soul, was also invaluable in working with all the contributors and creating every part of this book.

My final words are for Billy Graham, whose good-natured kindness has stayed with me throughout all these years. I remember when I was still in my twenties, reading his books and preparing questions in anticipation of my meeting with the world's most famous preacher. When the time came, the man I met was more than that. He seemed almost unaware of his own fame. We spoke as if we were old friends. As the conversation progressed, with just the two of us talking, away from the crowds and the adoring spotlight, I could sense the gentleness of his spirit. "The greatest demonstration of a true Christian is that he loves people," he told me. In these pages you will find 101 stories about a man who loves people, and the people who love him back.

·1·

LAMAR ALEXANDER

*U.S. Senator (Tennessee), former Secretary of Education
and former Governor of Tennessee*

I've known Billy Graham a long time. It goes back to 1979 when
the Billy Graham Crusade came to Nashville. I was in my first
year as governor then, and I was asked to play the piano for the
singing. There was a crowd of about 35,000 people at Vanderbilt
Stadium, and Cliff Barrows, Billy Graham's song leader, was
warming them up. They invited me over the night before to
prepare for it, and I found out later that they were really trying
to find out whether I could actually play the piano or not! But I
did, and it was a lot of fun.

Afterwards, Cliff Barrows asked me if I was any relation to
Charles M. Alexander. I told him yes, he was my dad's older
cousin, and he'd grown up on a nearby farm in East Tennessee.
Cliff's face brightened, saying that he was the world's greatest
song leader in the early 1900s. "He did what I do today, and no
one has inspired me more." He told me how Charles Alexander
had traveled the world with famous evangelists, including R.A.
Torrey and J. Wilbur Chapman, and how he had roused crowds
across England, Australia, China, and Japan.

A month later, Cliff sent me one of two books that he had

about Charles Alexander's life. When I opened the book, I found a signature on the front page. It said, *Charles M. Alexander, Timothy 2:15.* I opened our family Bible to that verse when I'd been sworn in as governor a few months earlier, knowing it was my father's favorite verse, but I never knew the reason. So when I opened the book Cliff Barrows sent me, I found out why my father loved that verse.

I'd seen Billy Graham at meetings over the years, but that crusade in Nashville in 1979 was when I spent the most time with him. I've always been impressed with his lack of pomp and circumstance, and with his sincerity. About twenty years ago, I got on the elevator at the Mayflower Hotel in Washington and somebody said, "Hello, Lamar." I turned around, and it was Billy Graham. It was such a simple greeting. He was just pleasant and friendly, never putting on airs. That is a characteristic of his that I've always admired.

You can't *try* to be yourself. You have to *be* yourself. When you're not, people can see through that pretty quickly, particularly in the television era. Television has its good and bad sides, but one thing television does is permit you to size up people pretty quickly—their personality and their sincerity, or lack of it. And so Billy Graham's naturalness has always helped him on television, even with people who haven't believed in his message.

TV is a very intense medium, and it reveals a lot about anyone who's there. That's why presidential debates are so important on television. I've seen them firsthand, and I know that it's not so much what the candidates say, it's how they conduct themselves. It gives viewers a chance to size them up. So to be able to survive for fifty years using such an intense medium is really a great compliment to Billy Graham's sincerity. On television, it's hard to fool people for fifty seconds. I've rarely known anyone who doubted Billy Graham's sincerity—agnostics, atheists, intellectuals at Harvard University, where I taught before being elected to the Senate, even people who disagree with him. Everyone respects his sincerity and authenticity. He may not always have changed their minds, but he earned their respect.

I remember the time someone asked him: "What has been the most remarkable thing about your life?" Billy's answer was that it goes by so quickly. It's as if he's always known this, since there's always been a sense of urgency about his teaching, and this has inspired people to act on his message. Throughout his many decades of preaching, people were able to see Billy's integrity and unwavering sincerity, which reflect the teachings of that verse cherished by my father, his cousin, and myself: "Be diligent to present yourself approved to God, a worker who does not need to be ashamed, rightly dividing the word of truth" (Timothy 2:15).

·2·

JUSTIN ALLGAIER

NASCAR driver and 2008 ARCA Re/Max Series Champion

The first time I heard about Billy Graham, I was pretty young, probably about ten years old. I grew up in the Church, and they talked about him a lot at Sunday school. The two teachers who taught me were big Billy Graham fans. He actually went to Wheaton College, just a three-hour drive from where I lived in Riverton, Illinois. Even though I was young, I felt close to him. I think the part that impressed me was that a lot of roads were paved because of him. Compared to the average community church, his crusades helped make evangelical Christianity more mainstream. Even if there were tens, hundreds, or thousands in a congregation—or however many might go to a local church—there really wasn't anybody out there like Billy Graham, whose preaching reached millions around the world.

I had achieved personal success as a NASCAR driver, already winning titles at fifteen, which had made me a celebrity while I was still in high school, but it was Billy Graham who allowed me to see that one person's voice can make a real difference.

I think the biggest thing that I like is that he wasn't afraid to go anywhere with his teaching, even to communist countries like North Korea and the Soviet Union. A lot of people just go with what's politically popular. When Jesus dwelt among us, He preached everywhere, to anyone who was willing to listen.

Billy Graham's preaching during the Vietnam War also influenced me, inspiring me to stand up and talk about what I believe in. When Billy Graham visited the troops, many critics wanted him to take a political stand on the Vietnam War. Those who protested against it demanded that he side with them. Those who supported it wanted the same. As he wrote in his autobiography, when reporters asked if he was in favor of the war or against it during one of his trips to Vietnam, he told them, "My only desire is to minister to our troops by my prayers and spiritual help wherever I can." I just thought that was very cool, and some of the things he said were pretty powerful, even though they were very controversial at the time.

When I moved to North Carolina in 2008, it was amazing to see the following that he had. I was already a fan, and with him having gone to school in my own home state of Illinois and my now living in Charlotte where the Billy Graham Evangelistic Association is headquartered, it is as if he's been a continuing presence throughout my life. But to actually arrive in Charlotte and see the following that he has here is unbelievable. It seems like there aren't many people in the community who haven't been touched in some way by him. It's like everybody you run into has a story about him. You don't normally have that effect on a big city.

Religious figures typically come and go. Their popularity peaks quickly, whereas Billy Graham has been popular for decades. I think that speaks volumes about the person he is, and how cool it is that he could have done that. I'm twenty-six years old, and Billy Graham is in his nineties, and I've been very lucky to be alive at the same time as him.

·3·

DANNY AYALON

Deputy Foreign Minister of Israel and member of the Knesset;
former Israeli Ambassador to the U.S.

Today, with extremism and intolerance in every corner of the world, Billy Graham's words, thoughts, prayers and life teachings, throughout his great career, have served a great purpose for bearing love and acceptance of others. As a former member of the Israeli Defense Forces and a current representative in the Knesset, Israel's parliament, I have seen how Dr. Graham's words provide us all with direction towards mutual respect and understanding.

From the first time I heard Billy Graham on TV, I have felt he speaks the truth; that he speaks from his heart. I have been very moved by his faith. As a proud Jew and Israeli, I have been deeply encouraged by his steadfast support for Israel and, I think, for all the people of Israel. He understands that we are here because of a grand plan, God's design, first and foremost to work for God's glory, to bring God's Word to the world. I believe Billy Graham has felt this same responsibility in the Judeo-Christian heritage.

I didn't hear Dr. Graham speak until after I was already married in 1980. My wife and I met in Israel, but she came from a family in Ohio. They were very devout Christians. Her father once told me how as a young man, he went to one of Billy Graham's services, and there became reborn, with new meaning and purpose in his life.

I will never forget hearing Dr. Graham say that one of the most exciting developments of the century was the rebirth of the nation of Israel. He then talked about this new land, scarcely more than 150 miles in length and nine miles in breadth, so big in history, the cradle of civilizations and the birthplace of the Ten Commandments, which were imparted just south of Sinai. I was so inspired!

Billy Graham has often spoken of Israel, preaching that Israel is the land where Jesus was born and raised as a rabbi—that it is here in this holy land that He brought about His miracles. Dr. Graham deeply affirms the unbreakable bond between Jews and Christians. Of course, we cannot hide the major theological differences between Judaism and Christianity, but Billy Graham's words are a testament to our common Judeo-Christian heritage and legacy, which brought about Western civilization with its justice, morality, and code of law.

It is no coincidence that my wife, who grew up watching Billy Graham, shares his embrace of our shared values. She is the president and co-founder of The Galilean Campus, a major project located in Migdal, on the shores of the Sea of Galilee. Its mission is to give Christians a greater understanding of the Jewish roots of their faith, and God's plan for His nation Israel. It will be a place for Christians to experience a spiritual renewal with God in the very land that both traditions cherish.

Today, we see the great biblical prophecies of Isaiah, Ezekiel and Jeremiah being fulfilled. Our return to Israel has given Jews, and also Christians, free access to all our sacred places—whether in Jerusalem or the Galilee—for the first time in 2,000 years. In the Bible, throughout Isaiah, we have the prophecies for the glory of Zion with Jews coming from all corners of the earth for the restoration of Israel, and for the Messiah to come. These are promises from God, and we Israelis understand this great responsibility to build our country and defend ourselves in our faith as part of God's plan.

Israelis appreciate Billy Graham not only because he has supported our country, but also because he has always been positive and forthcoming—never offensive. He has never tried to proselytize Jews, respecting instead our traditions while also highlighting our common values. He has done so much for Israeli-American relationships in general that President Nixon offered to make him the U.S. Ambassador to Israel. However, understanding his work and sermons were more important, he chose to pass up political opportunity and stay in the spiritual realm—a decision which has clearly benefitted millions of people all over the globe.

·4·

CLIFF BARROWS

*Mr. Graham's devoted friend and his longtime music and program
director, and radio host of* Hour of Decision

I've had the joy of working with Billy Graham most of my life,
from the time I was twenty-two years old and first met him in
North Carolina in 1945. On our honeymoon my new wife and I
went to a Bible conference. It was a youth meeting on a Saturday
night and the place was full. But the director of the conference
said they couldn't start the meeting because they didn't have a
song leader. The man who had taken us there said, "I can help
you. I have a young couple here. He leads the singing and she
plays the piano." He turned to us and said, "You'll help out,
won't you?" I said, "If we can, we'll be happy to do so."

Billy Graham was standing there and he said, "Well, come on
Cliff. We won't be choosy! Let's go!"

We started the service and had a wonderful time. That was
the beginning of our work together. At the time I thought I might
want to go on to seminary, but my wife and I prayed that the
Lord would show us the right path. He definitely did and assured
us, "You will be happy leading the singing for Billy, and I'll take
care of the preaching end."

A year later on a bright morning in Philadelphia, I told Billy about this. He put his arm around me, smiled, and said, "Cliff, this is wonderful! Let's pray that the Lord will keep us together till He calls us home, or until He comes again." I said, "I'll be happy to go anywhere. I'll carry your suitcases. I'll do whatever you want me to do. I'll just be grateful to be in the ministry with you."

That's how Billy and I began our work together in those early days in Youth for Christ meetings. It wasn't until 1950 that the Billy Graham Evangelistic Association was formally created and we began broadcasting the *Hour of Decision* radio program.

It's been almost seventy years since then. We've been together all that time, and I never once doubted this was what the Lord wanted me to do. We've been in 185 countries and territories around the world, speaking to 215 million people face to face, and nearly three million have come forward in a public commitment to make a decision for Christ.

There are so many stories I could tell about the wonderful things that have happened in those years, but two stories come to mind right now.

It was 1966 and we were to travel to England shortly for our meeting at the Earl's Court Arena in London. We had been in London twelve years before at the Harringay meetings, which were outstanding and touched the whole United Kingdom and also much of Europe.

Billy had been reading *The Times* and other newspapers so he could get up to date on what was happening in England and make his message relevant to the people. Some of the young reporters were recalling the meetings in Harringay. They'd heard about the big response when hundreds of people came forward at the invitation. They also knew that we sang the song, "Just As I Am," and automatically attributed the response, not to the preaching, but to the emotion generated by the song.

With this in mind, Billy called me on the phone from his home in Montreat. He was disturbed by what he had read. He wanted everyone to know that it was not the music, but the Spirit of God, that spoke to the hearts of the people. He said to me, "I have a suggestion. Let's prepare the choir to sing or not sing. You have the choir ready and if I want the song, I'll say we're going to sing 'Just As I Am.' But if I don't want it, I won't call for it. So don't begin the song until I call for it."

That first night at Earl's Court Billy preached his heart out. There was a real sense of the presence of God. When he finished he said, "We are not going to have any music tonight. There'll be no singing. But if the Spirit of God is speaking to your heart, then right where you are, just stand in your place, and make your way out to the aisle. Come down to the center through the side aisles and stand here in front of the platform." He stood back and said, "Now, you come."

For about fifteen seconds nobody moved. And that's a long time. Then all of a sudden a seat squeaked, and then another, and another. Then hundreds of people began to stand. They walked to the aisle, shuffled down the long wooden floor that had been put down to cover the turf, and stood at the front.

We went thirty nights without a single note of the hymn, "Just As I Am," which has been the signature tune of our crusades through the years. We had never done that before. When the reporters began to write about the invitation at Earl's Court, they said that all they heard was a shuffling of feet on the floor. "Bring back 'Just As I Am!' The silence is killing us!" they wrote.

I think this is very significant because Billy was always concerned about not giving an appeal at the end of his message that would awaken people's emotions and get them stirred up. He didn't want them to make an emotional decision but a clear-headed one, based on the message they had heard. He wanted the Spirit of God to speak to their hearts. He pointed out that Jesus said, "Whoever therefore shall confess Me before men, him will I confess also before my Father which is in heaven" (Matthew 10:32). Billy emphasized that need for a public decision all through the years I've been with him.

The second story that comes to mind took place nearly two decades later in 1984. We were again in England but this time in Sunderland. We had a mission across England that year called "Mission England" and we took the crusade to various cities.

Sunderland was just off the North Sea, and this was the coldest crusade we ever had. I'm talking about weather! The wind came off the sea and it was freezing. Billy had on his long johns, suit, sweater, overcoat, hat and gloves most of the time. He had never preached like that before but he did during that crusade.

On the last day of the crusade in the afternoon there were two beautiful elderly ladies, obviously very dear friends, who came early so they would have a good seat. They sat up in the balcony under the cover, carrying a little tea basket. Of course, for the English, high tea was one of the prime times of the day, and these two ladies took the time to unwrap their cookies and sandwiches. They got out their tea, poured it and were enjoying it when the service began.

Toward the end of the service, these two ladies began to put their papers and wrappings back in the basket. When Billy gave the invitation, one of them got up to come forward. "What are you doing?" the other lady said. The first lady replied, "I'm going to go forward and give my heart to Jesus." And the other lady said, "Wait, you can't go to heaven without me! I'm coming too!"

And they both came down to the front. It was so beautiful. They were such dear friends, obviously knew each other very well, and did things together. They made that journey to the crusade in Sunderland together as a real outing.

People did that. They came early to get a good seat, brought a little lunch or snack, and would sit on the grass or the beach until it was time for the service to begin. Often they would come back the next day and bring their friends. We've heard story after story of people who went to a crusade, brought their friends the next day, and then those friends came to Christ.

That is the way we are with our Christian witness. When God has done something for us, we let that be known to our friends, and we bring them along. Some of them are "found" because we invited them and showed an interest in them.

All these years it has been such a privilege to work with Billy Graham. Like the apostle Paul, who wrote to the Corinthians, "Our heart is enlarged... be you also enlarged" (2 Corinthians 6:11-13). Billy too is a man with a heart enlarged for the world. His only desire has been to preach the Gospel everywhere, to preach the good news that there is hope for the lost. I have tears of joy and gratitude to the Lord for the privilege of working with such a man who cares so deeply about people, who has a passion for saving souls, and who, over the course of his long life, has given his heart to the world.

·5·

MARK BATTERSON

Bestselling author; pastor,
National Community Church, Washington, D.C.,
named one of the most influential churches in the U.S.

I put my faith in Christ for the first time when I was five years old. I had watched a Billy Graham-produced film called *The Hiding Place* at a church in downtown Minneapolis, and somehow God used the medium of a film and the story it told to impact me deeply. When I came home after seeing *The Hiding Place*, I told my mom I wanted to ask Jesus into my heart, and she fully encouraged me to go ahead. It took some courage for me, but I felt a prompting to make sure I was in the right relationship with the Lord, even though I was so young. Mom kneeled next to my bed, as she usually did when we prayed before I went to sleep, and I prayed what I would call a "genesis prayer." That was the beginning of my spiritual journey.

My life is a work in progress. I think we grow into a holy confidence. Hopefully, now in my forties, I have a greater understanding of and deeper surrender to the Lord than when I prayed that night. However, after Billy's film, I made a five-year-old's profession of faith, and the Lord honored that. No matter what our level of knowledge, experience or maturity, He always meets us where we are.

I remember being transfixed by the movie, which was probably a bit beyond typical five-year-old fare. For instance, at moments it graphically displayed what happened in the Nazi concentration camps. The story of Corrie ten Boom's faith and endurance in the camp suffused my heart and spirit in a way that differed from simply listening to a preacher offer the Gospel message in words. I often marvel that God could use a woman named Corrie ten Boom, who was born decades before me, to reach me through a screen. The film is a testament both to the commitment to the Gospel and its creative communication that have been demonstrated by Billy Graham over all these years.

I think that we tend to try to reach people for Christ the way that we were reached. Perhaps that's why, as a pastor and preacher, the best compliment I can receive is to see a junior high kid listening to the entire message and getting something out of it. Interestingly, the Lord used a Billy Graham film to change my life, and I am now the pastor of theaterchurch.com, a church that meets in six movie theaters around the Washington, D.C. area. We have a media department that produces short films, as well as trailers for our sermon series. The medieval church used stained glass to communicate the Gospel story in pictures to an illiterate society. In our post-literate culture, movie screens are like post-modern stained glass, which we can use to communicate the Gospel message. I see Billy Graham and his films as being on the cutting edge of this approach.

My other encounter with Billy Graham's ministry was at a crusade at County Stadium in Milwaukee, Wisconsin, in 1979, when I was ten years old. It changed my life not because I went forward in an altar call to give my life to Christ, but because I brought a friend who went forward to accept the Lord. That truly formative experience helped me understand the importance of sharing my faith with other people. The crusade was a memorable testament to the power of the Gospel and Billy Graham's ability to communicate it. My experience there gave me my first excuse to be evangelistic, to invite friends that I knew needed a relationship with the Lord.

Pastoring a church in the nation's capital over the past fifteen years and having members of Congress, cabinet members and people that are part of every administration as part of our congregation has been incredible. Our church started with nineteen people and now has six locations around the D.C. area. In many ways, I feel like God has called me to our nation's capital to influence influencers and to be a voice to this nation, to this generation. In that respect, I am inspired by the example Billy Graham sets, because when Billy speaks, I am always confident that he will speak the Gospel in a way I can fully endorse, and there are not many people like that. Billy Graham possesses the ability to share the simple Gospel in a way that allows the Gospel to do all the heavy lifting. He preaches so that the Gospel itself does the work, which is one of the gifts that the Lord gave him.

I know that Billy Graham would never compromise the Gospel or his integrity. He is someone who says what he means, means what he says and always speaks the truth with love and in an uncompromising way. Billy has a long track record of consistent character. Even when he was at the White House praying with a president, it didn't change him. He never sought out relationships with the famous or powerful because of their positions. He lived for an audience of one, concerned only with what God thought.

Washington, D.C. has many people who fear other people more than they fear God, which is a dangerous thing. Billy Graham always had a healthy fear of God that helped him overcome his fear of people. It supported his ability to connect with millions of people around the world, the young and the old, the poor and the powerful. Everyone resonated with the purity of his love and his intention.

·6·

A.R. BERNARD

Founder and pastor of the 36,000-member congregation of the Christian Cultural Center in Brooklyn, New York

In 2005, I had the opportunity to chair the Billy Graham Crusade in New York City, which Dr. Graham said would be his final crusade. We did a press conference together, and for a community leader such as myself, the founder and senior pastor of the Christian Cultural Center in Brooklyn, appearing alongside Dr. Graham was an outstanding moment.

Reporters from nearly every media outlet imaginable questioned this outstanding statesman of evangelical Christianity. As he took question after question, Dr. Graham was able to concisely answer each one. He did not allow the journalists to lead him in a direction that he did not want to go. He was very polished, very respectful, but he stood by his convictions. Of course, I sat there amazed.

"I am going to refuse to answer questions on subjects that maybe twenty years ago I would have answered," Dr. Graham told the reporters, anticipating that some might try and entangle him in a political controversy of one kind or another. "I think that at my age, that I have one message," he explained. "And that is that Jesus Christ came, He died on a cross, He rose again. And He asks us to repent of our sins and receive Him by faith as Lord and Savior. And if we do, we have forgiveness of our sins."

Dr. Graham did not waver. He expressed love and compassion to all in every community regardless of the particular things that they were wrestling with, but he remained consistent on the overall plan and purposes of God and the calling upon his life.

Dr. Graham understood that every interview was his interview, no matter what the question. He knew the interview was his opportunity to get his message across, and if he could do so by answering the question, then so be it, but if not then he would focus on taking advantage of that platform, that opportunity, and I thought he did that amazingly well.

It is often difficult to stay on task. New York City is the media capital of the world. As a person of color who is the pastor of a mega-church with a multicultural ethnic body of 36,000 members, I deal with journalists and politicians on both sides of the aisle. We have liberals here, and we have the extremists. Believe it or not, we even have some Republicans. To navigate through all of the differing factors without getting trapped or losing composure takes a lot of skill, maturity and experience. Dr. Graham has set the example for the rest of us.

When you're strongly rooted in your convictions, you can sit at the table with people who disagree with you, who differ in their beliefs, who differ in their values, and you don't feel shaken. Dr. Graham modeled that strong foundation for me.

There are some Christians who become unraveled when they're dealing with people who have a different opinion, especially if they're very strong in that difference of opinion. But Dr. Graham didn't. The principles that Billy Graham lives by are eternal. They remain the same. They remain constant. They are obviously the anchors of his soul.

Dr. Graham's principles didn't change with fashion and pop culture. In 1957, he invited someone like Dr. Martin Luther King, Jr. to share the platform with him at his revival in Madison Square Garden, which was to become the longest of his career, extending it to sixteen weeks from its original schedule of six. "A great social revolution is going on in the United States today," Billy Graham told the gathering. "Dr. King is one of its leaders, and we appreciate his taking time out from his busy schedule to come and share this service with us." He had asked Dr. King to present a greeting at a time when segregation and racism were very strong. And yet he was willing to cross that line and take some of the heat. Not everyone was willing to take that kind of risk, but Billy Graham was. I'm sure he did not know at the time that Dr. King would become a global icon of the civil rights movement.

President Bill Clinton spoke of such moments when we both shared that stage with Dr. Graham during his final crusade in New York. Addressing an audience of more than 70,000, the President recalled: "When I was a young man and he came to Little Rock, we had just had a terrible crisis. The schools were closed over school integration. And all the powerful white people tried to get Billy Graham to speak to a segregated audience. And he said Jesus doesn't want me to speak to a segregated audience. I'm not coming unless everybody can come to my crusade. And I was just a little boy. And I never forgot it. I've loved him ever since."

As I told the crowd that night, Dr. Graham is "one of the most respected icons of Protestant Christianity in the twentieth century." Throughout his more than sixty years of preaching, Billy Graham has been an incredible statesman for the body of Christ. He has left an indelible mark on my heart, my life, and my ministry.

·7·

TONY BLAIR

Former Prime Minister of the United Kingdom;
Middle East Peace Envoy and founder of
the Tony Blair Faith Foundation

I remember my first spiritual awakening. I was ten years old. That day my father—at the young age of forty—had suffered a serious stroke. His life hung in the balance. My mother, to keep some sense of normality in the crisis, sent me to school. My teacher knelt and prayed with me. Now my father was a militant atheist. Before we prayed, I thought I should confess this. "I'm afraid my father doesn't believe in God," I said. "That doesn't matter," my teacher replied. "God believes in him. He loves him without demanding or needing love in return."

That is what inspires: the unconditional nature of God's love. A promise perpetually kept. A covenant never broken.

And in surrendering to God, we become instruments of that love.

I was, of course, to become a Catholic.

Blessed John Paul II wanted the Second Vatican Council to "transmit doctrine, pure and whole, without attenuations or misrepresentations" so that "this sure and immutable teaching... is elaborated and presented in a way which corresponds to the needs of our time." I have sometimes wondered if, perhaps, he should have consulted Billy Graham, who had been doing just that from within the Evangelical tradition since the Second World War. Perhaps he did. The number of famous men influenced by Billy Graham has been prodigious and it would not surprise me.

I shall always think of Billy Graham as the master of communication, radio, television and the evangelical mass rally. He has the right voice and the kind of delivery that can raise the hairs on the back of your neck. A politician would give his right hand for that voice and those skills. He was one of the founding fathers of the quite extraordinary growth of the evangelical churches around the world and modern techniques for preaching the Gospel in the twentieth century.

Today we are barely surprised that the daily *Focus on the Family* radio show reaches 220 million listeners or the Campus Crusade for Christ operates in 190 different countries. But Billy Graham's sermons topped them all, according to some sources reaching 2.2 billion people in his three score and ten years of active preaching.

I remember his Mission to England in 1984. Huge crowds in football stadiums in one of the more secular countries in Europe, large numbers coming forward, and the well-honed harvesting of converts that was the hallmark of his Evangelistic Association. But despite this global outreach he is quintessentially American, growing out of the great Southern Baptist traditions, fighting the good fight throughout the Cold War against communism.

Most important for me was his ability to develop his theological thinking and respond to the demands of simple justice, pulling away from the conservative attitudes of his southern background on civil rights, refusing to allow social action to be marginalized in the expression of his faith, but with a clear vision of the dividing line between faith and politics. His own spiritual journey reflected that of the wider evangelical community, accompanying and sometimes leading it, forging the Christian culture of countless Americans and others around the world.

Billy Graham, for all those who love America, is a living expression of what is best in its Christian traditions. We all stand in awe of his commitment, perseverance and skills, a Christian life lived full of the energy and spirituality that faith can bring, a global voice that spoke to the needs of our time.

·8·

KEN BLANCHARD

Bestselling author, business management and leadership consultant,
co-author of The One Minute Manager
and co-founder of the Lead Like Jesus ministries

In July 1957, just after I finished high school in New Rochelle, New York, my mother took me to Billy Graham's enormous celebration at Yankee Stadium. An estimated 100,000 people attended, the largest crowd the stadium had ever held. The event was part of Billy's New York crusade, in which he preached six nights a week for sixteen weeks in Madison Square Garden, reaching maybe two million people. The crowd at Yankee Stadium was so huge that people could not come down to the stadium floor to make their commitment as they usually did. Instead, people had to raise their hands.

My mom, who was faith-based and thought Billy Graham was special, made sure we left early so we could get in. Despite the numbers, the atmosphere was amazingly peaceful and polite, quite unlike the crowd at baseball games, where people did a lot of pushing and shoving and tooted their horns.

I am a very active believer now, but I was struggling with faith at the time. I was named after a Presbyterian minister and went to Sunday school. However, nobody got me too excited about

Jesus when I was young, so in junior high I switched to the Methodist church because it had a better basketball team. I had drifted away by the time I was eighteen, but going to that meeting made me really think about my faith. Even though I had partly turned my back on the church, I had never turned my back on God. Hearing Billy's love for the Lord and experiencing what he was doing at the stadium had a powerful impact on me. That fall, I went off to college and separated a bit, but I never forgot that time in the stadium and the way Billy Graham mesmerized the crowd.

My wife and I married when we were in our early twenties. We were idealists and, having witnessed a lot of hypocrisy in churches, we turned our backs on the church. I didn't reunite significantly until my book *The One Minute Manager* came out in 1982. Spencer Johnson, my co-author, and I appeared on the *Today* show on Labor Day in 1982, and the next week our book made the *New York Times* bestseller list and stayed there for two or three years. People started asking why the book was so successful, and I could only answer, "It must be God somewhere." The book was wildly popular, and I knew it was not because of me. That's when I remembered Billy Graham's humility.

He is one of those people who act as if nobody else in the world matters when you are with them. He focuses completely on you and what is happening in your life. Some years ago, I was on a program with Billy and I had a chance to sit with him at lunch. I was traveling a lot at the time, and asked Billy how he remained so faithful to his marriage, given all his time away from home. He told me that his wife was his best friend. Also, he had a rule that he would never have lunch or meet with a woman without a third person present. He said he did not want to give even a hint that something was going on, which impressed me deeply.

My wife and I recently celebrated our fiftieth anniversary, and

I have found that when you recognize your spouse as your closest friend, your relationship flourishes. My conversation with Billy made it clear that he and his wife were best buddies.

I saw Billy at a second crusade at Qualcomm Stadium in San Diego in 2003 and once again, the atmosphere blew me away. It had been over fifty years since I had participated in one of those gatherings, and I witnessed the same peacefulness in San Diego that I had at Yankee Stadium. Though he was much older, Billy radiated the same spark, excitement, and compassion as when I first saw him.

In contrast to many other speakers, Billy's sermons were never canned; they came from his heart. He loved God and Jesus absolutely and wanted to share that with people. He wanted everybody to have the joy that he felt in receiving the Lord's grace and realizing that God so loved us that He sent His Son down to die for us.

I have been around only a few people of Billy's stature who are truly selfless. No matter how many people admire him, he never lets that get in the way. He has remained a child of God. When he finally graduates, a lot of people in this country—no matter what their faith—will be sad, because they are raving fans of this humble man.

·9·

PAT BOONE

*Bestselling singer and television star; member of the Gospel Music
Hall of Fame and the Christian Music Hall of Fame*

For Shirley and me, one of the grandest blessings in our richly
blessed lives has been our friendship with Ruth and Billy
Graham. Though our times together have been few and far
between, they stretch from our first meeting in Beverly Hills for
the tribute to the famed country/western stars, Roy and Dale
Rogers, to visits in Hawaii and Beverly Hills, to my participation
in crusades with Billy, and a visit just a few years ago at their
mountain home in Montreat.

A God-ordained mutual appearance on national television
tops my list of memorable moments with Billy Graham. It was in
1972 on the popular *Dick Cavett Show*, and Billy was the main
featured guest. I was going to sing a couple of my hit songs after
Billy and Dick had their conversation, and was listening in the
"green room" while a somewhat cynical, skeptical Cavett asked
Billy some very direct questions. "Reverend Graham, do you still
adhere to your belief that there should be no sex outside
marriage?"

Predictably, Billy answered with something like, "That's not
my idea, Dick... it's God's directive." And then, impulsively I

guess, he went further. "In fact, let me tell you something, Dick. When I met and fell in love with Ruth, I was a healthy, normal young male, twenty-six years old, off a dairy farm in North Carolina. We married, had beautiful children and have enjoyed so many years of happiness as a married couple. And I can tell you honestly, Dick, that I never had sex with anyone but Ruth, before, during, or since our wedding day."

And the audience laughed!

I don't mean they snickered; they laughed out loud, as if Billy had told a funny joke. And Dick just looked at the camera, shrugged as if to say "it takes all kinds," and went to commercial.

I sang my song after the commercial break, and sat down next to a red-faced Billy Graham. He hadn't expected that kind of reaction from the audience, and I imagine he was wondering if he should have been so forthcoming. And Dick started right out asking me, "Have you been listening to the conversation? Do you agree with these things Billy has been saying?"

I nodded and said, "Billy and I may not agree on every single thing, I don't know; but I think I do know why you and the audience laughed when he said that about no sex outside marriage."

And I heard the audience start tittering and getting ready for another joke. Another big laugh at the outdated notion of fidelity in marriage. But I went on: "This young audience, and you yourself Dick, applaud dedication and commitment in other areas of life. Business, sports, politics—all these things reward commitment. But in one of most important areas of life, marriage, commitment is considered funny."

Nobody was laughing, not knowing quite how to react, so I went on. "But I'm just thinking about the one person in America tonight, in this vast viewing audience, who doesn't find what Billy just said funny — Ruth Graham."

He couldn't think of anything to say but "I think it's time for another commercial." And Billy and I hugged after the show, feeling that God had set Dick and his audience up for a one-two punch. Billy dropped the first shoe, and I got to drop the second.

·10·

VONETTE BRIGHT

Co-founder, Campus Crusade for Christ,
which has a staff of 27,000 plus 225,000 volunteers in 190 countries

My husband Bill and I first met Billy in early 1949 when he came to Los Angeles to discuss the possibility of a campaign. Along with the influential evangelical leader, Henrietta Mears, we met him for lunch in Hollywood.

We met again in August when he came to Forest Home for a College Briefing Conference, where Billy made the critical decision to faithfully preach "the Bible says…"

When he returned to Los Angeles to begin his crusade on September 25, 1949, Bill invited Billy to dinner at our home. I was a new Christian, having committed my life to Christ in August 1948. Soon after, I married Bill Bright, a young entrepreneur who was active at Hollywood Presbyterian Church. We lived in a little English-style cottage in Hollywood.

As a new bride I hadn't prepared a meal for a large group. The only dishes I had enough of were what are now called "Depression glass." I insisted to Bill that we get something else, because it would not do to serve dinner to Billy Graham on those plates. So we went to a pottery outlet and I chose plates that were about fifteen inches in diameter. They were huge! I don't know what I was thinking. You needed an enormous amount of food on those plates to make it look like you had something to eat.

When Bill returned from the meeting with Billy he said, "Well, we may have a few more people, honey." And in walked Billy, George Beverly Shea, Cliff Barrows, several other people including western entertainer Stewart Hamlin and his wife! I was a bit overwhelmed, but it turned out to be a wonderful evening I will never forget. The laughter and storytelling left precious memories. I learned a lesson that has stayed with me to this day—it isn't what you have; it's the spirit of your hospitality that makes the difference. I certainly didn't have a home I considered elegant, but God used what we had, and that was the important thing. If you depend on God to meet your needs it's amazing to see how He does.

When Billy Graham came back a few years later for another campaign in Hollywood, Bill and I volunteered to become counselors, Bill was qualified to do it but I still felt like a brand new Christian. I went to some training sessions, but I was nervous and felt underprepared. On our way to the Billy Graham Crusade, I said to Bill, "If they call on me to be a counselor, what do I say?" I felt very insecure. Bill told me to take down a few verses from the Bible about how God loves you, that you are a sinner, that Jesus is the way, the truth, and the life, and that He stands at the door and knocks.

I wrote down the relevant verses in the back of my Bible. Sure enough, as the first woman made her way to the front, I was motioned to come forward as a counselor. I was still uneasy about my ability. But with the lady I was assigned to, I just went through the basic verses about how to be sure you are a Christian. Then I said, "Now would you like to receive Christ as your personal savior?" And she said, "Oh yes, I would." I was thrilled. To myself I said "you would?" It was just too wonderful to be true!

We prayed together, she was sure that Jesus Christ was in her heart, and I sent her on her way. I was in glory to think that I had had this marvelous opportunity. This was the first person that I had been able to lead to Christ.

Each night during that sixteen-day Billy Graham Crusade in 1951, I counseled more and more people. It was a wonderful spiritual experience and the beginning of my confidence that God could use me in the lives of other people.

Another turning point for me came in 1974, when Billy Graham asked me if I would represent women on the continuation planning committee of the Lausanne Committee for World Evangelization, which Billy had started years earlier, in 1966. My husband was a part of the original planning committee. It was an honor and made a great change in my life. My husband had included me in the formation of Campus Crusade for Christ beginning in 1951 and my experiences had equipped me to step up to this challenge. I had organized what became the National Prayer Committee, and then along with Ruth Graham and three other women, we initiated the Great Commission Prayer Crusade. Our goal was to mobilize women in the United States to pray for spiritual awakening. We had committees all over the country, and I went to about twenty cities for prayer rallies. This allowed me to take a greater leadership role in mobilizing prayer groups all over the nation and the world. It was Billy Graham who gave me the opportunity as a woman to have greater visibility in a position of leadership on a committee comprised of forty-seven men and three women.

In the early 1980s I was working with the National Prayer Committee, and we had been able to mobilize people from different denominations and prayer groups and bring them together. We had a structure designed to mobilize such groups, particularly women. I became the chair of the Lausanne

Committee's Intercession Advisory Group. All the members of that group were prominent people of prayer in their nations. We talked about an International Prayer Assembly for a couple of years but it just wasn't happening. Billy was a great encouragement and gave $25,000 that allowed us to move forward. He gave me the inspiration I needed. The result was the 1984 International Prayer Assembly for World Evangelization, which took place in Seoul, Korea. Seven thousand people came from seventy countries to join with 100,000 Koreans. It was fantastic to see what happened. It was the beginning of a worldwide prayer movement that has grown tremendously and continues to thrive.

Mr. Graham has played an important part in promoting women. Many women have been platform guests. His daughter Anne is a perfect example of this in her ministry. Billy opened the door for me, and he certainly encouraged prayer around the world. Ruth Graham remained a constant encourager and dear friend.

When my husband and I first launched Campus Crusade for Christ there was little cooperation among churches. Our prayer was that God would use Campus Crusade as a catalyst in helping to bring the denominations together. The organization now has locations on more than 1,100 colleges, with over 74,000 students involved, having ministered to hundreds of millions of young people. It was Billy who had the visibility and willingness to help accomplish this goal back when we first began nearly sixty years ago.

Through the congresses he organized, he too wanted to bring the churches together. I think he has promoted the message and the vision to so many people in terms of what they might be able to do by bringing people together and letting them share their techniques, materials, and what they have accomplished. He has given many different organizations the opportunity to present their points of view and to bring the whole body of Christ together. That is one of the greatest contributions he has made.

Billy Graham has been a good friend. He and my husband were very close and very supportive of each other. Billy was always available to come when we called. When we first began our ministry, we were paying the bills with the money we earned from our own business. When our savings ran out, it was Billy who gave us $1,000, the largest donation we had received.

He is a very godly man, and there has been a sweet relationship between our families. We've prayed together and we have seen God do such miraculous works. It's been a wonderful time. There is no man in the world my husband loved more than Billy Graham.

·11·

DR. DAVID BRUCE

Executive Assistant to Mr. Graham,
Billy Graham Evangelistic Association, Montreat, North Carolina

Of all the special moments I have had with Mr. Graham while serving him, his organization and his family for twenty-five years, one impactful encounter surpasses them all and opened a window into the soul of this American icon and faithful preacher. In one sentence, Mr. Graham not only summed up the meaning of his worldwide ministry, but also revealed his unique and counter-intuitive humility.

Several years ago, a broadcast organization announced its desire to present a life-achievement award to Mr. Graham in honor of his role in founding a radio ministry that today covers a several state region with a signal emanating from the highest point east of the Mississippi River. The award was to be presented on the occasion of the fortieth anniversary of the station's founding by both Mr. and Mrs. Graham—a little known addendum to a long and faithful evangelistic ministry. As the banquet date approached, Mr. Graham fell ill, meaning that he would disappoint the audience since he was not well enough to leave home.

Mr. Graham had often remarked in both private and public

moments that he was troubled by the presentation of awards honoring him. He never sought them and was quite challenged by receiving them, never feeling that he deserved any recognition. His finest response at such a heartfelt dilemma is what he spoke on the floor of the United States Capitol, standing under the great dome when receiving the Congressional Gold Medal with Mrs. Graham in 1996. On that occasion, he spoke eloquently to the Vice President, Congressional representatives, diplomats and Congressional aides who had gathered to honor him when he stated: "As Ruth and I receive this award we know that some day we will lay it at the feet of the One we seek to serve."

On this occasion, too sick to attend the radio banquet, Mr. Graham called me to his home to ask a favor. Approaching his bedroom and study, I found Mr. Graham lying flat in bed—covered with blankets up to his chin. Speaking softly, he motioned for me to take a chair near him. I strained to listen to him—weak as he was, as he declared to me that he could not make the banquet. "David," he said, "please go in my place tonight and accept this award. I just don't have the strength to go. Give those wonderful folks my deep apologies, and thank them for thinking of me. Remind them of the reason the stations were first established, and encourage them to continue the strong Gospel witness which has been part of the stations' forty years."

Of course, I was privileged to stand in for Mr. Graham. I promised I would tell the assembled guests everything he said, and I would do my best to represent him by thanking them for the honor. With that promise, I excused myself and encouraged him to rest. As I left the room, I glanced back at him and noticed his eyes were trained on the ceiling—I could see Mr. Graham was deep in thought.

I walked away from his bedroom through his study—walking

slowly down the long hallway that runs the length of his home, pondering what I would say and the greetings that I would bring from him. Mr. Graham was the only one at home that day—Mrs. Graham had traveled into town. The only sound was the creaking of the antique wooden flooring beneath my feet.

Just before I reached the end of that hallway in the Grahams' log cabin home, I could hear the sound of struggle—like someone pushing covers away and attempting to get out of bed. I heard the sound of something hitting the side of the bed—and I knew immediately that Mr. Graham was attempting to stand.

I stopped in the hall just as I heard my name being called—"David, David!" I turned to answer and began to walk back down the hall toward the bedroom. Just them Mr. Graham came into sight. He had pulled himself out of bed and made it to the door of his study just outside his bedroom.

As I turned back, Mr. Graham spoke with a strong voice and a determined posture. "David—I forgot something. Tell those people tonight when you stand to receive the award—tell them to give God the glory! Don't forget to give God the glory!"

"Don't forget to give God the glory!" In that split second, I stood transfixed looking at this man. I knew in that instant I had seen the soul of the man, the heart that made his ministry endure for decades without failure, and the hallmark of a faithful man who knew that he could not share any of God's glory no matter what an adoring public said. This man knew that if it took all of his energy and strength, he could not let me leave his house that day until I had heard that directive—till I understood that this sentiment was pivotal in his life. I knew I would never be the same again after witnessing what I consider a poignant and powerful illustration of why God entrusted an incredible worldwide ministry to Billy Graham all along—Mr. Graham's incredible understanding of his place before Almighty God.

Someone once said that as Christians we should live to be forgotten while pointing all the time to a Savior who is to be remembered! This is what Billy Graham sought to do throughout his life and ministry. And because he lived that way, conscious of his standing before God and faithful with the message of Jesus Christ... Mr. Graham inevitably will never be forgotten, and God would be pleased with this amazing life yielded totally to Him. "Don't forget to give God the glory!"

amazon.co.uk

Thank you for shopping at Amazon.co.uk!

Ellen ML Turner DQs8V4ZDN/-1 of 1-/econ-uk/7039544 B1

Invoice for
Your order of 1 September, 2013
Order ID 203-5511003-9353156
Invoice number D8H1VHZsN
Invoice date 1 September, 2013

Billing Address
Ellen ML Turner
2 Stanley Drive
Bridge of Allan
Stirling, Stirling FK9 4QR
United Kingdom

Shipping Address
Ellen ML Turner
2 Stanley Drive
Bridge of Allan
Stirling, Scotland FK9 4QR
United Kingdom

Qty.	Item		Our Price (excl. VAT)	VAT Rate	Total Price
1	**Chicken Soup for the Soul: Billy Graham and Me: 101 Inspiring Personal Stories from Presidents, Pastors, Performers, and Other People Who Know Him Well** Paperback. Steve Posner. 1611599245 (** P-1-A92E173 **)		£13.10	0%	£13.10
	Shipping charges		£0.00		£0.00
	Subtotal (excl. VAT) 0%				£13.10
	Total VAT				£0.00
	Total				£13.10

Conversion rate - £1.00 : EUR 1,16

This shipment completes your order.

You can always check the status of your orders or change your account details from the "Your Account" link at the top of each page on our site.

Thinking of returning an item? PLEASE USE OUR ON-LINE RETURNS SUPPORT CENTRE.

Our Returns Support Centre (www.amazon.co.uk/returns-support) will guide you through our Returns Policy and provide you with a printable personalised return label. Please have your order number ready (you can find it next to your order summary, above). Our Returns Policy does not affect your statutory rights.

Amazon EU S.a.r.L, 5 Rue Plaetis, L-2338, Luxembourg
VAT number : GB727255821

Please note - this is not a returns address - for returns - please see above for details of our online returns centre

0/DQs8V4ZDN/-1 of 1-//DOM_UK/econ-uk/7039544/0904-16:45/0903-16:51 Pack Type : B1

·12·

GEORGE H. W. BUSH

41st President of the United States

The Bush family has been privileged to know and cross paths with Billy Graham on numerous occasions through the years.

One of the most memorable occurred when my mother—whose faith was strong, whose knowledge of the Bible was great, and whose life was full of Christian love—invited Dr. Graham to walk across from our house to her little bungalow for a private breakfast. Billy had always been so kind and considerate to my beloved mother. The two of them sat quietly and read some Bible passages, and Billy said a prayer. Later that day Mother said to me, "That was the most glorious time in my life." She loved the man. All Bushes do.

The day I was sworn in as President, my ailing mother was watching the parade from the window of the Queen's Bedroom in the White House. Dr. Graham saw her and left the parade to sit next to her and keep her company.

Billy came to stay with Barbara and me at the White House on the eve of the air war against Iraq. I told him what I was then having to do—our diplomacy and our quest for a peaceful solution having failed. I told him when the first cruise missiles would hit Baghdad, and we watched in wonder as the war to liberate Kuwait began. Just the three of us were there. Billy said a little prayer for our troops and for the innocents who might be killed. The next day we attended a church service at Fort Meade. His very presence brought great comfort to the people in uniform who were praying at that special service.

I cannot begin to tell what Billy's presence and his faith meant to me as President and as Commander in Chief. His own beliefs and abiding faith gave me great strength.

As other Presidents can attest, Billy was always considerate of administrations in Washington, not wanting to cause problems by traveling to places where a visit from him might complicate our foreign policy or relations with a specific country. Once he called me about a trip to Russia he was planning to take and asked, "Do you think the trip would make things more difficult for the administration?"

Of course I said, "No, go on your trip." He went and indeed I truly believe that visit gave hope to those in Russia who craved religious freedom. He did the same in China and Korea. His message of faith and love resonates wherever he goes.

The Bush family is indeed blessed to call this great man a friend. We love him as a brother; our sons and daughter love him as a father; and all of us love him as a wise counselor.

·13·

GEORGE W. BUSH

43rd President of the United States,
and co-founder of The Clinton Bush Haiti Fund

Until I met Billy Graham, religion had always been part of my life, but I really wasn't a believer. I was baptized in Yale's nondenominational Dwight Hall Chapel. When I was young my parents took me to First Presbyterian in Midland, St. Martin's Episcopal in Houston, and St. Ann's Episcopal in Kennebunkport.

I went to church at Andover because it was mandatory. I never went at Yale. I did go when I visited my parents, but my primary mission was to avoid irritating Mother. Laura and I were married at First United Methodist in Midland. We started going regularly after the girls were born, because we felt a responsibility to expose them to faith. I liked spending time with friends in the congregation. I enjoyed the opportunity for reflection. Once in a while, I heard a sermon that inspired me. I read the Bible occasionally, and saw it as a kind of self-improvement course. I knew I could use some self-improvement. But for the most part, religion was more of a tradition than a spiritual experience. I was listening but not hearing.

In the summer of 1985, we took our annual trip to Maine.

Mother and Dad had invited the great evangelical preacher Billy Graham. Dad had asked him to answer some questions from the family after dinner. So there we sat, about thirty of us—Laura, my grandmother, brothers and sister, first and second cousins—in the large room at the end of the house on Walker's Point.

The first question was from Dad. He said, "Billy, some people say you have to have a born-again experience to go to heaven. Mother [my grandmother] here is the most religious, kind person I know, yet she has had no born-again experience. Will she go to heaven?" Wow, pretty profound question from the old man. We all looked at Billy. In his quiet, strong voice, he replied, "George, some of us require a born-again experience to understand God, and some of us are born Christians. It sounds as if your mom was just born a Christian." [*I don't think Billy meant this literally. It seemed to me that he was saying that some people find their faith through a dramatic "born again" experience, while others come to it more gradually over a lifetime.*]

I was captivated by Billy. He had a powerful presence, full of kindness and grace, and a keen mind. The next day, he asked me to go for a walk around the property. He asked about my life in Texas. I talked to him about the girls and shared my thought that reading the Bible could make me a better person. In his gentle, loving way, Billy began to deepen my shallow understanding of faith. There's nothing wrong with using the Bible as a guide to self-improvement, he said. Jesus' life provides a powerful example for our own. But self-improvement is not really the point of the Bible. The center of Christianity is not the self. It is Christ.

Billy explained that we are all sinners, and that we cannot earn God's love through good deeds. He made clear that the path to salvation is through the grace of God. And the way to find that grace is to embrace Christ as the risen Lord—the son of a

God so powerful and loving that He gave His only son to conquer death and defeat sin.

These were profound concepts, and I did not fully grasp them that day. But Billy had planted a seed. His thoughtful explanation had made the soil less firm and the brambles less thick.

Shortly after we got back to Texas, a package from Billy arrived. It was a copy of *The Living Bible.* He had inscribed: "To my friend George W. Bush, May God bless you and Laura always." He included a reference to Philippians 1:6: "And I am certain that God, who began the good work within you, will continue His work until it is finally finished on the day when Christ Jesus returns."

I am blessed to know Reverend Billy Graham, and I am forever grateful to this remarkable, humble, decent man.

❧

Adapted from Decision Points *by George W. Bush © 2010 by George W. Bush. Used by permission of Crown Publishers, a division of Random House, Inc.*

·14·

DICK CAPEN

Former U.S. Ambassador to Spain and publisher of
The Miami Herald; *business consultant, author and speaker*

It has been my privilege to be associated with Billy Graham both professionally and personally for over forty years. Friends often ask me what Billy Graham is like: one-on-one, off camera, while not preaching. They are curious about who this man is up close and personal.

How do you capture the essence of the most respected leader on the world stage? How do you sum up such a powerful man of God who has written more than thirty books and preached to millions on five continents over a span of seven decades?

Well, the answer is amazingly simple. Whether he is preaching to a live audience of 100,000 or sitting in my living room, Billy Graham remains the same: loving, unselfish, gentle and humble.

Billy Graham is absolutely self-effacing.

He simply does not fully comprehend the enormity of his legacy—it transcends time and geography. When conversing with him it is difficult to look beyond the inspiring aura his presence projects so that you can absorb the reality that you are talking with the most respected, influential religious leader of our time. Instead, he comes across as your closest friend.

Billy is down-to-earth, clear thinking, always interested in others and reluctant to talk about himself. His influence cuts across politics and poverty. His message is timeless. He describes his life's work this way: "I am a simple proclaimer of the Gospel of Jesus." In his eyes, all the glory belongs to God.

Over the years I have had a front row seat on Billy's ministry. I have marveled at how profoundly he has given hope to millions around the globe who have no hope. Through what he would describe as God-given responsibility he has led people out of the depths of depression and the ravages of natural disaster. He has offered freedom of the soul for millions trapped behind the Iron Curtain during the Cold War while uplifting thousands of people held as political prisoners suffering unbelievable brutality at the hands of dictators.

Billy's ministry has leveraged Internet technology allowing access to his message in the most remote jungles of Africa, in huts on mountaintops high in the Andes and in isolated Alaskan villages. He has consoled our nation's leaders in the loneliness of the Oval Office. He has led our nation in prayer in times of crisis and inspired our best during Inaugural transitions of power. Though for years he has been considered one the world's most respected leaders Billy insists that the credit for it all belongs to God.

Billy Graham has been called "God's Ambassador" for good reason. He has preached to more than 215 million people in live audiences in 185 countries and territories spanning five continents around the globe. Hundreds of millions more have heard his message on television, radio and via satellite. Today, sermons he delivered as long as fifty years ago have been lip-synced into more than eighty different languages and dialects. These translations flow beyond any boundaries of culture, tradition or restrictions on religious expression.

Even as his physical energy wanes, Billy's mind remains sharp. He continues to write books, pray for those in need, and plan yet another major outreach of God's love. This one is tied to his upcoming ninety-fifth birthday year.

As I read through the stories by so many familiar names in *Billy Graham & Me*, from the good folks at Chicken Soup for the Soul, the words to describe this humble man sound like a massive choir singing a chorus of trust, respect and faithfulness. That simply is who he is.

When I served as publisher of *The Miami Herald*, I met regularly with Billy Graham. For me Billy was an enormous source of inspiration, love and commitment. With his insight and encouragement—and what an encourager he is—we greatly expanded our newspaper's coverage of religion news and ran interesting profiles on individuals who led faith-based programs in South Florida.

I cherish my personal friendship with Billy, which dates back to early 1969 when I served as a key assistant to the then Secretary of Defense Mel Laird. Billy traveled to Washington and came to the Pentagon to dedicate the Memorial Chapel in the Pentagon. From that time forward our association has grown closer.

At my invitation Billy met with dozens of families of Vietnam POWS and missing men, a cause I led while in government. His involvement was comforting to all those affected by this prolonged war that we worked hard to end.

Over the years Billy sought my advice on media matters and issues of international diplomacy. He asked for my help in reaching more of the senior media executives in America, whom he believed could do much more to underscore the faith-based foundation of our nation.

At his invitation, I have served for many years on the board of the Billy Graham Evangelistic Association, the organization he founded in 1950. He insisted that his ministry be managed with absolute integrity. At that time, 215 million dollars or more was raised annually from ordinary people who gave on average about thirty dollars a year in support of his ministry. His dedicated volunteer board of men and women usually had to plead with him to accept even modest increases in salary.

In 1992, despite recovering from a major illness, Billy insisted on flying to Washington to pray with some 500 friends and government leaders who had gathered at the State Department for my swearing-in ceremony as U.S. Ambassador to Spain. My wife Joan held for this occasion a special leather-bound Bible that he had given us years earlier. Billy, President George H. W. Bush and Juan Carlos, the King of Spain, each signed that Bible in honor of my appointment.

Billy and I have prayed together in both good times and bad. When our grandson died five years ago, he was one of the first to step forward and offer prayer for our family. He is always there for his friends and family, especially in times of loss or illness, showing sincere warmth and concern.

Billy contributed the foreword for my book on faith and personal values, *Finish Strong*. When I ran *The Miami Herald*, the annual convention of newspaper publishers was held in South Florida. This is an organization accustomed to hearing from world leaders, including heads of state, corporate chiefs and the like. But inviting a religious leader on their program? Never in my memory. Billy's keynote address was a first for the group—and for Billy. To this day, almost thirty years later, publishers recall Billy's presentation as one of the most inspiring ever.

I have attended many of Billy's evangelistic crusades over the years. On several occasions, I was invited to sit on the infield platform behind him. It was overwhelming to look out at the overflowing crowd of as many as 90,000 people packed into the stadium from ground level on up to the third upper deck. Many came with needs and deep hurt. They listened intently as Billy spoke. Part of Billy's gift rests in the sense that one gets that he is speaking directly to you.

It is a powerful moment when those present are invited to step forward in front of the podium to make a faith commitment. Hundreds—sometimes thousands—make that long walk from high above, down dozens of steps and through long hallways, onto the field to humbly confess their decision to follow Jesus. Billy has touched each soul. In the span of his public ministry, more than three million individuals have come to The Lord in this way.

Untold millions more watching these meetings as they are broadcast on network and syndicated television get on their knees in the privacy of their living rooms to similarly accept God's offer of love and forgiveness. Billy has spoken directly to them too, all through the powerful, yet humble, message delivered by one of the most charismatic preachers of all time.

For over fifty years Billy Graham has lived in a small log home located on a remote mountain in western North Carolina. This is where his wife Ruth committed early in their marriage to provide him with a loving home and family while he evangelized the world. Today he lives there alone with caregivers. Ruth died several years ago and her loss to Billy is profound.

Though in his mid-nineties, each day—with the help of his incredibly devoted assistant Reverend David Bruce—Billy prays, reads the Bible and works on the manuscript for his next book. He finds his greatest joy in knowing that Jesus Christ has promised him eternal life, one without pain, where he will one day be united forever with his Savior and his beloved partner, Ruth.

·15·

JIMMY CARTER

39th President of the United States,
Nobel Peace Prize winner,
author and founder of The Carter Center

I first became associated with Billy Graham about forty-five years ago, when I was in Sumter County, Georgia. Anyone who knows anything about Georgia would recognize Sumter County, and particularly Americus, as having the strongest John Birch Society in the South. In those days it had almost 100 percent membership among white men and the White Citizens' Council. Andy Young and the Reverend Martin Luther King, Jr. both said that Sumter County was the worst place in the United States to be put in jail.

Someone called me on behalf of Billy Graham and asked if I would lead a Billy Graham Crusade. I said, "Yes I will, if Billy Graham comes." The representative replied, "Well he's not coming, but he'll send a motion picture, and we want you to put the event together." Then he added, "And the first thing you have to realize is that all over the world, the Billy Graham Crusades are absolutely and totally racially integrated."

I somewhat reluctantly agreed to do it, knowing the South as I did. Then we tried to find a place where we could have a biracial planning meeting. However, and I hate to report this, not a single one of the Christian white churches would let us meet on their premises. So we had to find some secular place to meet, but the planning went on. The name of the movie was *The Restless Ones*. During the crusade, we showed that film in the movie theater, two hours each night, and at the end of the film, I gave a short presentation about the Gospel message. During the completely integrated ceremony, 650 people accepted the call to accept Jesus Christ. This event, sponsored and orchestrated by Billy Graham, was a major breakthrough in severing the distinctive separation between our African American and our white citizens. It helped to integrate our county in a major way, because whenever anyone went forward in that theater, black or white, to accept Jesus Christ, they were embraced by the leaders of the segregationist churches as Christian brothers and sisters.

The first time I actually met Billy Graham in person was when I became governor of Georgia in the early 1970s. I invited him to come down and lead a prayer breakfast. He came and I was delighted. We had big crowds, as you can well imagine.

The next time I saw Billy Graham was when I was invited as a governor to go to the White House for the National Prayer Breakfast sponsored by President Nixon. That was a special event for me not only because I saw Billy Graham there, but also because it was the first time I had ever met a U.S. President.

While I was President, Billy Graham performed another important service that had an influence on the secular as well as religious world. He was the first evangelist of any stature who penetrated the Iron Curtain. In 1977, he went to Hungary, then ruled by a communist government, and he preached — so the CIA told me — to hundreds of thousands of people who came to hear his message. Wanting to downplay the impact of the visit, the Hungarian government said that maybe a thousand people showed up! Later, in the 1980s, Billy Graham did something else that was profoundly significant: he met with Pope John Paul II. Both this meeting and his trip to Hungary were criticized by some devout Christians as "going to the communists" and "going to the Catholics," but that was the kind of thing that Billy Graham did.

In 1994, I decided to go to North Korea to help improve relations with that country during a difficult time. It was very difficult to obtain any accurate information about North Korea from the CIA or State Department, so I had a conversation with Ruth and Billy who had just before that visited Pyongyang, the North Korean capital. As you know, Ruth attended high school in Pyongyang, North Korea, for several years. I learned a lot from what they told me.

That visit turned out to be a very wonderful occasion for me because I discovered something quite unexpected about Kim Il-Sung, a communist dictator whom I had despised ever since I served as a submarine officer in the Pacific during the Korean War. I learned that he not only had a great affinity for Billy Graham but also for Christians generally. Several times he expressed to me his appreciation for Christians. He said that Christians had saved his life when he was imprisoned by the Japanese.

I'll conclude by giving a report on an interview I had with Fox television. It was a special program about Billy Graham. The question was, "Who has been most influential in your spiritual life?" My response was: "Billy Graham." He was constantly broad-minded, forgiving, and humble in his treatment of others. He has reached out to all people—black or white, American or foreign, man or woman—for opportunities to serve God. My testimony is that I am just one of tens of millions of people whose spiritual lives have been shaped by Billy Graham.

⟡

Adapted from remarks delivered at the dedication of the Billy Graham Library on March 31, 2007.

·16·

STEVE CASE

Chairman and CEO, Revolution LLC; co-founder, AOL;
chairman, The Case Foundation

I first met Billy Graham in early 1998 when he spoke at a technology conference called TED. After the conference we talked, and I was quite taken not only by his message but also by his simplicity and humility, and the passion he brought to an audience made up mostly of technology executives focused on building companies.

About a month later I visited him at his home in North Carolina, and about a month after that I went to a crusade in Toronto and heard him speak there. We struck up a quick friendship and I've probably been with him about fifty times since then, including between six and eight crusades. Every two or three months I'll fly down to North Carolina and spend an afternoon with him just to talk. On his eightieth birthday we invited him down to our house in Florida, and when my wife and I got married in the summer of 1998 he agreed to fly to Virginia to be the pastor at our wedding, which was sweet.

In a friendship that has developed over about fifteen years, we've had a lot of conversations about many different topics. If I had to pick one representative quality about him it would be humility. He is one of the best known and most respected people in the world and has met with and counseled thousands of people, including all the presidents over the past half century. He has been a trusted advisor to so many people and such a powerful voice globally. Yet despite all that, he carries himself with tremendous humility. There is a certain softness and sweetness about him that I've always admired.

Most people are a little in awe of the opportunity to spend time with him. I don't think he fully appreciates the impact he has had because he is not focused on that. I'm deeply honored to be able to spend some time with him, but he can't believe, given my busy schedule, that I can find the time to be with *him*! His humility is remarkable.

The touchstone of Billy Graham's life has been simplicity, both in his message and his personal life. Because of that, it is hard not to have your faith deepened when you talk to him. It's not just the sermons he preaches but the everyday life he leads. This is what draws people to him. I remember a dinner at the Clinton White House that my wife and I attended. Billy and Ruth were among the many high-powered people there, and I remember at the end of the evening, Bill and Hillary basically wanted to pull them aside and find a quiet space upstairs where they could just chat. That shows how people valued the wisdom he had, and his patient, nonjudgmental approach to life.

A few years later, in 2002 or 2003, President Bush hosted a family dinner for Billy at the White House on his birthday, and again you got to see the deep connection there. Everybody just feels better being in his presence and benefiting from his wisdom.

I noticed this when I first met him at the TED conference. I also appreciated the skill with which he delivered his talk. Most of the speakers at the conference talked about technology, but he took things to a different level. It was a mixed audience. Some people had strong faith, while others had none. Some were surprised he was there and wondered why he wanted to come, or why he had been invited. It was one of those situations where nobody quite knew what to expect. Probably he most of all because it was a different crowd for him. But his talk was mesmerizing, both for me and many others. It's viewed as one of the legendary TED talks. It was very well crafted in that it was not the kind of message he would deliver at a crusade. He recognized that he had a more diverse and probably skeptical audience so he was not preachy. That's not to say there wasn't a strong message embedded in his talk, but I don't think anyone would listen to it and refer to it as a sermon, although in fact it was. But it was a subtle approach. One of the themes was that technology is an enabler. It is a tool that can bring people together but it also carries the risk of separating people, and you need to be careful that you don't get so focused on it that you lose sight of more important things. It was an important message to any group but certainly to that one.

In retrospect, it was not surprising that Billy Graham would want to address the TED conference. He has always tried to push the envelope in terms of new ways to reach more people with his message. He told me that when radio first came on the scene, he was on some radio stations in Hawaii (where I am from). He realized intuitively that this new-fangled thing called radio would allow him to reach new audiences, particularly people who would not likely show up in church or at a crusade. Similarly, he embraced television early and used it as a way to extend his reach, particularly to the unconverted, which has always been his desire.

He also saw the Internet and technology generally as an opportunity. When I was running AOL in 1995 we hosted an online national interactive chat with him. We take things like that for granted now but it was a new idea then. The fact that he accepted our invitation, in conjunction with *TIME* magazine, to be our special guest and interact with the audience, demonstrated a willingness on his part to embrace these technologies because they were new ways to reach people with a message.

There are a couple of remarkable things about Billy Graham in his later years. The first one that strikes me is that he is not a man who fears death at all. If he's fearful of anything it is having to deal with the frustrations of getting older. The book he wrote, *Nearing Home: Life, Faith, and Finishing Well*, is instructive in that respect. The second thing is that even to this day he possesses an extraordinary memory. He has a much better memory than I do. The stories he can tell! If you just mention some topic he will say, oh, I remember when this happened, or that happened. It's almost like a *Forrest Gump* movie about someone who has managed to be present at every pivotal moment in history for many decades. Billy Graham was a witness to history, and he has thousands of stories to tell because he has been with so many people in so many places over so many years. It's been a remarkable life, and I feel privileged to know him.

·17·

JOHN CARTER CASH

Grammy Award winner, country music singer and songwriter,
music producer, author

I have known Billy Graham since I was a young boy. He has been a steady, constant source of inspiration for me throughout my life. I'm still amazed when I hear him speak or see clips of the crusades. I'm drawn to him. I still visit him to show him respect and express appreciation for all that he has done for me.

My father met Billy in the 1960s. Billy used to say that he had gotten in touch with my father because his son Franklin was a big Johnny Cash fan! They formed an immediate connection through their faith and quickly became very good friends. I think they also saw the possibility of working together, forwarding their own personal missions, based on their Christian faith. Also, they just liked to hang out with each other.

As a young boy, although I knew Billy was a preacher, to me he was just a friend of my parents, and I loved him to death. I thought he was the greatest guy in the world because he was so comfortable to be around, so tender.

He and Ruth sometimes came to stay at our house in Montego Bay in Jamaica. They went to the beach and swimming pool and just relaxed with my parents. They all had a lot of fun together.

I was very comfortable with Billy. He was at our house not long after I learned to swim, so he would watch me in the pool and sometimes we would swim together. He was a dear man.

My parents and Billy and Ruth were together in the Caribbean quite a few times in the 1970s and 1980s. Billy and my dad also corresponded regularly. There were some tough times in my father's life; when he was a bit lost and searching he knew he could always reach out to Billy, because Billy would never condemn him. That's the kind of person that Billy Graham is. He is not a condemning person; he is a Christian in the real sense of the word. He has a very simple, kind nature.

My father and mother also participated in many of Billy's crusades, and I went along too. I remember being overwhelmed by Billy's strength as a speaker, but at the same time it didn't seem unusual to me that this was the same man that I was swimming with and hanging out with. There was something about the way he related his message. It wasn't like he was forcing it on anyone. His power as a preacher was actually just another expression of his kindness, his desire to be of service.

Whenever I've had a chance over the last fifteen years or so, I've gone to see Billy at his home. I remember one visit just a few years ago that had particular significance for me.

I wanted to find out more about my father's relationship with Billy. I had often felt that there must have been something amazing about it, some secret that these two great men shared that enabled them to do God's work so powerfully together. After all, they both had a kind of charisma and you felt it even when they walked into a room or in Billy's case preached to fifty thousand people. What was it that bound them together in this magical kind of way?

I sat around with Billy and we talked for a couple of hours. I asked him, "What was the basis of your relationship with my dad? What made it so strong?" And he replied, very simply, "We were Christian brothers."

The simplicity of his answer was a revelation to me. I discovered that there was, after all, no great secret to the strength of their relationship; there was just that one great, simple truth, that they were Christian brothers. They were joyful in their spirit; they had joy for Christ. And that was what bound them together as good friends. And it's what had a resounding influence on so many people throughout the world as shown through Billy's crusades.

This realization was an eye-opener for me. Before, I think I may have been putting their relationship on a pedestal, thinking there must have been some complex secret to it because it had the power to influence so many people. But now I saw there was no need for any complicated explanation. Sometimes the most beautiful thing about the truth is its simplicity, and that's what I discovered on that visit to Billy.

I discovered something else on that visit, too, because I also asked Billy about his own greatness since I have never been in doubt that he is a great man. He shook his head and replied, "I'm just a servant."

That too was an eye-opener for me in my own faith. It put me back in contact with my own personal salvation; it reminded me of what Christianity is. I've heard a thousand times that the least shall be the greatest, and that the greatest is the humble servant. But hearing it from his mouth was a special thing for me.

And that's Billy. He can't help but be a powerful, compelling person, but he is truly a servant and has been since he began his ministry. His mission is, first of all, to serve. In spirit he is washing people's feet. Whether they know it or not, that's what he's doing and has been doing for so long. It's what Christ did.

There are so many people that have other agendas. Billy has no agenda other than to serve and bring people closer to God.

I also realized that God had used the simple Christian brotherhood of Billy and my dad for His own purposes. They just happened to be amazingly charismatic men, but they hadn't used their own power for anything; on the contrary, it was God who had used them.

So I looked at things differently after I talked to Billy that day. Simplicity, Christian brotherhood, and service. That was what clicked with me. It grounded me, and there was nothing mysterious about it. Just the simple truth, and you never need anything more than that.

·18·

ROSANNE CASH

Grammy Award-winning singer and songwriter, author,
daughter of Johnny Cash

Billy Graham was a very good friend of my father, Johnny Cash, and my stepmother, June Carter Cash. I first met Billy when he and Ruth visited my dad and June at their house in Jamaica. They were frequent visitors, and June christened one of the bedrooms "The Billy Graham Room." It was at the back of the house, with two beds and beautiful windows, and nobody ever stayed in that room without June saying, "Well, this is The Billy Graham Room."

I found Dr. Graham to be the most tolerant, nonjudgmental person of anyone that I've ever met. He was extremely kind, and he had what you would consider true Christian qualities of being openhearted, and loving. I always appreciated that in him. I never heard him say an unkind word about anything.

One time, my dad was playing in Las Vegas, and Billy and Ruth were there for a ministry event. It was kind of adorable because they just observed all the goings-on at the casinos with equanimity. They never judged it for a second. My stepsister Rosie and I were fifteen and eighteen—too young to gamble—but my father would give us money to go anyway, and then he'd pretend that he didn't know what we were going to do. Rosie and I would get all dressed up to go to the casino, and Billy and Ruth just giggled at us so tolerantly. It was very sweet.

My father's spiritual life did not fit into any religion. He had a lot more mysticism in him than fundamentalism. He and Dr. Graham had many discussions about theology and divinity, and I'm sure they spoke about the differences in their beliefs. My dad was a historian. He read Josephus, the first-century Jewish historian, as well as books about Christianity, from its early beginnings up to contemporary times. But regardless of their views about history and doctrine, where Billy and my father came together was through love—just a basic sense that love is the true Christian value.

Ruth was the same way, and she was just a doll. Ruth and Billy knew how to have fun—they weren't all about religion all the time. Billy was probably more singular in that way. I think it was just in the forefront of his thoughts all the time. But Ruth would go shopping with June and sit by the pool and play. They had a lot of fun together.

Like Billy, Ruth was just beautiful—openhearted, kind, and loving. You know, even if other Christians around her would say something judgmental about someone—she wouldn't join in. I never saw either one of them do anything negative at all. I wish more so-called Christians would pay attention to the way they lived.

I was in my teens and early twenties when I spent time with the Grahams. I thought they were a standard for what Christians should be. Getting to know them made me relax a little bit about religion, I think. I had been raised Catholic, but then I purposely left the Catholic Church and tried a lot of things. Although I don't ally myself with any specific religion, I was always a spiritual seeker, and I still am. And if Billy and Ruth represent Christianity, then I respect that. Billy didn't use fear to manipulate people, which happens a lot. I think people felt safe with him. They feel that he has some kind of divine connection, and that his essence is love and compassion. I think they are right.

·19·

BILL CLINTON

42nd President of the United States, founder of the Clinton Global Initiative and co-founder of The Clinton Bush Haiti Fund

For more than fifty years, including wonderful encounters and encouraging phone calls and letters when I was governor of Arkansas and after I left office, Billy Graham has blessed my life. But the story I like to tell best about Billy Graham happened when I was a twelve-year-old boy in Arkansas, and my Sunday school teacher drove me to Little Rock for Billy's 1958 crusade at the War Memorial Stadium. Schools in Little Rock were closed at the time due to the Central High School integration crisis, and racial tensions in the city were running high. Arguably because of these tensions, which they exacerbated, the White Citizens' Council suggested that Reverend Graham restrict the crusade to whites only. A lot of less radical whites agreed. But Billy refused. He said that all people deserved to hear God's Word and that, if he couldn't preach to everyone, he wouldn't preach at all.

So the crusade happened as Billy wanted it, with tens of thousands of people, black and white, pouring into the stadium where the Arkansas Razorbacks played. When Billy finished preaching and issued the call, inviting us to rededicate our lives to Christ, thousands, black and white together, some smiling, some crying, went down to the field to answer the call. It was a moment in Arkansas history after which nothing would be quite the same for those who were there and those who knew the stand Billy had taken. And Billy didn't have to preach one word about integrating the schools. All he had to speak was God's Word to all God's children. It may seem easy now, but back then, fifty years ago, it was an act of moral courage and deep faith.

At the time, I didn't fully understand it, but I felt it. After all we'd been through, I was thrilled to see an integrated crowd actually living their faith. I had been a Christian for only about three years then and was still questioning everything, trying to sort out what being a Christian really meant for my day-to-day living. Through Billy's example I began to see how faith was not just something to affirm on Sunday; it was something to be lived. Only a man who lived his faith could do what Billy did in Little Rock, could tell people in word and deed both to forgive those who sin and to love their neighbors. I was so moved by his stand that I decided to send him a little bit of money each month from my small allowance.

Another three decades would pass before I'd have the privilege of meeting and befriending Billy Graham. When I was governor, Billy came to Little Rock for another crusade, and we traveled together to visit my pastor, W.O. Vaught, who was dying of cancer. I'll never forget their conversation—about faith and fears, life and death. It was my first real glimpse of Billy the private man. He went to the home of my pastor and offered him comfort, saying that he too had lived a long life, and would see him again soon "just inside the Eastern Gate." He lived his faith when no one was looking.

This extraordinary kindness and concern has remained constant throughout the more than quarter century I've known Billy Graham. It remained true when he visited Hillary and me in the White House, just as he visited other presidents before and after me. And whether he was speaking to our nation after the terrible tragedy in Oklahoma City or speaking to me privately in the Oval Office, he embodied St. Paul's maxim that of all the virtues, faith, hope, and love abide, but the greatest of these is love. It can bring redemption, healing, and new beginnings.

The other lesson of Billy's that I've carried with me is the notion that living with faith requires a fair amount of humility. To be faithful we need to acknowledge what we don't know, admit our vulnerability to sin and errors. I guarantee that any person in power who's tried to live by this has found it easier said than done. Yet it's essential to the honest governance, constructive criticism, and principled compromise necessary to build a "more perfect union." When you recognize that no one has all the answers, you know you need to work with others to find solutions. *How* you work becomes as important as *what* you work on. For my part, I've tried to build my Foundation on the idea that we can bring very different people together to share their knowledge, experience, and resources to solve problems, knowing that in this life, perfection is impossible, but doing better is a moral responsibility.

When I think back to what the world looked like in 1958, when I first encountered Billy, I know Billy's crusade didn't abolish racism or the prevailing vestiges of segregation. But he showed us that by following our faith we would move the rock up the hill. The Scripture tells us that faith is "the assurance of things hoped for, the conviction of things unseen." That faith is Billy Graham's great gift to the world. He has given it to millions in public and only the Lord knows how many in private. I'm grateful I got to experience it both ways.

·20·

DOUG COE

As part of the National Prayer Breakfast family,
works with friends around the world, including political leaders,
who gather around the person and teachings of Jesus

I was just fourteen years old when I first heard Billy Graham speak in 1943 at a Youth for Christ rally at Waters Field in Salem, Oregon. After hearing Billy Graham preach, my mother wanted me to attend Northwestern Schools (now Northwestern College) in Minneapolis, where he served as president. She figured I could learn from the evangelist what it meant to be a man of God, but that didn't happen. I do recall, however, a special all-school convocation held in the fall of 1949 upon his return from his historic eight-week crusade in Los Angeles.

As I sat listening to the report and watching the films of people responding to Billy Graham's preaching, I was skeptical of both the person and the process. I was a mathematics and physics major, still trying to figure out faith in my head — not my heart — and I was a long way from being able to relate to his transformational message of God's love and forgiveness.

But through the providence of God our lives have intersected in many ways and on numerous occasions ever since: as a mentor, a partner, a brother, a great example, and a dear friend.

I first met Billy Graham personally in the early 1950s through Oregon Senator Mark Hatfield. The Senator and I had become close friends, having met Jesus together, and learning to pray and read the Scriptures together. Mark Hatfield loved and admired Billy Graham and always wanted to help him as much as he could. I then worked on a number of crusades, more deeply in the Portland, Oregon crusades where Senator Hatfield was greatly involved. I began to know Billy Graham more closely because of his friendship with Dawson Trotman, founder of the Navigators.

But it wasn't until I moved to Washington, D.C. in 1959 to begin my life's work with the National Prayer Breakfast family that I came to really know Billy Graham as a brother, and to observe and embrace his unique, inclusive perspective as ambassadors of Jesus Christ's love. Until that time, I thought the work of God was evangelism, but I soon realized that the only person I could evangelize and disciple was myself. I learned from Billy that the Gospel message isn't three or five "points," it's a Person—Jesus. He would also preach that God is love, and since Jesus is God, then the Gospel is also love.

Throughout his life, Billy was transparent and accessible to everyone. He loved all the sinners Jesus came for, and included himself in that group. He didn't have a judgmental spirit, but rather a supernatural love for anyone he met, regardless of their religious background, or none. And he was always fully present, focused and engaged with anyone—whether a President or Senator or a waiter or bellman at the hotel.

Billy also had openness to the study of Jesus. Even though his crusade outreach was always church-based, he worked hard to overcome the pressures and influences of religion. "The greatest need of the Church," he once told me in one of our many conversations, "is to set it back 2,000 years to the time of Jesus."

Billy kept growing in his understanding of Scripture. That put him way ahead of his time. He didn't preach about a Christian Jesus, but rather the universal message of Jesus of Nazareth, Who came for all mankind. He always spoke publicly and privately about "Jesus is the way, the truth and the life. Jesus is not *a* way, He is *the* way." He said, "It's not information about Jesus that's the way; Jesus Himself is the way, the truth, and the life."

When Billy started traveling the world, he found people who never had heard the word Christian, but whom he knew he would see in heaven because of their faith in, and relationship with, Jesus. Once, while singing "Jesus Loves Me" with a group of Chinese children at the Great Wall, an elderly man in his nineties came up to him with tears streaming down his face and said, "I've known Him all my life, but I didn't know His name."

Billy once told me, "I became born again as a teenager, attended a Bible school, graduated from a Christian college, served as a Christian pastor, was appointed president of a Christian university, and eventually answered the call to become a Christian evangelist. Eight years later, I finally met Jesus, in a new and more personal way."

What may sound like a distinction without a difference to some was vividly reinforced for me during Billy's 1994 crusade in Tokyo. I was traveling in India at the time, but read his farewell press conference. I was amazed.

A Japanese reporter asked, "Mr. Graham, Christian missionaries have been coming to Japan for 150 years, and you have just completed your second crusade here. Yet Christians represent less than .5 percent of our population. Is there something wrong with Christian religion or with the Japanese people, that they don't respond?"

Billy replied to her and all of the assembled media, "The

answer is clear. Most pastors, teachers, and missionaries have equated Christianity with Jesus—and there is a vast difference, you know."

Along with Senator Frank Carlson and Abraham Vereide, Billy had a major role in the founding of the National Prayer Breakfast in the early 1950s by encouraging President Eisenhower to attend the first of what has become an annual gathering. He was the main speaker at most of the first fifteen, and has said a prayer or read Scripture at many others.

Though renowned for his public evangelistic crusades, Billy was one of the few leaders I have known who had the vision and heart not only to equip laypersons, but as best as possible to turn the work over to them. In this he followed the example of John Wesley. Whenever he met with members of the House and Senate weekly prayer groups, and other leaders throughout the world, he would encourage them to give leadership by talking and thinking about Jesus, having genuine fellowship together, and praying together, without depending on a professional religious leader to do it.

One day, Billy was speaking about these prayer fellowships with Senator Sam Nunn, who exclaimed, "Billy, the Lord has used you to bring millions to faith in Jesus Christ and it is a privilege to partner with you."

Billy replied, "Senator, most of what you are saying is not true. I am thrilled to be used by God as an instrument, but if you as a layman would teach the Scriptures, it would be far more effective."

When Senator Nunn told Billy he was just being humble, the evangelist grabbed him by the lapels and pulled him close. "Senator, thousands of people already know what I am going to say," he said. "But millions want to know what you would say."

God has honored Billy Graham's faithfulness, through his

consistent focus on Jesus, his exemplary public and private humility reflecting the Spirit of the One he serves and in his empowerment of laypersons to do the work of evangelism. Just as chicken soup helps heal the body in times of physical illness, Billy's unfailing fidelity to his calling has enabled millions of individuals suffering from spiritual sickness to find nurturing for their soul. I don't think we will see another like him in our lifetime.

·21·

BOB COY

Pastor of Calvary Chapel Fort Lauderdale,
one of the largest evangelical churches in the U.S.,
and host of The Active Word *broadcast ministry*

I had never met Billy Graham before he agreed to ordain his grandson Stephan at our church, where he had been serving. Naturally, I was honored and thrilled, and when we got together in my office, I said, "Dr. Graham, if there's something that you'd like to share or anything you'd like to say beyond the ordination, I know our congregation would love to hear you speak."

He graciously replied, "Bob, I came here to hear you preach today." I felt so moved by his humility.

Whether Billy communicated with one person or a billion, he was always genuinely humble. In every encounter I had with Dr. Graham, his focus was fully on me. He had no thoughts for himself; it wasn't important how he was feeling. His only concern was for my needs. That's the heart of the Lord. The Lord is interested in where you are today, and I saw that concern in all my exchanges with Billy Graham. For instance, one time when I was at the Cove, the Billy Graham Training Center in Asheville, North Carolina, his grandson and I went to the house. He was ninety years old, but received us so warmly, remembered my wife's name and knew about the church, even though we had not met often. He was totally engaged.

Years ago, I had the privilege of taking part in a global outreach that Billy Graham was hosting in Puerto Rico. I was astounded by the enormity of the electronic system set up to transmit his preaching to a huge number of people, perhaps eventually a billion worldwide. It was a feat of technological genius. More importantly, just prior to the beginning of the crusade, I seized the opportunity to ask the president of the Billy Graham organization, "So who's going to be the next Billy Graham?" His answer was something I'll never forget. "The next Billy Graham won't be sitting in the seats watching Billy Graham. He's going to be reaching out to a homeless person, giving a glass of water to a thirsty child, or lovingly sharing God's forgiveness through His Son Jesus Christ," he explained. "He's going to be so occupied in doing the ministry that he's not even thinking about becoming the next Billy Graham."

Billy Graham changed the way that I live my life in a number of ways. He has been a tremendous role model for me, always remaining faithful to the Word of God, always using Bible stories, Bible references and Bible verses. The Modesto Manifesto also had a huge influence on me. The manifesto is a set of principles and agreements, rather than a physical document, that has been adopted by a large number of preachers and has become a template for how we operate here at Calvary Chapel.

By 1948, Billy Graham was becoming fairly well known as an evangelist in Protestant, fundamentalist and evangelical circles in the United States. He was receiving more and more invitations to hold citywide evangelist meetings. However, evangelism had gained a bad reputation with much of the general public, because of real and alleged misdeeds and corruption. During his November 1948 meetings in Modesto, California, Dr. Graham joined with his co-workers and friends, George Beverly Shea, Grady Wilson and Cliff Barrows, at the motel on South 9th Street where they were staying, to face these problems head on. They determined the most common criticisms of evangelists and developed working principles for their own missions, so their behavior would always be above reproach.

For one, they agreed to avoid even the appearance of financial abuse. The men vowed not to emphasize the monetary offering and to have the local campaign committees oversee the offerings and disbursements of funds. They would accept a straight salary regardless of how high the offerings were. Second, they promised to avoid even the appearance of any sexual impropriety. From that point on, Dr. Graham made it a point not to travel, meet or eat alone with any woman other than his wife. Since evangelists had gained a reputation for overestimating their congregations, the group also assented to being honest and reliable in their publicity and reporting of results. Finally, they knew that evangelists often criticized local pastors and churches from pulpits, and they vowed not to do this, or criticize pastors who openly criticized them.

When I visited Billy in 2004, he was bedridden, recovering from a physical setback. He had just watched the movie *The Passion of the Christ*, and was deeply excited about it, wondering how many people would see it and get energized about Jesus. He was eighty-five at that time and still full of zeal, something I saw many times through the years. He never lost his love or sense of burden for the lost or his hunger for the Word. It was always there.

We have a huge historical wall down one of our church's main hallways, and it includes photos of the day Billy Graham came to ordain his grandson. In one, I am looking up at him with an adoring face, as if to say, "Oh, my goodness, I can't believe the guy is here." A sconce light glows behind me, which makes it look like the light is illuminating my head while he is talking at the pulpit, which is in the shape of a cross. No one can miss the integrity and the passion in his heart, even in a photo. It suffused everything he did every day of his life.

·22·

JIM CYMBALA

Bestselling author and pastor of Brooklyn Tabernacle Church,
a multi-racial congregation with 10,000 members

I saw Billy Graham when I was growing up, and I heard him preach. Like millions of other people, I saw his integrity, his humility, his faithfulness to the Gospel. But I had never met him until the spring of 2012, when his grandson Will took me to see him. That meeting had a profound effect on me. I didn't say twenty words to him, but something happened that explained to me in one single sentence why God used him in such a profound way over all those years.

I had been invited by the Billy Graham Association to speak at some pastors' conferences and prayer rallies in four cities where Billy Graham's son, Franklin, was to go that summer. I went to Rochester and Buffalo, New York, and the Association let me minister as I saw fit. They wanted me to try to bless and encourage and unify the pastors and give an inspirational word.

A day after I had been to Buffalo and Rochester, I flew down to Asheville, North Carolina, where I was to be the speaker for a couple of days at the Billy Graham Training Center at the Cove. It was an honor for me to do that. While I was there, Will

Graham was my escort. I'd never met him before, but I knew that he was Franklin's oldest son, an evangelist in his own right, doing all kinds of things, keeping up the great, godly, blessed family line.

The first night I spoke, Will was in the front row. I noticed as I was speaking that he was taking notes, which sometimes people do. I sure hoped I would say something productive to bless him.

I preached from Mark 3 about how Jesus called His first disciples. Jesus called the twelve disciples to Him—just twelve. He had dozens, maybe hundreds of disciples. We know He had seventy others He sent out, but He appointed these twelve that they might be with Him and that He might send them out to preach and to have authority over evil spirits (Mark 3:14). My point was that the first calling on our lives as pastors and as Christians is that we might be with Him, not do anything, not preach, not write a book, not travel. The first thing the disciples were called to do was be with Him. That meant eating meals, walking on the roads, talking, unloading their hearts, listening to His words, many thousands and thousands of words that we don't have in the Bible. They were with Him for three and a half years.

We know Christianity is about relationship. That's what Dr. Graham has done all these decades, called people into relationship with Jesus Christ, to make Him their personal savior. But this was what relationship should lead to—intimate communion and fellowship with Christ.

The day after preaching that message, I was in the bookstore signing a new book I wrote called *Spirit Rising*. The Association was nice enough to say, "We're going to sell it. Would you autograph it?" There was a long line in the bookstore. Suddenly, Will came in and said, "You've got to leave now. Folks in the line, you go back. He'll get you later tonight." I said, "Will, these people have been waiting a long time." He replied, "No, Pastor Cymbala, you come with me. We've got to do stuff." So I said, "Okay, Will, you're running the show."

As we were walking out, Will said, "My dad thinks it's important and so does my grandpa. You've got to meet Grandpa Bill. You're representing us, and he wants to meet you." But knowing that Dr. Graham was somewhat failing and that his wife had passed away, I felt uncomfortable with the thought of bothering him. I said, "Will, I don't really feel like doing that." As much as I wanted to meet him, I felt it would be an imposition on him. I'm no one special to be meeting Dr. Graham. What if he was not having a good day? But Will was determined. "No, come on," he said.

We drove to Montreat. Inside the house a lunch and cake-cutting ceremony was in progress for a long-time employee. I think it was being held at the house because they wanted to bring Dr. Graham out of the bedroom so he could be around people, just to enliven his day.

I walked in with Will and a friend on my staff. We met everyone. Dr. Graham was in a wheelchair, sunglasses on, white hair. Next to him, also in a wheelchair, was George Bev Shea, who told me quickly, "Oh, I know who you are. Your wife's choir has sung with us. Tell her I'm still singing and I'm 103." It was surreal. I thought, Where am I? What's going on here? The man is 103 and he still wants to sing for Jesus. Dr. Graham was quiet.

After a while, Will thanked everyone and people started leaving. Eventually, I was left alone with Will and Dr. Graham. I said hello, but I felt awkward, so I didn't say much. I just sat in a chair next to him. I didn't want to bother him, and didn't feel like saying much beyond "Nice to meet you and let me get out of your way so you can get on with your day."

Will spoke very loudly so Dr. Graham could hear: "Daddy Bill, you know Pastor Cymbala is at the Cove speaking. He was up in Buffalo and Rochester helping Daddy with those events up there." Dr. Graham looked at me and said, "Thank you." I said it was an honor to do it. Will continued, "You know, Daddy Bill, Pastor Cymbala preached a message last night that really touched my heart. I needed to hear that message. That was an important message for me." Dr. Graham looked up and asked, "What did he speak on?" Now it was getting ridiculous. Will Graham is explaining to Billy Graham my message.

Will continued, "Well, he preached on our first calling, everyone, especially ministers' first calling." Dr. Graham looked up and said, "What's that?" Will continued, "He preached from Mark 3 and said that Jesus called the disciplines that they might be with Him, that He might send them out to preach and that they would have authority over evil spirits, but, see Grandpa Bill, he said the first calling—and I need to hear it as a young evangelist because I've got so many things happening—is to be with Him, not to preach, not to travel, just to be with Jesus. I needed to hear that, Grandpa Bill." Then came the words that explain everything. Dr. Graham's head bolted up and he said, with a broken voice, "No, I need to hear that, because I need more of Jesus, and I'm ninety-three years old."

He could have said, "Yeah, I know that. I can preach better than this man over here." He could have said a lot of things, but in his humility he said, "No, I need to hear that. I need more of Jesus." His words struck a deep chord within me.

After that, we left, and I contemplated those words of Dr. Graham's that were so full of meaning for me. In the ministry today, a lot of people think it's about them and the spotlight is not always on Jesus. Dr. Graham has been so different in that respect, and I realized that is why God used him, because he's small in his own eyes. It's like a surprise to him that God used him.

When you're conscious of Jesus it's very hard to walk around full of yourself. When we lose contact with Jesus and don't fellowship with Him our lives slide quickly into the flesh. Thank God that Dr. Graham has maintained that simplicity and humility. You'd see it even when he would preach. Sometimes his tie wouldn't have been tied the right way. The knot wasn't right. I would notice that and say, "He's sure not into a perfect image." It was rather, "Hey, I'm here to tell you about Jesus. So let me get to it." Amazing.

Dr. Graham was never a prince of preachers, a great orator. He was a simple man preaching from his heart. God blessed him and the Holy Spirit anointed him because he believed what John the Baptist said, speaking of Jesus: "I must decrease, and He must increase." For Dr. Graham, it's always been about Jesus.

·23·

JIM DALY

President of Focus on the Family ministry,
and host of its radio broadcast

Growing up in a broken home, I often found myself longing for a hero. My parents divorced when I was five. My mom was my rock, but she passed away when I was nine. Loneliness swept over me. There were days when I would have given anything to have a dad who kept his promises, but my father was tragically seized by the wicked grip of alcoholism. He passed away when I was twelve.

So, unable to find that bright light of hope and guidance within my own family, I turned my attention outward. It was the later part of the 1960s and several professional athletes grabbed my attention, as did the astronauts of the famed Apollo 11 moon landing. Yet through the 70s and 80s as I matured in both my faith and my professional interests, I began to admire from afar two giants of my day: California Governor Ronald Reagan and Dr. Billy Graham.

Little did I know at the time that they were dear friends and shared many of the same characteristics. Their history together was more than simply interesting to me. It was instructive.

At the time Dr. Billy Graham and Ronald Reagan first met in

1953, both men were rising stars, one in the pulpit and the other in a pseudo-political role. Mr. Reagan was on the verge of signing a lucrative deal as a corporate spokesman for General Electric, a move that would not only make him a good living, but also put him in everyone's living room for the next eight years. Still, Dr. Graham's future appeared even brighter. The great Los Angeles Crusade in the fall of 1949, held under a hot Ringling Brothers circus tent, had made Billy Graham a household name all across the nation. By the hundreds of thousands they were flocking to stadiums and arenas to hear his crisp and lilting Carolina drawl. With enthusiastic and robust evangelical fervor, the tall and lanky Graham was single-handedly sparking spiritual revival all throughout post-World War II America.

That first meeting was memorable for another reason. They met for the first time in Dallas to help raise funds for a retired film actor's home. On the dais with the two men was Dr. W.A. Criswell, the senior pastor of First Baptist Dallas, one of the country's largest and most influential Protestant congregations. The forty-four-year-old Criswell was known for strong opinions, both in and out of the pulpit. With Graham looking on, the Southern Baptist clergyman was true to form. Movies were of the devil, he told Reagan. Graham was incredulous. All the while, Mr Reagan listened politely. He then proceeded to share with Criswell his perspective on the upside to the movie industry and just how many good, wholesome films were being made out in Hollywood. To his credit, the fiery pastor absorbed the thoughtful response. When it was over, he spoke. "I'm going to start going to some movies," he replied. "And I'll tell my congregation that it's not a sin to see certain types of movies."

The incident greatly impressed Dr. Graham, who marveled at his new friend's keen ability to navigate cantankerous criticism. "Ron had not only changed a man's mind," he would later write, "but he had done it with charm, conviction, and humor — traits I would see repeatedly as I got to know him."

These same traits and shared interests pulled and kept the Reagans and Grahams close through the years. The close ties also put the evangelist in a tough spot when Mr. Reagan was running for president in 1980. Just prior to the Republican Convention, Dr. Graham crossed paths with Reagan during a trip through Indiana. The polls were tightening, and Mr. Reagan said he especially needed help in North Carolina, the Grahams' home state. Would Dr. Graham be willing to say a kind word about him? It was the first time he had ever asked for political help, and he was only doing so because it could very well make the difference in the race.

"Governor, I can't do that," the Reverend Graham told him. "You and I have been friends for a long time, and I have great confidence in you. I believe you're going to win the nomination and be elected president. But I think it would hurt us both, and certainly hurt my ministry, if I publicly endorsed any candidate."

Mr. Reagan said that he understood, though his aides appeared frustrated. Still, just like that, the tension between the two quickly faded.

This wasn't the first time Dr. Graham had been forced to navigate the confluence of politics and religion. Over the years it had become a predictable and, in many ways, unavoidable source of tension for the evangelist, and how could it not? To be sure he wasn't always entirely successful at steering clear of partisan activity. By his own admission he occasionally strayed too close for comfort. But when he did, he quickly adjusted and apologized. And in his course correction, Dr. Graham demonstrated strength of character: He bluntly and boldly admitted error.

For a man of his stature to be so candid and forthcoming about his own faults reflects a humble spirit as well as a confidence in the truth of the Gospel he so proudly and unapologetically has professed all these years. The church of Jesus Christ would be stronger if more of its leaders acknowledged their own weaknesses, echoing the words of the apostle Paul. "I will boast all the more gladly of my weaknesses," he wrote, "so that the power of Christ may rest upon me... For when I am weak, then I am strong" (2 Corinthians 12:7,9).

Now I am President of Focus on the Family and host of our daily radio show which reaches over 220 million people around the world, and I continue to thank God for the life and ministry of Dr. Billy Graham, a great man whom the Lord called to do even greater things. He has modeled God's truth with Christ's heart, inspiring and challenging millions all across the globe—this former orphan among them.

·24·

CHARLIE DANIELS

*Grammy Award-winning country music singer, guitarist and fiddler,
and member of the Grand Ole Opry*

I started hearing Billy Graham's name when I was just a child. He was preaching the Gospel of Jesus to a changing world entering the nuclear age, with all the inherent fears and rampant rumors that went along with it.

It was a strange and confusing time, just a few short years after the national nightmare of the Second World War and we were already facing a new enemy with a whole new vernacular like "Cold War" and "Iron Curtain," a belligerent, godless enemy who stared down a war-weary America and held on to vast territories in the Balkans and Eastern Europe.

For the first time, man had a weapon capable of destroying civilization.

America needed God and needed to be reminded of it.

Billy Graham preached with a fire, enthusiasm and common Gospel sense that touched the down deep part of man that nothing but the blood of Jesus can reach, and thousands came to accept salvation at his crusades.

In 1949, Mr. Graham held a crusade in a tent in a parking lot in Los Angeles and for reasons that are not completely clear, attracted the attention of media mogul William Randolph Hearst, who instructed his national chain of newspapers and magazines to promote Billy Graham.

The now legendary crusade ran for eight weeks and the rest of the nation learned what the people in the Southeast had known for some time. Billy Graham was here to stay and he was bringing the Gospel of Jesus Christ with him.

I've been performing for over sixty years, reaching the top of the charts, producing albums, writing for Elvis, playing at the Grand Ole Opry, and meeting many famous people that I admire, everyone from President George W. Bush to Bob Dylan. Yet I cannot name a public figure I respect more than Mr. Graham. When we received an invitation to play at a crusade, we were honored and accepted with gratitude and humility.

The night arrived, the choir sang, the invited speakers spoke, we did our songs and then it was time for him to speak.

Mr. Graham's message usually contains some humor, some acknowledgement of the area he's in and a few lighter statements, but no matter the preamble, he is always headed in the same direction, bringing the message of hope, forgiveness and love and explaining the simple process of making a decision to accept Jesus Christ.

To sit on that stage when the invitation is given and watch the first person come to the front, then the trickle, then the deluge, as thousands of people come down from the heights of a massive stadium to seek salvation, is a sight like no other I have ever experienced.

Billy Graham is a humble man. Though he has been spiritual advisor and confidant to several presidents, foreign dignitaries and international celebrities through the years, from his Western Carolina accent to his unpretentious manner, it's evident that he is still just "one of us."

I remember a night in Charlotte when the governors of North and South Carolina were there to present proclamations honoring their local boy, Mr. Graham was gracious as always in accepting, but quick to tell one and all, "This is not about Billy Graham."

He refused to let anything distract from the fact that he was on a mission to win souls—nothing else mattered, just the souls that would come forward to accept Jesus that night.

That's the laser-like focal point of this great man of God we call Billy Graham and this world is a much better place for having him pass through it.

I am much blessed for having known him.

·25·

DANIEL DE LEÓN

*Pastor of Templo Calvario, the largest Hispanic congregation in the
U.S. with seventy-five satellite churches*

Our church, the Templo Calvario in Santa Ana, California,
is one of the few Hispanic churches in America in which
Billy Graham has preached. In 1985, he came and preached to
our ministry. It was an incredible blessing for us and something
we'll never forget.

It all started when my wife Ruth and I were in Orlando,
Florida, where preparations were being made for the dedication
of a beautiful church edifice called Carpenter's Hall. We noticed
on a flyer the names of all the people who would be speaking and
ministering at the dedication, and it included some of the top
names in the nation. I remember my wife saying, "How come
God doesn't bless us with something extra special for our
dedication?" We were also building our new sanctuary at the
time.

Months passed, and then I received a call from England. It
was from one of Billy Graham's assistants, and he said, "Would
you like to have Billy in your church?"

That was an incredible moment. I can't even describe how I
felt, hearing that Dr. Graham was willing to come to our church.

Here we were, ministering to the Hispanic community in Santa Ana, a city that one study said was the hardest place to live in America when compared to others of similar size. It still has the highest number of gangs per capita in the entire United States. And Billy Graham, who was on his way to Southern California to conduct one of his famous crusades, decided to take the time to visit our little-known Hispanic church in Santa Ana.

A couple of weeks before Billy's visit not only the local police but also his crusade logistics people and maybe the FBI or some other agency came and checked out the facilities and the route he would take. It just impressed the daylights out of us, making us realize, if we didn't already know, that this was not just an ordinary preacher but a world figure, and that he was coming to our church!

The night before Billy's visit to our church, a special banquet was held for all the people who were part of the crusade. This was when we first met him. In the receiving line he was there with all his staff, and my wife and I were way back, maybe about 100th in line. Then a young lady came up to me and said, "Are you Pastor Dan de León?" I said, "Yes, I am." She said, "I just want to let you know that Dr. Graham has requested that you and your wife sit at his table."

We were floored. We couldn't believe it, but they took us up to the table. Ted Engstrom, head of World Vision, was there, and so was the president of the crusade and a couple other important people, and we were... well, who were we?

One thing Ruth and I noted, as Billy Graham conversed with the people at the table he would always make sure that he included all of us. He'd turn and look at each one of us as he was answering a question or making a comment or conversing. He would make sure that we were all included. What humility and graciousness. It impressed us very much that he was concerned about making everyone feel comfortable in his presence.

On the day of the actual dedication, there were local policemen scattered throughout the area he would pass through, which I am told is typical in any crusade city. They were on walkie-talkies... he was three minutes away... and two minutes away... and one minute away. And we were standing there like a bunch of kids gawking. I said, "My God, what a blessing it is for us that this man is coming."

You can imagine what it was like for our staff. We were all on our best behavior. People were just waiting and waiting, very patiently. The sanctuary was filled to capacity and then it overflowed. People were sitting everywhere, outside the doors, all over the place, waiting for Billy.

Finally he came in, and we had a receiving line for him. It was made up of just the church staff. Billy's organization wanted to make sure that we as a church were made to feel important, so there were no dignitaries or city officials there. It was just us. That's how they had planned it.

At the end of the line my wife Ruth stood with a Bible. We asked him if he would sign it, and he was very gracious in doing so. Then Ruth asked him, "Would you consider, Dr. Graham, taking a picture with our family? My boys are just going crazy; they want to take a picture." He said, "Of course." We took the pictures later, after Billy finished a news conference and turned to my wife and said, "Where are the boys? I want to take that picture!"

So we went and had the service, the very first at our new facility. The place was jam-packed. There was no room for anybody else. People from all races, people from the community, and of course the news media were there in numbers. We had been pushed for time in our preparations and didn't have the carpet on the floor yet. Nor did we have the lights set up, so we had to use temporary lights to light up the stage. Obviously, things were not yet where we wanted them to be, but Billy Graham didn't seem to mind anything. He just made everybody feel so welcome.

And he did so despite his own discomfort. Just a few weeks before his visit, Billy had fallen and broken two or three ribs, and his crusade staff weren't sure he would be able to make the trip. But he had said, "No, I want to be there, and I'm going to be there." He didn't speak for long—maybe twenty minutes. He was obviously in pain and he also had to conserve his energy for the crusade. But the fact that he fulfilled his commitment in spite of adversity showed the kind of man he is.

For my wife, Billy Graham's visit was the fulfillment of her prayer in Orlando, Florida, when she watched that grand ceremony at the dedication of the new church at Carpenter Hall and wondered, "Why can't we have a dignitary come and speak at our dedication?" The answer came when Billy Graham became the first preacher to speak at our new facility.

When Billy Graham came to our church, many people came up to me and asked, "Is he the head of the evangelical church?" Of course, that's not our tradition, and Billy would never make such a claim. But those questions showed how people viewed him, how significant Billy Graham was to them. Even today, some people can't believe that Billy Graham preached here. "Billy was at your church?" they say. And we proudly say, "Yes, he was."

A few years ago, I attended a special gathering, and Billy Graham was there. I went up to him and said, "Dr. Graham, do you remember visiting our church in California and speaking at our dedication?" He said, "Of course, I do. I would never forget it." We won't either. Our ministry is now the largest bilingual

Hispanic congregation in the country, with seventy-five satellite churches across the U.S. and Latin America. And Billy Graham is part of our church history. But he is also part of my history, and my family's history. We still hold dear that picture we took so long ago of him, my wife, and our three boys, and me, on that day when Billy Graham came to celebrate with us at the dedication of a little-known Hispanic church in Santa Ana, California.

·26·

RICH DeVOS

*Businessman, author, co-founder of Amway and owner of
the NBA Orlando Magic basketball team*

I have been fortunate to meet many times with my very good
friend Billy Graham and get to know him personally as a man
of great wisdom and deep conviction, integrity, a talent for
effectively raising funds to spread the Gospel, and, of course, a
gift of a preacher's voice that has reached millions of souls for
Christ.

Despite his hectic schedule and heavy demands, Billy has
always found time to share his wisdom with me in private talks
that I will always cherish. I remember one particular meeting
when Billy was in Edinburgh during a crusade, and I happened
to be in Scotland's capital at a hotel where Amway, the company
I started with Jay Van Andel in 1959, was holding an event. Billy
visited me at my hotel and suggested we meet for tea at "a nice
quiet spot where we can just sit and chat for a couple of hours."
We spent that special time discussing evangelizing people
worldwide, his methods versus other methods, how he raised
money, and many other things. I also shared my thoughts about
how the Amway business reaches out to new people and brings
them in. Billy listens, is open to ideas, considers and discusses.

He pays attention to details, which I believe is one of the reasons he has been so successful. Unlike some evangelists who simply want to preach to crowds, Billy takes great care with all the elements of his organization.

I also remember a meeting in my office when Billy was seeking financing for a worldwide evangelism program. As with many of his causes, I helped out because I knew him as a man of integrity. He wasn't afraid to ask for money and to raise money. He is totally easy to talk to and deal with. He's equally easy to say no to. Some fundraisers can almost make asking for money awkward—being pushy and making a potential donor feel guilty for not giving. Billy never makes anyone feel uncomfortable.

Billy is also smart enough to get really good people around him. Although he has played a role in fundraising, he never touched the money he raised. No one could question that money was sidetracked or going into Billy Graham's pocket. Billy was smart enough to keep fundraising and fund management separate. He just received a salary. He set a new standard that way. He has always lived simply and humbly before the Lord.

Billy used to hold crusades in my hometown of Grand Rapids, which is a religious community where he had successful events. He once spoke in my town at a reception for President Gerald Ford, who also was from Grand Rapids. The reception was a big event for a lot of our friends, who were thrilled to meet Billy and shake his hand. President Ford highly respected Billy and was equally easy to chat with and be a friend to.

Like so many people, I also am captivated by Billy's preaching voice. In person, Billy speaks quietly in a soft voice, but his preaching style reveals his extremely powerful, but still very pleasing, voice. A voice like Billy's is a gift from God—sweet, strong, warm and enriched by that North Carolina twang.

Billy's voice, his style and his conviction all make him a

compelling preacher. He believes in his message and wants to deliver it to you without pushing it at you. His goal is for people to meet Jesus, but he wants his listeners to be the ones who make the decision. And that's why he is a great preacher. He makes it easy for people to listen to him.

Billy is a very wise man in all that he does. He is what you would call a good old southern preacher—a great guy and a man of integrity. Everybody loves him, and it's been my privilege to know him over the years.

·27·

E. ROLLAND DICKSON, M.D.

Emeritus Professor of Medicine, Mayo Clinic;
personal physician of Mr. Graham

Doctor Graham and I first met thirty years ago at the Mayo Clinic in Rochester, Minnesota, when his physician at that time, Dr. Carl Morlock, transferred responsibility for Billy to me. That turned out to be one of the greatest gifts anyone has ever given me! While I served as Billy's physician, we also became close friends. In fact, I consider him one of my best friends.

Taking care of Billy's health has been a tremendous privilege and, at times, a bit of a challenge. I recognized how important he is to so many people and I felt responsible for providing the best care possible. I have valued both aspects of our special relationship; serving as his personal physician and enjoying the depth and treasure of our unique friendship.

Billy is genuine. He often visited in our home and with my family. On some occasions he would come into the living room, stretch out his six-foot two-inch frame, take off his shoes, and sit on the floor with my two sons, Mark and Rolland. He was completely open with them and allowed them to ask him questions that, at first, I thought might be a little uncomfortable.

They talked openly about everything from girls to drugs, smoking, and alcohol.

Billy's authenticity is real and young people recognize this quality even more than adults. Billy's visits became important to my sons and they often asked to bring their friends when he planned a trip to Rochester.

The influence and intimacy of Billy's relationship with our family was made clear by an event that took place when Mark was in eighth grade. He came home one day with a bruise on his cheek, bringing with him his good friend, Rocky. Some classmates had made fun of Rocky for wearing a cross necklace. Mark and Rocky had gotten into a fight defending this symbol of his faith and Mark was concerned about how Dr. Graham would view fighting and wondered if he would be disappointed in them.

I replied, "No, you were standing up for something you believed in and Billy would have approved of that."

I was blessed to have known Billy's children and his late wife, Ruth. Billy and Ruth adored each other and were a wonderful match. They met in college and I think Ruth is the only woman that Billy ever truly loved. She was warm, talented, gracious, and beautiful.

We have wonderful memories of visiting Ruth and Billy in their Montreat, North Carolina home. Because Billy loved the apple pies my mother-in-law baked, we made it a point to bring one with us whenever we visited their home. During our stay, I routinely would review his medical status and then share time just talking. We both appreciated this special time together and consider the hours a memorable blessing to both of us.

When my wife, Susan, and I visited him a few years ago, we found him sitting on the front porch of their beautiful, log cabin-style home. It sits at the top of a small mountain at the end of a long, winding single-lane road that is not easy to navigate. When he was young, Billy ran up and down the road for exercise. He was a good athlete and in excellent physical condition most of his adult life. I told Billy that I worried a little about the house's remote location, but he said he would never leave. It was "their home" and he loved it!

Whenever I arrive and depart, he has a special prayer with me. He also has written me letters that I will always cherish. I have kept them all in two three-ring notebooks. People often ask each other what they would save in case of a fire. I would save some pictures and the notebooks with Billy's letters to me.

Billy is always modest and unassuming. As he headed out to a ballgame in Florida once, he told me, "Rollie, I'm going to wear a baseball hat and sunglasses and nobody will recognize me."

I responded, "Are you serious? Billy, everyone will know who you are, so just be prepared for that." Despite being one of the most visible, recognizable people in the world, he was modestly convinced that the baseball cap and sunglasses would assure that no one would recognize him.

Speaking of being recognized, wherever he went, he was always generous with his time and willing to speak with anyone. People would approach him and ask, "May I just shake hands with you?" or "Would you sign my Bible?" and he would give his undivided attention to each of them. Often, when we would go out for dinner, people would stop and comment, "You've changed my life" or "You've been an inspiration." He was never irritated or impatient. I, on the other hand, would be impatient to sit down and start dinner while Billy would continue visiting, graciously sharing himself with others. He is a true celebrity who never thinks of himself as a celebrity.

Another example of his lack of self-importance. My wife, Susan, and I were attending one of Billy's crusades at the Coliseum in Los Angeles. We were seated with his wife, Ruth, and shortly before Billy was scheduled to deliver his address, we were notified that Dr. Graham would like to see us. They put us in a golf cart and whisked us down to an area underneath the stadium where Billy was sitting quietly. He welcomed us with a big hug.

When we sat down, I looked at my watch and said, "Billy, we don't want to stay too long." He inquired, "Why not?" I answered, "You're on in seven or eight minutes." "Oh, but I'm enjoying this," he explained. I was looking at my watch, nervously thinking that he had to be on the podium preaching to 120,000 people in only minutes but, for that moment, he was just happy to see us.

One of the things I have found most impressive about Billy is his acceptance of everyone, irrespective of race, nationality, or religious beliefs. He was one of the first individuals to make his religious events open to people of all races and all nationalities. He was an early supporter of the civil rights movement and desegregation.

Mayo Clinic has a broad network of patients and visitors from around the world, from royalty, heads of state and Hollywood celebrities to ordinary, everyday people. As a Mayo physician, I have had the privilege of meeting and serving a wide and diversified number of individuals. However, I have never met anyone who has been such an inspiration and the source of hope to millions of people around the world.

Billy Graham's message is simple and straightforward: "God loves you." He is the most Christ-like person I have ever known.

·28·

TIMOTHY MICHAEL CARDINAL DOLAN

Archbishop of New York

It's tough to get a private audience with the Pope...
In the happy years I worked for the Vatican Embassy in Washington D.C., we'd get dozens of requests for such an honor every day, from political leaders, government officials, and movers-and-shakers from business, communication, military, and ecumenical endeavors.

We took them all seriously before we passed them on to Rome. The word was out that Pope John Paul II enjoyed meeting people from all over the world, Catholic or not, so we were trying to do our best.

However—unless you were the President—our reply was always the same: no private audience can ever be guaranteed. You tell us when you plan to be in Rome, and where you can be reached; then we'll pass on the request to the appointments people who will let you know the day before if an audience is possible. No exceptions... Except one! Guess who?

Dr. Billy Graham was going to be in Geneva for four days of

meetings. Through us in D.C. he requested a private audience with Pope John Paul II.

Same reply from us: "Thank you, Dr. Graham. Happy to help. Tell us when you plan to be in Rome, and where the papal offices can reach you, and you'll hear if and when the audience can be granted when you're in Rome!"

Came back a courteous response: "Thank you. But, Rome is not on Dr. Graham's itinerary. He would fly from Geneva to Rome once you can let him know if and when His Holiness can receive him."

Uh oh! Now what? We were under strict instructions that the protocol was not to be broken except for heads of state. This could be embarrassing....

We sent it over anyway, by cable, and held our breath. Within two hours the wire came back from the Holy Father's private priest secretary: "The Holy Father would be delighted to meet with Reverend Graham. What day would be most convenient?"

We could hardly believe it! We checked for a misprint. We had never seen this before!

Blessed John Paul II knew what the rest of the world knows: Billy Graham is one of the most beloved and effective preachers of the Gospel since St. Paul. (Which, by the way, is what Dr. Graham remarked about the Pope when he died in 2005.)

I had the honor of meeting him only once, in company with a dozen or so seminarians. One of the future priests blurted out, "Dr. Graham, any advice for us?" The famed preacher replied, "Never, ever say anything without mentioning the Name of Jesus!"

In that spirit, recalling Reverend Graham's life with awe and gratitude, I'll borrow Blessed John Paul II's favorite saying: "May Jesus Christ be praised!"

·29·

TONY DUNGY

NFL Super Bowl Champion coach, *bestselling author,*
NBC Sunday Night Football *analyst*

In 1998 I was coaching the Tampa Bay Buccaneers. Our new Raymond James Stadium had just been built, and it was a fantastic thing for the city and for the team. But the first event we had in the new stadium wasn't a football game. It was a crusade, and we were very excited to have Dr. Graham coming.

The stadium was filled to the brim and it was a really exciting day all around. I had been involved in the organization of the crusade and that day I had the privilege of introducing Dr. Graham on the stage. I'd met him a couple of other times, briefly, but I had never before been able to spend time with him.

Dr. Graham delivered his typical, simple Gospel message. He just put it all in a nutshell and presented it so clearly. Then he asked people, "If you have heard this message and it has touched your heart and you want to respond, come down."

It was like being at a game when the game had just ended. Everyone got up. It was amazing to sit there and watch and see the upper decks totally emptying and people coming down onto the field. It was one of the greatest thrills of my life.

I think the reason so many people came down was partly due

to the preparation and the prayer that went into the crusades, and partly the simplicity of Dr. Graham's message. It was plain but very vivid and he was so sincere. The message was, if you want to be redeemed, if you want to be helped, now is the time.

I'm used to altar calls at the church in which one person will stand up and then another person will come, but I had never experienced anything on this scale. This was a mass movement. Everyone came at the same time, everyone responded, and to see it from the stage, on the field, looking all around in this big new stadium, was just breathtaking.

For myself, I feel the Lord has given me a different kind of platform, but in many ways I try to do a similar thing. When you are involved in professional sports such as the NFL, people know who you are, and you can get large audiences. I've done press conferences with thousands of people watching and accepted a Super Bowl trophy with an audience of over 100 million people. I never expected to have that kind of audience for anything that I did, but it was there, so how was I going to use it? How was I going to let my light shine so people could see that what was really important to me was serving the Lord?

There is a verse in the Bible that says, "Whatever you do, do all to the glory of God," so I looked at it that way. I didn't separate my sports career from who I was. Who I am and what I do is much the same thing. When I was coaching I told a lot of Bible stories. We'd be talking about a situation and I would say, "This reminds me of something that happened in the Bible," or "This is how Jesus handled this type of situation." I definitely let my team know where I was spiritually. I didn't expect them all to have the same beliefs as I did but I thought that a lot of the examples could help us, and they did.

Growing up in a small town I never imagined I would meet the people I have been privileged to meet through the NFL, including Presidents—Clinton, Bush, and Obama. It's been exciting. I'm particularly grateful to Dr. Graham for his continual inspiration over the years. He was so impactful and effective, and his message changed so many lives for the better.

I have also been privileged to meet some of Dr. Graham's family members. Clyde Christensen, an assistant coach on my staff, went to the University of North Carolina and got to know the family well. It was Clyde who introduced me to Anne Graham Lotz and her husband Danny, and to some of the Graham children. Clyde always talked about Dr. Graham's simplicity and his humanness, how down to earth and genuine he is, and that is what has struck me in the times I have been around him. It's like going to visit your uncle.

I really feel Dr. Graham has a calling. There are people in the Bible whom God touched and used to spread His message, and I think Dr. Graham is one of them. Paul had that gift, and so did John the Baptist, as well as others. I put Dr. Graham in that category of people who had the right words and the right personality and the right spirit that enabled them to have a real impact on so many different kinds of audiences.

·30·

GERALD DURLEY

Civil rights leader, pastor emeritus of Providence Missionary Baptist Church, Atlanta, Georgia; NAACP Board Member

I have not been a lifetime follower of Dr. Billy Graham. As an African-American man who participated in the civil rights movement, my perspective of Dr. Graham was quite different. I moved from Colorado in 1960 to attend college in Nashville. This was during the era of segregation in the South where African-American people lived under oppressive racism. It was a time when people like city official Bull Connor unleashed fire hoses and attack dogs on peaceful demonstrators in Birmingham. Sheriff Jim Clark sent a posse of mounted police to beat a crowd of unarmed peaceful marchers at the Edmund Pettus Bridge on the outskirts of Selma. One of those brave "Bloody Sunday" marchers was John Lewis, who was hospitalized with a fractured skull and eventually went on to become a U.S. Congressman from Georgia, and who, like me, praises Billy Graham in the pages of this book.

In Nashville, during those days, there were people who prayed to God during the day and lynched people at night. For years I was skeptical about the Billy Graham Crusades, because their message was conspicuously silent on the atrocities against God's people. African Americans had their own needs in the South, and my personal thinking about the crusades was that they went into a city and put on the crusade like a grand concert, and then they were gone. Nothing changed for *faith-filled* believing African Americans. The crusades didn't make a difference to the city, the racial and economic conditions didn't change, nor did anything else related to the plight and souls of Black people. We were fighting for voting rights, and this Graham movement—as I saw it at the time—was "just about saving the soul," not the changing of the attitudes of those who oppressed Black Americans.

Many years later, in 1994, the Billy Graham Evangelistic Association planned to conduct a crusade in Atlanta. Their frontrunners met with me to discuss the anticipated crusade. I was a dean at Clark Atlanta University at the time, and I was also the pastor of Providence Missionary Baptist Church. I challenged the Graham crusade organizers as to what they wanted to accomplish. I was not an easy convert to assisting in this endeavor since I did not feel the sincerity of the group for addressing African Americans' concerns.

I expressed to the planners my view about the crusades coming and going without making a significant racial, social, or economic contribution to the city. They said, "We want to have a lasting impact on the total lives of those we are called to serve. If we come to Atlanta, we are not coming just as a white-Christian, evangelical movement. We're here to reach all of the people in the cradle and melting pot of the civil rights movement."

I continued to remain skeptical. My attitude was, "Whoa, prove it to *me!*"

A few months later I met Dr. Billy Graham. He was graciously taking the time to meet with people, to address their personal concerns, and spiritual issues. When I initially met him, I felt his strong physical presence. He was tall. His eyes were piercing. His jaw was set. His handshake was firm. His eyebrows were bushy, his smile disarming, his voice captivating, and his message genuine.

He said, "Hello, how are you? I've heard so much about you." I shook hands with him and he said, "We need your help to complete God's mission here in Atlanta. We want to include all races and cultures. Can we depend on you for your support?"

I was completely disarmed, and all of a sudden, I felt like putty in his hands. I was literally mesmerized by his godly sincerity. I was ready to work for God through Dr. Graham to improve the lives of people in Atlanta, Georgia.

The important characteristic about Dr. Graham personally was his unassuming demeanor. He never tried to impress me. He did not act like a man who expected to be treated in a special way just because he had traveled all over the world and was world famous. His attitude was, *I'm a servant of God, here to do what I can, and I would like us to work together. I'm not coming to your city to tell you what you should do. I am coming to learn and to work along with you and your ministries here for the cause of Christ.*

He shared from his heart what he wanted to happen in the birthplace of the civil rights movement. It was a very genuine and transparent revelation and changed my life forever. He commented, "This is something that I feel the Lord has laid on my heart. What we want to share is not only important here in Atlanta, but all over the world, and for all of God's people."

These were simple, yet profound, words. Dr. Graham was doing what God had placed in his heart and mind to do. It was now up to me to decide how I could be of assistance in sharing the Word of God.

Looking back on the first meeting that I had with Dr. Graham, it was one of those *kairos* moments when you have certain preconceptions in your mind about an individual or an organization—then you meet the person and they are totally different. Immediately, I thought to myself, *Wait a minute! I have believed and accepted some of the myths and misperceptions about this man and these crusades, just as some people had the wrong perceptions about those of us in the civil rights movement. Back then many wrongly stated that we were trying to disrupt "the system" when in reality all we were seeking was "justice for all."*

After meeting with Dr. Graham, I got involved in the Atlanta Crusade of 1994. I was put in charge of what was called the Love in Action Committee. As preparations got underway, I called a group of African-American ministers together in Atlanta. I brought them together to meet with Dr. Graham, since he requested inclusivity.

Dr. Graham and his team went to a church that was one of the larger congregations in Atlanta. The minister there, whom I knew, was the administrator for hundreds of churches throughout Georgia, as well as the pastor of his own congregation. He was somewhat skeptical about the prospect of a Billy Graham crusade, because of the perception of the BGEA's insensitive nature to the plight of Black Americans.

As I sat there with Dr. Graham in the waiting room of the church, I was struck by the oddness of the situation. I thought, *Dr. Billy Graham is patiently waiting for an African-American pastor to invite him in to a meeting.*

While we were waiting, one of the secretaries asked, "Would you like some water?" Dr. Graham replied, "I would appreciate that very much." I was deeply impressed, because he was so genuine and profoundly appreciative.

Thirty minutes passed and Dr. Graham never became impatient. Finally, when we entered the pastor's office, the introductions were made, and we laughed and talked for more than an hour. Just before we left, the pastor said to Dr. Graham,

"Will you please forgive me for your having to wait? I had an emergency." And then this minister, who had been so unenthusiastic about the crusade, and who had kept Dr. Graham unexpectedly waiting, walked Dr. Graham to his car and pledged the support of his entire network of pastors to assure the success of the crusade. Dr. Graham had all of us on his team and he never disrespected any of us.

That same minister, the skeptical one, became one of the major motivators for the entire crusade. He became one of the most influential organizers. He even canceled the revival he had planned at his own church, and encouraged everyone from around the state to come to the Georgia Dome. He was there every night, sitting with us on the stage.

There was one remarkable situation that I observed during the crusade here in Atlanta. I did not know that Dr. Graham was experiencing some minor physical challenges. At times, he would twitch. I was in the group with him just before he came out to speak, and I noticed that he was visibly shaking, and somewhat unsteady. However, when he approached the podium, I could see the apparent empowering of God take over his entire body and dominate his voice. He was powerful, strong and resolute each night as he shared God's Word. True to his word, Atlanta was changed.

When Dr. Graham stood at the pulpit preaching, he did not shake at all. He spoke adroitly, he spoke forcefully. His hands did not shake; his mouth did not quiver; and his eyes were like an eagle's eyes piercing the crowd. He gave life to those who were around him, and all those gathered in the Georgia Dome.

When he finished preaching, I could see once again that he was physically challenged; however to this day I am amazed how God used him to preach and profess His Word boldly. The only explanation I can give to this phenomenon is that he is an anointed servant of the Lord who gave his message life — it came through him, and was so powerful that it enabled him, in those moments, to overcome the physical challenges of his body and bless thousands.

I discovered one more valuable detail during the immediate aftermath of the crusade message — *that what the crusade had promised was true.* They did not just come into a city, preach and leave it unchanged. After the crusade, the Billy Graham organization bought, for the City of Atlanta, a mobile health unit, which would go into poor areas and provide medical screening to the least, the lost and the left behind. That medical unit is still in service to the poor today. Dr. Graham's crusade did not just pay lip service to the idea of leaving something with the community. It actually did it.

I accepted the truth and reality that Dr. Graham changed the internal spiritual nature of all those who listened, believed, and came forth regardless of color. Many people were changed when the crusade concluded. I had a different perspective of Dr. Graham. I viewed him as a man who remained true to his calling, because not everyone does. There are evangelists who are more engaged in politics than religion and a few who seem to become larger than God's Word. Dr. Graham always kept the appropriate perspective of his relationship with God intact — that's the secret formula for Dr. Graham's longevity for success, *his right relationship with God.*

When you are with Dr. Graham you realize that you are in the presence of a man who knows God but does not pretend to be God. This is at the heart of what the Billy Graham Crusades are about. My experience with him was that he was transparent and honest to his calling. He never became larger than that which God called him to be. My working for the crusade in Atlanta paved the way for my ministry to touch the lives of all of God's children regardless of race, creed, or faith.

To this day, nearly two decades later, one would be hard pressed to find any of us, here in Atlanta, who would have a negative word to utter about Dr. Billy Graham. Doubters we may have been, but during that crusade, he won us over and we, Atlanta, and the world are better.

Thank you, Dr. Billy Graham.

·31·

YECHIEL ECKSTEIN

Rabbi, founder and president of the International Fellowship
of Christians and Jews

Thirty-five years ago, as a young Orthodox rabbi, I started the first Evangelical Christian-Jewish dialogues. Together with the Bible Chair at Wheaton College, which was Dr. Graham's alma mater, and the Dean from Trinity Evangelical Divinity School, we put together the first Evangelical-Jewish conference. More conferences followed, and before I knew it, it had become my career, my ministry, and my mission. Today we have 1.1 million Christian donors to our ministry. We raised $120 million from Christians, and we have offices of the International Fellowship of Christians and Jews around the world. We work with all segments of the evangelical community, including Pentecostals, Charismatics, Fundamentalists, and Southern Baptists.

I see Dr. Graham's greatness in terms of the Jewish community in two ways. First, he came to represent the face of a more open, moderate Evangelicalism not just to the Jewish community but to America and the world. As Dr. Graham receded from the public scene, his role as the face of Evangelicalism was taken over by other increasingly popular television evangelists who did not always share this message of inclusiveness. As a result, whatever positive impression of Evangelicalism that Jews and others had received from the image of Billy Graham was put into question by the some of the more strident fundamentalists and politically conservative Evangelicals. Billy Graham was overtaken by that change, and the image of Evangelicals in the public sphere and among the Jewish community became different.

Second, Dr. Graham was one of the first people, at least in America, to start to turn Evangelicals toward a favorable view of Israel. Billy Graham, who was Mr. Evangelical for the world and the Jewish community, was very friendly toward the nation of Israel. Later, as Evangelicalism embraced a more political role, championed by such figures as the Moral Majority's Jerry Falwell, the Christian Coalition's Ralph Reed, and the Southern Baptist Convention's Paige Patterson, it gave rise to the Christian Zionism of Pastor John Hagee. But I attribute the American evangelical movement's turn toward support of Israel to the favorable place that Billy Graham gave the Jewish people. This was very similar to what Dr. Martin Luther King, Jr. achieved in terms of the stance of the African-American community toward Israel, noting that there's an inherent closeness theologically and spiritually with Israel.

I'm not sure whether the Christian Zionism of the late nineteenth century would have emerged if Billy Graham had been anti-Israel, or anti-Jewish. He was pro-Israel in a deeply spiritual way, choosing not to get involved in the strong political activism that characterized Christian Zionism. But he opened the door for that next generation of Evangelicals to adopt a passionate embrace of the Jewish nation.

A few years ago, I brought a group of leaders to the White House just to talk about Israel. That would not have happened during Billy Graham's time. But on the other hand, it might not have happened at all had he not in those earlier years pointed toward reconciliation with the Jewish people and Israel. It's not that he gave pro-Israel sermons or anything like that. He would not have gone to the White House to plead, say, against F-16 fighter planes being sold to Israel's adversary, Saudi Arabia, but on the other hand it was no secret that he was friendly to Israel.

Dr. Graham established a dialogue with the Jewish community, even though his commitment to evangelism was absolute. That was a unique quality that led to the dialogues that I was able to start. It is interesting that I started these dialogues at Wheaton College, where Dr. Graham went to school. Initially, the college was very circumspect about hosting interfaith Christian-Jewish dialogues. At the time, Wheaton officials did not even want the press to know about it. But they were open to it because Billy Graham was seen as a friend of the Jews and a friend of Israel.

Dr. Graham's mission was not to develop a theology to deal with the conflict between the commitment to evangelize the world and the Jewish absolute commitment to remain as Jews. He just naturally knew this was possible, often insisting that you can't be anti-Semitic and claim that you are a good Christian. Over the years, I have worked to develop my own theology that reconciles the Christian's commitment to the Christian message with a respect that supports the decision of those who wish to embrace their own path. But I couldn't have done this without the ground that Dr. Graham had already covered. He never compromised on his absolute commitment to Evangelical Christianity but somehow he was able to handle the delicate question that every reporter and news show asked him, about whether Jews are saved: *If you believe that Christ died for our sins, what about the people in the Holocaust? Are they going to hell?* He was the first who was able to be nonjudgmental but at the same time to be committed absolutely to his evangelical mission. This enabled him to be friends with the Jewish community.

Seen in this light, it was Dr. Graham who established a beachhead that led to further dialogue between Jews and Evangelicals over the past thirty years. There are others who have assumed much of that role, urging all believers to respect one another. But today there is no one who fills Billy Graham's former role as the worldwide face of Evangelicalism.

As a leader in the Evangelical-Jewish movement for reconciliation, and Goodwill Ambassador for the State of Israel, I have spent thirty-five years trying to achieve many of the same goals that Dr. Graham has worked to accomplish. He was the father of that whole movement in America that has been able to bring faith into the public square uncompromisingly but in a sensitive, tolerant and modern way. I would have liked to work with him personally, but nevertheless, through his work I see the heart of this great man.

·32·

PHIL EHART

Co-founder, drummer and manager of the rock band KANSAS,
creators of the classic hits "Dust in the Wind" and
"Carry on Wayward Son"

What could the Reverend Billy Graham and a drummer in a rock band possibly have in common?

Though I've never had the honor of meeting Dr. Graham, he was definitely in my life as a young man growing up. I remember his sermons on the television, his many books around our house, and the distinct sound of George Beverly Shea singing "How Great Thou Art." My parents even sang in the choir at one of Dr. Graham's crusades. So at an early age, and into young adulthood, Reverend Graham had planted the lessons of God and the Bible in my soul.

It was at this time that the band KANSAS, a band that I help start in Topeka, Kansas in the early 1970s, was beginning to see success on a national level. We had signed a recording contract with music mogul Don Kirshner and released our first album in 1974. We went on tour from Topeka to open for bands like The Kinks, Queen, Bad Company, the Eagles, and KISS. It was an incredible time for a group of six small town young men from Kansas!

As we continued to tour, our fame increased and radio airplay on the FM stations around the country was building a solid fan base for the band. In 1976 we released an album called *Leftoverture* that contained a song called "Carry On Wayward Son." This song shot up the charts on pop radio and became a huge hit for the band around the country, and the world. We became headliners in many venues in the U.S.

Success with the band did not slow down. In 1977 we released an album entitled *Point of Know Return* that contained two more hit songs, including the title track "Point of Know Return" and the acoustic smash hit "Dust in the Wind." The band was now selling out 20,000-seat arenas everywhere. Our time had come!

With all this success, drugs and alcohol were everywhere in the music business and in the 1970s culture in general.

But through all this success and craziness, I chose to do no drugs and drink no alcohol. It went all the way back to my days in high school and playing in bands then.... I drank no alcohol and did no drugs... ever. But why? Why did I make that choice? To be perfectly clear, I was a sinner, but I never looked down on anyone who drank and did drugs. I never sat in judgment of them. In fact, I really never gave it much thought! I just chose not to partake! But I didn't know why I made those choices! It's not like I had some personal abstinence agenda that I was pushing on everyone! Why, through all those years, did I choose to do no drugs and to never have a drink?

As the years went on, our popularity started to wane, and the band started to lose members, with different incarnations of KANSAS starting to appear in the 80s, 90s and 2000s.

It was at this time that my wife Laurie was having a discussion one day with my mom, Martha. Laurie had mentioned to my mom that so many people found it so odd that through all the years of playing in a world famous rock band, that I had never succumbed to the music business pressures of drinking and doing drugs. My mom didn't miss a beat. She said, "Laurie, when Phil first started playing in bands, I went to my knees every night and asked the good Lord above to protect him from those pressures around him. I asked the Lord to please never let the world tempt Phil with drugs and alcohol or influence him in a sinful manner. I knew Phil had Jesus in his heart and would be okay... it was those in the music business that I was worried about!"

When Laurie came in and told me what my mom had said, it hit me like a freight train! IT WAS THE PRAYERS OF MY MOTHER! All these years people had been giving me the credit for abstaining from drugs and alcohol, but I knew down deep that I did not deserve the accolades. I wasn't that different from those around me, but the answered prayers of my mother made me different!

Over the next few days, I started to think back through all the many years, and never once, not once, could I recall anyone ever offering me a beer or mixed drink. No one ever offered me a joint or a hit of acid, or any cocaine. Never. Not once! The answered prayers of my mom!

And now, as the band's fortieth anniversary comes in 2013, I'm sitting here, humbly writing about how Dr. Graham touched my mom's life in those early crusades, and she in turn touched my life, in so many ways. And I'll try to pass on to my kids the lessons planted in me so many years ago, by Dr. Billy Graham.

·33·

JEAN FORD

Sister of Mr. Graham

There were four of us siblings growing up together. Billy is the oldest, and I'm the youngest. I also had a sister and another brother. It was a strong Christian home where every night at eight o'clock everything stopped and we had Bible reading and prayer.

As long as I can remember, Billy was interested in preaching. When he made a commitment of his life to God he was seventeen years old, which meant I was three or four. So as long as I can remember, he has had this commitment.

Billy worked in the dairy farm but he did not like that kind of work, unlike my other brother Melvin, who loved it. Melvin later took over the dairy farm and went on to become a very successful businessman. Billy, on the other hand, wanted to read. He read everything he could get his hands on. I remember him sitting in the living room biting his fingernails, reading.

Billy has always been there for me. He's always been a big brother. It's understandable that I should think of him in that way, given the age difference, but it was more than that.

I think of one particular incident involving Billy early in my life that still touches my heart, all these years later. It happened when I was eleven years old. I had polio. Polio was a common disease in those days, especially for children, and it could have devastating consequences. Billy and Ruth had left Charlotte only a short while prior, and they were in Chicago, where Billy had a little church. But as soon as they heard I had polio they got in the car and drove straight back down here. And that was a long drive back in those days, before the Interstate highways were built. When they arrived back home I was in quarantine so I couldn't see him, but his actions at that time made such a statement to me. It showed how much he cared. It turned out later that at the time they were fearful that I would not survive.

I have of course many other memories of Billy. I participated in his wedding to Ruth. That was sixty-nine years ago, and I doubt whether anyone else who was in it, other than Billy, is still alive. Billy and Ruth were married on Friday the 13th, and Ruth said that just as she walked up the steps of the church, a black cat ran across her path. But so much for superstition—they had a wonderful marriage! Ruth was a very strong woman. She has been portrayed as just being behind the scenes, but she had a lot of influence. She was very cheerful, always looking on the bright side of things.

Another wonderful contribution Billy made to my life was that he introduced me to my future husband. Billy met Leighton in Canada when Leighton was sixteen. When Billy came home he told me about him. And when Billy found out that Leighton and I would be going to the same college, he told us to look each other up. We did, and we fell in love. We were married fifty-eight years ago, and it was Billy who performed the ceremony. He was very nervous because he was not accustomed to doing weddings. I remember him saying, "Now Jean and Leighton are going to be sharing this rings." The audience laughed at the slip up. It was a sweet, amusing moment.

Just as Billy has always been a big brother to me, I think I have always been a little sister to him. When I visit him now, well into his nineties, he wants me to sit with him, and he holds my hand and calls me sweetheart all the time. He has never let me get beyond age seventeen! As far as he is concerned, I'm still his little sister. And as far as I am concerned, my big brother still looks so great, with that beautiful white head of hair. He is a loving, kind, gracious gentleman, he really is.

·34·

KEVIN FORD

Author, speaker, leadership consultant;
Chief Visionary Officer of TAG Consulting, nephew of Mr. Graham

My father is Leighton Ford, and my mother is Jean Graham Ford, Billy Graham's youngest sister. I have a sister, Debbie, and an older brother named Sandy who died thirty-one years ago. My family is from Charlotte, North Carolina.

While I was growing up I saw Uncle Billy at Thanksgiving and Christmas, typically once or twice a year. He was very loving and always gave me a big hug. We had a friendly relationship, but at the same time it was more casual. After Sandy passed away, our relationship changed in a unique way. It's been a warm and intimate relationship ever since.

Sandy was my hero. He was a very unusual brother. He included me in social outings with his friends and so forth. He was president of his high school class, which was one of the larger schools in Charlotte. When he ran for class president, he actually gave his testimony. He also competed as one of the top milers in North Carolina. He was an all-around great guy and a very strong Christian.

When Sandy was fifteen years old, he was diagnosed with a heart problem called Wolff-Parkinson-White syndrome, known as WPW. At Duke University Medical Center, he underwent open-heart surgery in order to sever an extra electrical pathway in the heart. The doctors thought they had corrected the problem, but five years later Sandy had a recurrence. He was running a track meet and collapsed thirty yards from the finish line. He then crawled his way across the line to win the race. It made the headlines of the Charlotte newspaper—it was a really dramatic thing.

Just after Sandy turned twenty-one years old, he went back to Duke for another open-heart surgery. At that time, I was sixteen years old and attending Windy Gap Young Life Camp in the mountains of North Carolina. I knew about the operation and assumed everything would be fine. I got a call on the evening of November 27th and found out there were complications with the surgery. I was told my Uncle Billy was coming to pick me up. I immediately sat down with a couple of the Young Life staff people and began to pray. Then, all of a sudden, I felt Sandy say, "Goodbye, Kevin. I love you." I remember looking at my watch. It was just after 7:30 p.m.

When Uncle Billy arrived at the camp I got in the back seat with him while someone else drove. He put his arm around my shoulders and said, "Kevin, your brother, Sandy, has gone home to be with the Lord." We both wept together. He took me back to his house in Montreat and kept his arm wrapped around my shoulders the whole time. He sobbed, and I sobbed. We prayed. He was not Billy Graham the evangelist. He was my uncle. He was a man who was deeply broken by what had just happened.

We found out the next day that Sandy passed away precisely at 7:37 p.m., which was about the time I felt him say, "Goodbye, Kevin. I love you."

Uncle Billy let me stay at his house for two or three days, listened to me, and prayed with me. He was just as dear as he could be. Then he took me to Charlotte for the funeral, which he helped officiate.

Those moments spent with Uncle Billy forever changed our relationship. I'm sure he had thousands of other things to do with his ministry that were probably far more important, yet he made me his priority. Since then, our relationship has stayed very close.

Sandy's death altered my view of life. At sixteen years old I no longer felt immortal. It suddenly hit me that I might die any day. My life became more intentional. Following Christ, wanting to be a support and servant to others, and wanting to be a better role model became my priority.

Uncle Billy has always been incredibly modest. Whatever car he was driving was at least twelve or thirteen years out of date, whether it was a Delta 88 or whatever. He never drove anything fancy. He did not see himself as an international celebrity. I'd hear him talk about a prime minister who he'd just had lunch with or the CEO of a multibillion-dollar company that he had met. He was just captivated and enthralled by these people. He never had a sense of being a world famous personality, even though he was often more well known and influential than many of the leaders that he was talking about.

Uncle Billy was non-judgmental and never got caught up in issues that could be divisive. He stayed focus on the Gospel. I remember one time I heard him speak at a convention and someone asked, "Dr. Graham, would you share with us your view on infant baptism versus believer baptism?" He walked up to the podium while 20,000 people waited to hear his response. His answer was very simply, "No," and then he sat back down. He never got into controversial issues and shied away from partisan politics. He honestly loved people, and he chose to be inclusive. As a result, some of the Christian population, whether on the far right or far left, viewed him with suspicion. They believed he didn't have a strong enough backbone. The conservatives thought he should be more conservative, and the liberals thought he was too conservative. My uncle simply stayed focused on the Gospel and did not judge.

Aunt Ruth and Uncle Billy had a wonderful relationship and enjoyed each other. She was very opinionated and had a quick wit. She was hilarious. She put him in his place. That may have been one of the things that kept him humble across the years. He knew he wasn't a celebrity at home.

People have asked me over the years what it's like to be Billy Graham's nephew. What I say is, "He may be Reverend Billy Graham to the world, but he's simply Uncle Billy to me."

·35·

LEIGHTON FORD

*Author, founded ministry that mentors future Christian leaders
and has preached worldwide, brother-in-law of Mr. Graham*

I was seventeen when I first met Billy Graham. I was in high school in my hometown in Chatham, Canada, and at the time I was the youngest local director in the world of a youth organization called Youth for Christ. We held monthly rallies and we had invited Billy Graham to come and be our speaker. It was 1949, and I remember it was a very cold January night. It was icy and the roads were very slick. But our high school auditorium was packed. We were excited because even then we knew that the young Billy Graham (this was before he became nationally known) was a powerful speaker and people responded to his message. So I assumed that everybody who came would say, yes, we want to follow Jesus.

Billy preached, and his voice was very strong. I can still hear that Southern drawl saying, "Prepare to meet thy God." And then came what we used to call the altar call, when he would ask people to come forward publicly as a sign of their commitment to Christ. I thought everybody would respond. We waited and waited and waited. No one came. Finally, one young girl, about twelve years old, came forward. She said she just wanted to be sure she knew the Lord. She was the only one. No one else stepped forward.

I was so disappointed. After the meeting I went off to the wings of the stage, and I was in tears. Billy saw me and he came over and put his arm around me. He said, "Leighton, I believe God has given you a concern to see that people know the Lord, and I am going to pray for you. If you stay humble I believe God will use you."

I never forgot that arm around the shoulder. Billy Graham wasn't thinking about the fact that people hadn't responded to his message that night. He was concerned about me.

I later learned that when he got back home to North Carolina, he told his kid sister Jean about this young guy he had met in Canada, so he was a bit of a matchmaker for us, too.

That same night in Canada he told me about Wheaton College, in Illinois, where he had studied. I had planned to go to the University of Toronto, but I liked what he said about Wheaton, so I applied there. Later he told Jeanie about Wheaton College, so she went there, too, and that's where we met and fell in love. I had just turned twenty-two when we got married in 1953, and we have been married fifty-eight years.

So the influence of Billy Graham on my life was very strong from the beginning.

He invited me to become part of his evangelistic work. I was ordained as a Presbyterian minister and evangelist and spent thirty years speaking around the world, both with Billy and on my own.

That arm around the shoulder meant a lot to me in future years.

Our older son Sandy, when he was a twenty-one-year-old junior at the University of North Carolina, died during surgery for a heart arrhythmia problem. He was an athlete, a strong leader, a strong Christian. The loss of Sandy was a major factor in the decision my wife and I made to change the focus of our ministry. I had been preaching to great crowds, which was wonderful, but we decided the next phase that God had for us was to identify and encourage the emerging generation of leaders, the young men and women who had a call from God. In part this was because we had lost a son, but it was also because I remembered that arm around the shoulder when I was discouraged that night, when Billy saw a need and encouraged a younger guy. I wanted to do that for other young people.

There have been many other times in my life when Billy had the same encouragement for me. In 1957, he was planning his first really big crusade, in Madison Square Garden, New York City, which lasted sixteen and a half weeks. Some time before the event, he asked me to drive up from Charlotte, North Carolina, where we were living, to his home in Montreat. We talked about the crusade, and he said, "Leighton, I'd like you and Jeanie to go there ahead of time and start working with the churches to prepare them and recruit them to be involved in the strategy of this crusade, so they get the benefits from it." I was in my mid-twenties and had just finished seminary. I look back on that time and I think, if that had been me, and I had been planning the biggest thing I had ever been involved in, would I have chosen a young guy like me and given him that big responsibility? Billy knew I had had a fair amount of experience by that time, but I think for him to take that risk, to entrust me with such an opportunity at such a young age, was a sign of very insightful and encouraging leadership.

Jesus of course showed the same kind of leadership. Out of the crowd He picked twelve people. They certainly weren't perfect but He saw their potential, and through them began to change the world. Any true leader is going to do that. He or she is going to encourage the next generation to come forward. I call it "aspen tree leadership," and I contrast it to "banyan tree leadership." There is a saying in India, "Nothing grows under the banyan tree." The banyan tree is so thick it doesn't let the sunlight through to nurture the seedlings at its root. There are a lot of leaders who are banyan tree leaders. They take up a lot of space and oxygen when they enter a room, and their vision is not reproduced because they do not nurture those seedlings. In contrast, the aspen tree grows underground. The second largest organism in the world is an aspen tree in Colorado that has 44,000 trunks, and it grows up from underneath, unseen.

I see Billy Graham's leadership in this light. When people think of him they may think of the vast crowds, the millions of people he spoke to, the conferences he organized, his television programs, and his books that have sold hundreds of thousands of copies. But what most people won't know of is those little private human touches by which he would offer comfort and inspiration and even change a person's life. Time after time he would see a need or a potential in an individual, and he would offer that person encouragement or opportunity, or both. That is true and genuine leadership—as I found out for myself that cold night in a high school auditorium in Canada over sixty years ago.

·36·

BILL GAITHER

Grammy Award and Gospel Music Association award-winning
Christian singer and songwriter

In 1976, Cliff Barrows invited my wife Gloria and me to perform at one of Billy Graham's crusades in Toronto. This was in one of those big stadiums with 60,000-70,000 people in attendance. We were a young married couple at the time, and our songs were catching on, but we hadn't performed at that level yet.

We arrived the night before and met some of the staff. I said, "Where is Mr. Graham?" I had seen him on television programs like Johnny Carson's *Tonight Show* in the 1960s and really admired him for his ability to articulate his message to a secular audience. On occasions like that, he wasn't preaching to the choir, he was talking to regular people.

Since I had never met him, I was excited by the prospect, but I still had to wait for a while. I found out that for security reasons his staff would not disclose where he was staying. They were smart. They protected him very well.

The next day, Cliff was rehearsing a 5,000-voice boys' choir. It was a pretty amazing thing. We went onto the platform, where there were a lot of dignitaries, including government officials and clergy, but still no Billy Graham.

Then I looked back and saw what must have been a Ford or a Plymouth sedan approaching, with another car behind. The car pulled up and Billy Graham got out, and from the second car four or five guys in raincoats emerged.

It was the first time I had ever seen him in person. He looked extremely tall and imposing—it was like Moses had arrived! He seemed like such an untouchable human being.

He came over to Gloria and me and was so gracious and kind. He said, "Thank you so much for doing this." We were moved that he cared that much.

Since then we've probably been involved in between twenty and twenty-five crusades over the years, including the last one Billy Graham did, in New York City. Over the years, we got to know him personally as well. He is one of the most humble, down-to-earth people I have ever been around.

We vacation sometimes in Asheville, North Carolina. We love the mountains and it's a beautiful place. Billy Graham lives not far from there, and I remember the first time we went to see him. His house looks like a log cabin. It's high on the mountain and has a beautiful view.

The first time we ever walked into his house it felt a lot like ours. We still live in the same house we did when we were both schoolteachers. It's a country home. We walked in and this giant of a man greeted us at the door.

When we first visited him, he said something that I thought was very typical of his gentle, humble spirit. "Bill and Gloria," he said, "I want to apologize for not spending more time than I've spent with you all across those years when we did those crusades." We understood completely why he had not had more time available. Obviously he was very focused on what he had to do and couldn't spend all his time socializing. You have to prioritize, and certain things have to take a back seat.

I remember one time as we left, Billy and Ruth were sitting out in their rocking chairs with their two dogs by them, waving goodbye to us. Gloria said, "Is that a picture?"

One of the last times we were there I called down to David, his scheduler, and asked if Billy would be up to seeing anyone that day. By this time he was about ninety years old. I was told to come on up, and I found Billy in the den, wearing a baseball cap. All around the den were pictures of his wife. I thought, *It's great to be a man who in his life has had such amazing public appeal, who lives to a great age, and is still in love with the lady he married.*

We talked briefly about him growing up on a dairy farm. I had grown up on a dairy farm too. In those days, before the invention of electric milkers, you milked the cow by hand. "Did you ever have cats in the barn?" I asked him. "You *did* grow up on a farm, didn't you?" he replied. He knew there were *always* cats in the barn. "Did you ever give them a drink?" I asked. "Oh, yes, straight from the source," he said. We were laughing about growing up on the farm, milking cows, and then he would talk about the love of his life, Ruth, and how much he missed her.

I was very touched. I had seen him in his prime in Toronto, and seen pictures of him with kings and queens and world leaders, but it was quite another thing to see him in old age, sitting quietly in his study, surrounded by pictures of a person he loved very much. He said he was proud of Ruth, and that it was tough being without her, because she was the rock of the home. "I really miss her," he would say. "I'm looking forward to seeing her again."

One of the greatest things that can happen to a person who has a hero is later to meet that man, become close to him, and find out he is exactly as you thought he was, and even more. And that has been my experience with Billy Graham. This is a great man. This is what I call a Moses.

·37·

ELA GANDHI

Granddaughter of Mahatma Gandhi; former member,
Parliament of South Africa; trustee, Gandhi Development Trust;
Honorary President, Religions for Peace

In recent years in South Africa I have followed some of the sermons presented by Reverend Graham and have seen the influence he has had on thousands of people. In a world where there is so much self-centeredness, breakdown of moral fiber, and violence, the Word of God is certainly an important vehicle for mobilizing people. It is equally important for people to move away from ritualistic, superstitious beliefs to values that determine the future of our lives.

Those who are able, through their own personal charisma as well as their faith, to mobilize masses of people need to very firmly and decisively communicate the message of our scriptures — that of love, compassion and of oneness of humanity and the universe, of the task assigned to us as humanity to care and labor so that the world can prosper in peace and harmony, as has been preached by Reverend Billy Graham.

Religious leaders, as Reverend Graham has pointed out correctly, need to set an example by respecting diversity without compromising on basic principles of love and caring. There is no place in our scriptures for hatred, violence, abuse of any kind or exploitation.

Coming from a different faith background, I believe strongly that faith communities are united in their belief in universal values. These values are the threads that bind us. I was honored to receive the Community of Christ International Peace Award, which likewise honors these values, and like my grandfather, Mahatma Gandhi, I believe that whatever different scriptures we may adhere to, whatever our beliefs in the process of birth, death and the hereafter may be, we adhere to the same basic values. That should be the uniting force. We, as religious leaders, have a responsibility to respect the rights of others to their scriptures and their beliefs. We must respect the right to differ. It is only when we can truly encourage this respect for diversity that we can lead our world towards peace and harmony.

Many wars have been fought in the name of religion. In hindsight all our leaders have condemned these wars. But there are some among us who continue to sow divisions. That has to stop because the world is diverse, society is diverse, scriptures and beliefs are many, and this will remain so because that is how we are created and that is the nature of humanity. We think differently and therefore we are different. Yet we have much in common that binds us and it is that commonality that we need to emphasize and loudly and clearly articulate for our world to change its course.

Reverend Graham has the power and the charisma to change the world for a better more tolerant world. May his followers continue to preach the message of peace, tolerance, compassion, caring and respect for all life.

·38·

JIM GARLOW

Bestselling author, pastor of Skyline Wesleyan Church in San Diego, California; host of daily radio broadcast

My first time going to a Billy Graham crusade was at the Aksarben Coliseum in Omaha, Nebraska, when I was a child growing up on a farm in Kansas. I invited a neighbor, a farm boy who lived down the road from us. His parents never went to church—they had a very low opinion of church—but for reasons I can't understand, they allowed him to go with us all the way to Omaha, a four-hour drive, and he was one of those who went forward to receive Christ. That's quite a thrill for me to look back on.

When I was an undergraduate in college, the Billy Graham organization started the School of Evangelism. The classes ran simultaneously with his crusades. One of the workshops was held at a large, old church in Kansas City. It was only for pastors and seminarians, so you had to be a graduate student, which I wasn't. But my Greek professor somehow prevailed upon them to allow a group of about ten guys from his class to attend. So we undergraduates got to sit in with all these pastors at this huge conference.

I can remember everything about this as if it happened this

morning. I remember where I was sitting in the balcony, listening to a talk about how, ultimately, ministry wasn't attached to the pastor. Ministry, properly understood, was lay ministry, that is, it belonged to all of God's people. It was so breathtaking.

I began to study this concept, and I kept studying it even when I went to graduate school and earned a Master of Arts from Southern Nazarene University, a Master of Divinity from Asbury Theological Seminary, a Master of Theology from Princeton Theological Seminary, and a Doctorate of Philosophy from Drew University.

Following the workshop at Billy Graham's School of Evangelism, I wrote to his organization asking, "Please send me instructions on how you organize a crusade." I look back and think did I really do that? Writing the Billy Graham team, asking how to organize a crusade when I was still just an undergraduate in college. I remember that the address was Billy Graham, Minneapolis, Minnesota. That's all the address you needed—just Billy Graham, Minneapolis, Minnesota. I soon received three pages of instructions.

In my hometown of Concordia, Kansas, I was part of a Wesleyan church. I am still pastor in a Wesleyan denomination today. The Baptist church was on the same street, about five or six blocks away. The two churches had some theological differences, but they had a great relationship. The Baptists asked me to become their youth pastor. I'd done a lot of youth work in our little town of just 6,000 people. I agreed, but I told them that I'd been dreaming of something. "I have these three pages from the Billy Graham organization on how to organize a crusade," I explained, "and I'm going to organize one in our town."

So I organized a crusade, forming committees just like the instructions said to do. I took youth groups to seventeen small towns around us, knocking on nearly every door. We handed out literature, blitzing everything until our town was abuzz about the upcoming crusade.

We also brought in a rancher-farmer who was a very good Youth for Christ speaker. Billy Graham was one of the founders of YFC. We had an incredible response the last night of the crusade—we did it just like the Billy Graham Crusade—in a football stadium, and we had 2,000 people, one third of our town!

People were so enthused, they began saying, "Let's do it again." I had started working on my master's degree in Oklahoma City, which was several hours away, so I had to organize it long-distance, but we had all the committees set up, and the town was so motivated. I did it all over the phone, making trips back and forth from Oklahoma City to Concordia. When it came time to get a speaker for the second crusade, I called a man who had been featured in Billy Graham's *Hour of Decision* magazine. He directed me to a young seminarian named Ross Rhoads, and we became friends from that point on. Little did I know that Ross would later become the chaplain of the Graham organization.

Billy Graham not only provided a model for how to organize a crusade, he was also a role model for many of us on how to conduct a ministry with integrity. One time, at one of Graham's crusades, a reporter told him to climb, turn around and wave at us as he was getting into the car, and so he did. His newspaper had also snapped a picture the night before at the crusade of the ushers standing with the offering baskets stacked so high. Then the editors took the two pictures, put them side by side, and wrote something like this, as I recall: "Graham 'Love Offering' Collected at Final Service."

Well, he didn't. He was a man of integrity, but he realized then that he had to form the Billy Graham Evangelistic Association. Everything was set up with an independent board, and his salary was established by others to avoid any question about how much he was earning from his ministry.

We used to be told when we were young that pastors, male ones that is, shipwreck on three things: gold, glory, and girls. As young pastoral students, we realized we were going to have to be careful about money and relationships with the opposite sex. I remember hearing the stories of the overtures that young women would make towards Billy Graham. He had to have guys around him to protect him. Billy Graham's model of ministry played strong in the hearts of young college guys—that we were going to have to be very careful in all that we did, that we needed to walk with integrity. So the model for us became, "Billy Graham did it; we can, too." And many of us follow that to this day.

Billy Graham would not allow himself to be tempted by women, riches, or power. Despite attempts to get him to run for President of the United States, he wisely realized that it would be a huge step down from his calling. He not only resisted these temptations, but he also was able to resist the intellectual challenges that had shaken the faith of many of his contemporaries.

During his early years as a preacher, many types of liberal academic approaches to the Bible were being discussed in U.S. seminaries and undergraduate institutions, such as redaction criticism, form criticism, literary criticism—all of them questioning the reliability of Scripture. Billy Graham began a profound intellectual struggle. Like many of his young colleagues, he was wrestling with basic questions: Is the Bible really authoritative? Is it really true? His answer came while at a Christian retreat center near Los Angeles, founded by the great Henrietta Mears. During a walk one night, he laid his Bible on a tree stump, and prayed something like this: "God, I can't understand all this," he cried out. "I don't know it all. I can't figure it all out. But I'm going to trust that Your Word is true." From that moment on, Billy Graham's preaching was punctuated by one phrase: "the Bible says..." That's the hallmark of Billy Graham.

Yet his friend, Charles Templeton, made a different choice. Templeton was one of the early young evangelists with Youth for Christ International, founded in 1946. He was a young, effective, ruggedly handsome evangelist, and partnered with Billy Graham as one of the organization's preachers. They traveled together, even introducing their new organization to pastors across Europe. But during his studies at Princeton Theological Seminary, Templeton decided to embrace much of the modern academic criticism, and he eventually became an atheist. He had lost confidence that the Bible was true.

So Billy Graham was not only a role model for organization and integrity, he became an intellectual model for so many of us who wrestled with these same academic issues. Billy Graham was the model for how to read the Bible, saying, "I can't understand it all, but I choose to cast my lot on the side that believes it is true." So many of us, like Billy Graham, have no regret that we did.

When we were young college students, everyone's goal was to sound like Billy Graham. Everybody tried to sound like him, and it was somewhat humorous. We all wanted to be like him. But it really was more than just imitation. We were honoring a wonderful characteristic, an unwavering faith that I'm still thankful for, since like Billy Graham, I still believe the Bible is true.

My favorite figure in the Bible is Thomas. Many call him the doubter. But, I don't think so. He was just a questioner. I too question things — a great deal. I've had struggles with doubt. But, the power that Billy Graham brings to his preaching is a model that has helped hold me and my generation of preachers to this day. Our faith is stronger than ever.

I was once told that before preaching, Billy Graham would spend the afternoon meditating. All he would eat was a piece of toast and some warm tea. He'd be alone the whole day. That had a big impact on me. I was so moved that Billy Graham—the great Billy Graham—had to be alone with the Lord before he would speak. Even the fact that he would limit his food intake showed such a deferential attitude toward his calling. I have found myself following similar practices before speaking at Skyline Church, where I serve as lead pastor here in San Diego, and before other speaking engagements.

In front of our church is a sidewalk that's nearly 100 yards long and 8 yards wide. Etched in tiles down the center of that walk are the top leaders in church history, from every century and from all six continents. Billy Graham is one of those prominently displayed alongside his devoted wife, Ruth.

I think back to those days when I was just a kid, sitting in the basement of our farmhouse, glued to the TV, watching Billy Graham's crusades. I look across the decades and see the impact he has had on me, my fellow pastors, and on so many tens of millions of others. It's as if God reached down, and said: "I'm going to pick a North Carolina dairy farmer—William Franklin Graham, and do something with him the world will never be able to explain." And God did.

·39·

KATHIE LEE GIFFORD

Co-host of NBC's Today *show and
co-founder of the Association to Benefit Children's Cassidy's Place
and Cody House child advocacy centers*

I was a young teenager when I saw *The Restless Ones*, one of the first movies produced by the Billy Graham Evangelistic Association. It was about a young girl who was at a crossroads in life. She questioned which path to take: the world's way or God's way. Seeing that movie was truly a defining moment for me. I distinctly remember hearing an inner voice say, "Kathie, I love you, and I want to make something beautiful out of your life. Will you trust me?" I then made the most dramatic decision of my life. I went forward in that little ramshackle movie theater in Annapolis, Maryland and I asked Jesus to come into my heart. It is by far the most important, the most profound, and the best decision I have ever made. In a sense, I owe my physical life to my mom and dad, who brought me into this world, and my spiritual life to Billy Graham which will lead me into the world beyond.

It has been a great privilege to become friends with Billy. I thank him every time I see him, for his faithfulness, which, in turn, brought me to faith. Billy has impacted millions and millions of people's lives. My whole family came to know the Lord through him and we are all deeply grateful.

A few years ago, a pianist friend of mine went to North Carolina to play a concert at the Montreat Conference Center. I asked him to please give my love to Billy and Ruth, who live nearby. When my friend returned home, I asked him, "Did you see Billy and Ruth?" He answered, "Kathie, I didn't see Ruth, but I saw Billy." Then I asked, "Well, how is Ruth doing?" With a look of concern, he explained that when he had asked about Ruth during his visit to Montreat, Billy had answered, "Oh, dear Ruth. She's not doing that well and is having a really hard time, so we continue our romance with our eyes." I was so deeply touched that soon after I wrote a song for Billy and Ruth's sixtieth wedding anniversary, "Our Loving Eyes," and later recorded it.

The last time I saw the two of them together was when they were both given the Congressional Gold Medal, the highest honor that the United States Congress can bestow upon a civilian. The service was in the Rotunda at the U.S. Capitol Building in Washington, D.C. It is a magnificent hall filled with busts of America's founding fathers, including Presidents Thomas Jefferson and James Madison. During his acceptance speech, Billy said something like, "Look all around you. We're in this auspicious hall with all of these incredible busts of amazing people. Do you know what they all have in common?" We all sat holding our breaths. "They're all dead," he continued. "In spite of their accomplishments and in spite of the place they hold in history, they are all dead. And do you know what everyone of us has in common?" Again, we held our breaths. "We're all going to die," he said. It was so profound. Then, after a moment of silence, Billy asked the questions, "Where are you going, and what have you left behind to impact the Kingdom of God?" That day, after all, for him was not about Billy Graham getting an award. It was about using every opportunity to turn people's eyes to what mattered, their personal relationship with the living God.

That evening, while changing for the black tie event to be held in honor of Billy and Ruth, I watched the news on television in my hotel room. The reporter said, "Billy Graham received the Congressional Gold Medal of Honor today." I then heard myself scream at the television, "So did Ruth! She received it, too!" Billy has said to me on several occasions that he could never, never have done what he did without Ruth keeping the home fires burning while raising their children at a great personal sacrifice. Sadly, she died not long after.

What will we have to cast at the feet of our Lord? It will be how we have loved others and served others. In Micah of the Old Testament, it says "To do what is right, to love mercy, and to walk humbly with your God" (Micah 6:8). As far as I'm concerned, Billy did exactly that. He did what was right. He loved the mercy and compassion of God. And he was a giant, a lion of a man, and yet he walked humbly with his God and he did it with a twinkle in his beautiful blue eyes. He brings out a lot of tears in me, tears of joy and tears of sadness, because we will never see the likes of him again.

Billy has said, "Every one of us has a calling from the Lord, but most of us don't respond to the call." Billy doesn't count how many lives he has affected. Instead, he looks for the next opportunity to share the love of God with someone who is hurting or lost. He doesn't look back. He looks forward. And now I'm happy for him that he's closer and closer to living in Paradise. If anyone has earned a place there, it's Billy. Ruth will be waiting for him, and they'll continue their romance with their loving eyes. I love you, Billy, and I am "eternally" grateful.

OUR LOVING EYES

We looked at one another so many years ago
And found something special in our eyes
We vowed to each other that
There would never be another
For if love is truly real, then love never dies.

Now here we are
Weathered by the years
Strengthened by the trials
Tethered by the tears.

No need to speak of all we share
It comes as no surprise
That we'll continue our sweet romance
With our eyes, our loving eyes.

No need to speak of all we feel
We know what's true, we know what's real
And until we whisper the last of our last goodbyes
We'll continue our romance
With our loving eyes.

We've dreamed our dreams together,
We've walked the narrow road
We've shared every burden side by side
And as we turned each corner,
We turned to God above
Depending on His grace to sanctify our love.

Now we sit by the fire
Weathered by the years
Strengthened by the trials
Tendered by the tears.

No need to speak of all we share
It comes as no surprise
That we'll continue our sweet romance
With our eyes, our loving eyes.

By Kathie Lee Gifford and Phil Sillas
Written for Ruth and Billy Graham in Celebration
of their 60th Wedding Anniversary

·40·

AL GORE

45th Vice President of the United States and Nobel Peace Prize
winner; founder and chairman of The Climate Reality Project

There is a special grace about Billy Graham, a gentleness of spirit, a presence so filled with his love for God that one can almost immediately feel the depths of his devotion. Moreover, he has led while taking himself out of the message—allowing people to feel the power of God through his humility and to be touched not only by his words, but by his actions as well.

I grew up worshiping at a Baptist church, and later studied at Vanderbilt University's Divinity School. I believed then, as I do today, that the greater purpose of life is glorifying God. I deeply respect and admire Billy Graham as someone who has indeed dedicated his entire life to that purpose—glorifying God.

For Billy, glorifying God also means honoring His creation. I once had a private dinner with Billy, where we talked for several hours about the global environment crisis and our shared belief that the earth is a creation of God, and to that end, we must be good stewards to insure that the planet is nurtured and protected. As he has explained, "The very first verse of the Bible says, 'In the beginning, God created the heavens and the earth' (Genesis 1:1). When we see the world as a gift from God, we will do our best to take care of it and use it wisely, instead of poisoning or destroying it. We don't worship the earth; instead, we realize that God gave it to us, and we are accountable to Him for how we use it."

When I was given a tour of the Billy Graham Library, his son Franklin likewise spoke about the environmental concern that he shares with his father. "As a Christian," Franklin said, "I am concerned about the planet that God has given to us. We have a responsibility to live on this earth and respect what He has given to us." Billy's Scripture-based interest in environmental issues was the basis for a workshop that we held here in Nashville, with 200 Christian ministers and lay leaders.

I have met many people of great power and celebrity during the course of my lifetime; yet, there has always been a special quality about Billy Graham. Billy's love for God, which he says must extend to all people—to all of God's creatures, and to the world that He has provided so that we may live in faith, health, and harmony—is a message that he has preached to millions across the planet—regardless of race, culture, nationality, ideology, or religion. He has worked to bridge the divide between liberals and conservatives, Republicans and Democrats, the rich and the poor—addressing issues that may separate us in order to unite us.

Simply put, Billy Graham is a man of integrity who has answered God's call to preach a message of inclusion and compassion so that we might cherish one another and the world in which we all live.

·41·

DEBBIE FORD GOURLEY

Niece of Mr. Graham, homemaker, entrepreneur, and mother of three

My mom and Uncle Billy are fourteen years apart but are extremely close. She adores him. When they were growing up, they lived on a farm off a little dirt road in Charlotte. She would often sit and wait for hours for him to come home, because she missed him so much.

I knew the more public Billy Graham as I grew up. When he came home to Charlotte, our entire family stopped what we were doing so we could hear about Uncle Billy's travels; the kids got out of school early, the adults took off work, and we usually met at my parents' house. We'd have perhaps twenty of us gathered in my parents' living room, listening to Uncle Billy's stories about meeting the president of this or the king of that. It was unbelievable. There were lots of personal stories, and often he told us things he couldn't repeat publicly. We heard about conversations he had with really famous politicians and world leaders. He talked with them about God, about faith and about spiritual things. We always knew that whatever he told us was a private matter.

Over the years, the Billy Graham crusades grew. As a thirteen-year-old girl, it was fun to go behind the scenes at the Madison Square Garden Crusade. At the time I remember asking myself, "Could all these people really be here to hear my uncle?"

I admire the stance he took during those years of strict segregation when he insisted that African Americans be included in his crusades. And he strongly supported the role of women. But he wasn't an issue-driven kind of person. It's not what he said; how he lived his message is what people will remember.

For me, one of my key memories about my uncle is how he helped me when I was going through a difficult period. I had breast cancer in my thirties and shockingly, I had a recurrence seven years later. My husband and I went to the Mayo Clinic in Florida to get a second opinion. Uncle Billy happened to be at Mayo at the same time. I didn't expect to see him but knew he was there, because when we got to our hotel room there was a big basket of flowers waiting for us that he had sent—it was so thoughtful and kind!

The next day I had a long series of scans and tests. Toward the end of the day, I went for another scan (to see if my cancer had spread) but I had to go without my husband. I was walking down a long hallway when a nurse said, "Come this way." She took me down another long hallway, and there at the end, I saw my Uncle Billy sitting in a wheelchair. He had asked people to go all over the Mayo Clinic to find me. Even though he was at Mayo undergoing tests, he wanted to see me. I was shocked! I ran down the hallway, sank into his open arms and tearfully said, "I am SO scared." He threw his arms around me like a father would, and he cried with me.

Even though Billy Graham was my uncle, he was also a famous and busy world figure, so I didn't get to see him very often. That day at the Mayo Clinic was such a tender moment.

He held me and he cried with me. To have his arms around me is something I will never forget. What I felt was incredible compassion and tenderness. His tears were for me and for my fear. I actually felt God saying, "I'm here with you, today. I am with you, through your uncle. I have put you together in each other's arms."

When I returned home and told my parents about my time with Uncle Billy, my mother was quite surprised. She said her brother rarely cries, and it was probably a really tender moment for him. My dad said, "That's probably the best sermon he could have preached. He was there to put his arms around you and bring you a direct message from God." It was a tender and personal moment, just between Uncle Billy and me. And it was a great example of Billy just living His message.

·42·

RUTH GRAHAM

Bestselling author and speaker; founder and president of
Ruth Graham Ministries, and daughter of Mr. Graham

I gave my heart to Christ at a young age as I knelt beside my bed with my mother asking Jesus to forgive me and come into my heart. It was a private moment. I had yet to make a public commitment, which Christ asks us to do.

My father's affection and unconditional love for me was a bedrock for my childhood. Though often gone, I knew he loved me. That built my confidence like nothing else.

Perhaps, most significantly for me, when I was ten Daddy took me to a revival at a Baptist church in Florida, where our family was wintering that year. My father's associate, Lee Fisher, was holding the revival in a nearby city, and Daddy attended in order to lend support. The sanctuary was small and we slipped into one of the pews in back so as not to attract too much attention.

Near the end of the service, Mr. Fisher ("Uncle Lee" as we called him) invited people who wished to make a public confession for Christ to come forward. The pianist was playing a hymn, and I remember feeling self-conscious standing at my seat. I wanted to go forward, but what would people think? I was already conspicuous in the little church—despite his best efforts my father drew attention wherever he went—and I did not want to make more of a scene by going to the altar. What if I embarrassed my father? I dreaded being noticed.

But whatever my fears, they passed quickly. The "yes" to go forward became stronger than the "no" holding me back. Overcoming the awkwardness, I walked to the front of the church and stood before Uncle Lee with my eyes shut tight and my head down. I could hear movement and the sound of footsteps—other people coming forward. Then, suddenly, I felt a hand on my shoulder. I opened my eyes and recognized my father's hand. He was standing with me in front of the congregation. The evangelist who had invited countless people around the world to commit their lives to Christ now stood with me, his daughter, as I responded and made that same public commitment.

My father's support has never waned. After my marriage of twenty-one years ended, my family encouraged me to make a fresh start. Thinking I would be nearer my older sister and a good church to both minister and be minister to, I moved from rural Virginia to the downtown of a southern city. I was out of my comfort zone trying to rebuild my life.

Soon the pastor and my sister introduced me to a handsome widower. We began to date and he showered me with attention. I was even told he had made a commitment to Christ at one of my father's crusades. He seemed tailor-made for me but my children didn't like him.

My family became concerned. My father called me from Tokyo to tell me to slow down. My mother called me from Seattle to suggest I wait. I thought they didn't know what it was like to be divorced and a single mother. I thought I knew what was best for myself and after dating him for six months I married him on a New Year's Eve. It wasn't twenty-four hours before I knew I had made a huge mistake. After five weeks I became afraid of him and had to flee. What was I going to do? Where could I go?

I had to go home and face the music.

It was a two-day drive. My questions multiplied with each mile. What was I going to say to them? I feared I was the weak link in a godly heritage. Would they be disappointed in me? Embarrassed by me? Would they tell me that they warned me? That I had made my bed and now I had to lie in it? What was I going to say to my children? I had let them down. What kind of example had I been for them? How could they trust me again? How could I trust myself again after making such a terrible mistake?

As I rounded the last bend in my parents' driveway, I saw my father standing there. I pulled my car to a stop and got out. As soon as I did, my father wrapped me in his arms and said, "Welcome home."

There was no "I told you so," no condemnation, no blame, just unconditional love. His grace changed my life and it informs my ministry today as I seek to pass that same godly grace on to those sitting in the pews with a broken heart—those whose lives are in tatters because of their own choices or the choices of others.

·43·

WILL GRAHAM

Executive Director of the Billy Graham Training Center,
grandson of Mr. Graham

In 2006, I left the pulpit of my church in North Carolina and accepted God's calling on my life to be an evangelist. It was not something I set out to do. Nor was it ever a guarantee that I would follow in the footsteps of my father and grandfather, just because my name was William Franklin Graham. Simply put, the day came when I felt very strongly that God was leading me to work full-time with the Billy Graham Evangelistic Association.

This was a daunting step, and not something I took lightly. I was comfortable where I was. I had a church that loved me, that supported me, that provided for me and my family financially. I was now leaving that sanctuary behind and—along with my wife and three children—stepping into a world of long hours, exhausting travel to the farthest corners of the earth, and higher visibility than I had ever sought.

Of course, when faced with this challenge, I turned first to my heavenly Father for guidance and then to my earthly grandfather for his advice. After all, Billy Graham had lived in the realm I was about to enter for more than six decades. He traveled longer and spoke with audiences far greater than I was likely to encounter in my ministry.

I knew he would have practical tips to help me in the pulpit. "Use hand gestures," he might say. Or, "Preach from these passages of the Bible." As I drove the long and winding road to his log home in the mountains—the one that he and my dear grandmother built from the ground up in the 1950s—I didn't know what nuggets of wisdom he would offer, but I knew I would take them to heart and write every one down so I wouldn't forget.

I met my grandfather in the living room where I had visited with him countless times. He was no longer the strapping firebrand of his youth, but a silver-haired veteran—a warrior who has seen the battles and survived the journey. His ears fail him and his eyes, though still piercing, are dimmed by macular degeneration. The man who once prowled the stage and was referred to as "God's machine gun" now moves slowly and deliberately with the help of a walker.

On that day, we sat together by the fireplace and I sought the wisdom I made the trek to receive. But there would be no lengthy list of do's and don'ts. I wouldn't need my pen and paper to chronicle every bit of advice.

"Will," he said softly. "Pray, pray, pray, and study, study, study. Looking back, I wish I had done so much more of both." That's it. From my earthly focus, I was expecting practical strategies to walk me from Point A to Point B to Point C as I began my evangelistic ministry. My grandfather, however, saw with greater vision the simple, yet profound, instruction to "Pray, pray, pray, and study, study, study."

I must admit that I was taken aback by his guidance. After all, as long ago as I could remember, whenever I entered his house, my grandfather was a) praying, b) reading the Bible, or c) watching

Larry King Live. (He was good friends with Mr. King, and loved to watch the program and learn about other people.)

How could my grandfather, who spent more time in prayer and study than anyone I had ever met, feel inadequate in those areas? His response: "I wish I knew the Bible as well as your grandmother does. She knows it better than anyone I have ever met," he whispered quietly. "And we could have done so much more if we had taken fewer speaking engagements and spent more time on our knees in earnest prayer."

Billy Graham, the man who spoke to nearly 215 million people in live audiences and watched as millions placed their faith in Jesus Christ, had come to realize that he could have done even more through prayer and spending time in God's Word. He wanted to make sure that I understood this at the beginning of my ministry. It was far more important than any checklist of instructions he could provide.

I'm now several years into my ministry and have preached on six continents, sharing the same message that my grandfather carried those many years. Not a day has gone by when I haven't heard those whispered words in my head and sought to follow his humble guidance.

Pray, pray, pray, and study, study, study.

·44·

CRAIG GROESCHEL

Pastor of LifeChurch.tv, the second largest church in the U.S. with fifteen locations and an Internet campus

In the spring of 2012, I visited Mr. Graham at his home along with Bobby Gruenewald, my colleague at LifeChurch.tv. Will Graham, Mr. Graham's grandson, took us there.

I was struck by the simplicity of where and how Mr. Graham lived. He greeted us warmly, like family. It was as if he were a granddad I'd known my whole life. He knew about our ministry, which surprised me, and he also knew details about me that a lot of my staff members don't even know, like where I was born. He had apparently prepared himself for our meeting.

At ninety-three, he was not able to hear well or see clearly, but his mind was 100 percent perfect in every way. Bobby and I gave him his first iPad. If Apple had been there with a video camera it would have been the best commercial in the world. He had never seen or heard of an iPad, and we had installed the free Bible app that we created at our church. He was blown away by it.

While we were with Mr. Graham, we put the Bible in the biggest font available so that he could make out the words, which he hasn't been able to do with a printed Bible for years. The verse that came up was John 3:16, and that was really moving to him: "For God so loved the world that He gave His one and only Son, that whoever believes in Him shall not perish but have eternal life." We also showed him how to change versions, from the New International Version to the King James Version to the American Standard Version along with 300 other versions.

When we told him we had given away over sixty million of these digital Bibles he got really choked up and said, "Do you have any idea what this means to the world, that you can give God's Word away for free? I don't understand all this technology, but I do understand this is something that is going to impact the whole world." He was visibly moved by having the Bible available in this new form, and he told us to keep preaching the Gospel and the Word.

I've met presidents, prime ministers, and other world leaders, but nothing has meant as much to me as meeting him. Everything else pales in comparison. He has been such an influential figure for me. His autobiography, *Just As I Am*, was the biggest faith-building book I've read outside the Bible. I was so moved by how God could take an ordinary man who was willing to remove himself from the picture and be completely obedient. It was wonderful to read of how God opened the doors, how God built his platform, and how God drew the crowds. Whenever his ministry had a need, God met the need; whenever there was an obstacle, God removed the obstacle. It felt like I was reading the Book of Acts, only it wasn't the first century, it was the century I live in. The same type of miraculous presence was working through Mr. Graham. Reading *Just As I Am* gave me the faith to believe that if God can do that through him, then maybe God can do something special through me as well.

Seeing Billy Graham's passion for preaching the Gospel around the world inspired me to do the same in a church setting.

I realized that you could invite non-Christians, people who were not normally churchgoers, to the service and preach the Gospel to them every week. That was a revolutionary idea to me at the time and it has resulted in lots and lots of people coming to Christ. It was Billy Graham who moved me to say, *No matter what, I'm going to present the Gospel.* We started a church inside a two-car garage and wound up establishing fifteen different LifeChurch.tv locations across five states, plus an Internet campus and more to come. I wouldn't have been able to do it without the influence of Billy Graham.

Before we left that day, Bobby and I had a photograph taken of us with Mr. Graham. In the photo, he holds the iPad we gave him, which itself is showing a photograph of him in his prime, holding his own Bible aloft as he preaches. It's a photo I will treasure as a reminder of a day when I met a man who brought so many thousands of people to Christ over so many decades and who refused to take any personal credit for it, offering all the glory to God. It was such an honor to meet him.

·45·

NATHAN HATCH

Author, historian, president of Wake Forest University
and former Provost of University of Notre Dame

I've known Billy Graham since I was a child because my father
and mother grew up in Charlotte, North Carolina and were
part of the same circle of young people in which he grew up. My
father was a Presbyterian minister and I went to Billy Graham
meetings as a boy and as a teenager. I know Leighton Ford, his
brother-in-law, and Jean, one of his sisters, well. I was always
deeply aware of what he was doing and followed his career
intently, even more so after I became a historian focusing on the
history of American religion.

So I have a personal connection as well as a more academic
connection to Billy Graham. It goes without saying that Billy
Graham was a huge phenomenon in the second half of the
twentieth century. I put him in the same category as another
important figure, Father Theodore "Ted" Hesburgh, a Catholic
priest who is of the same generation as Dr. Graham and was
president of the University of Notre Dame for thirty-five years.
Like Billy Graham, he was also a counselor to presidents. Since
I was privileged to work at the University of Notre Dame for
thirty years, as both a professor and provost, I came to know

Father Hesburgh very well. Both he and Dr. Graham are towering figures. Above all they are men of deep faith and generosity, unfailingly gracious to others, who see the best in people and live out their Christian faith in ways that are magnanimous and deeply appealing. Although one is in the Protestant evangelical world and the other in the Roman Catholic world, they have many similarities in their deep sense of calling, their deep compassion for people, and their ability to relate to people.

In a world where religion often takes a strident tone and can be at the heart of the culture wars, Billy Graham stands out in focusing on what is absolutely essential in terms of the love of God for humanity and how people can live lives of faith in the most meaningful way.

I think of him as a deeply generous person, and if there's anything else that characterizes his life, it's his deep integrity. Obviously, an organization as large as the Billy Graham Evangelistic Association has huge financial capacity, and yet Billy Graham never enriched himself. He lived on a salary and was scrupulous about everything he did, and that's in marked contrast to many evangelists. I think the generosity and the integrity of Billy Graham are absolutely striking.

Both Dr. Graham, a minister, and Father Hesburgh, a priest, are authentic witnesses to the love of God in Christ. What is so special about them is that there is no dissonance between what they speak about and how they live. What they believe is exemplified in how they live their lives and how they treat people. Their very lives draw people to their message. The closer you are to these two men, the more you admire them. Some leaders may be great leaders and get a lot done, but as you get closer you think, *I'm not sure I like all of that.* But in the case of Dr. Graham and Father Hesburgh, their lives and their messages are in harmony.

Billy Graham was a constant learner. There was a maturing over the years, particularly as he traveled abroad and listened and dealt with other cultures. In his youth there probably was a sharper tone in certain ways, but that was in the Cold War era, when Soviet communism was seen as a serious challenge to Christianity. His thinking on global issues such as the dangers of nuclear weapons and the benefits of arms-control agreements evolved over time. He came from a fundamentalist evangelical background but became a world Christian who engaged mainline Protestant, Catholic, Orthodox — any variety of Christian. He was able to see the world with that wide view and probably spoke to more people about Christianity than anyone in history.

Billy Graham always gave himself unrelentingly to the service of people, and he was not corrupted by power and acclaim. He refused to get sidetracked by things he thought were peripheral, and he saw himself as an evangelist of the Gospel. He was bringing good news, and he just stayed to that task. He has been a leader of extraordinary power and vision.

·46·

MIKE HUCKABEE

Former Governor of Arkansas, presidential candidate,
and host of Fox News Channel's Huckabee

In 1972, the Expo '72 evangelistic conference was held in Dallas, Texas, sponsored by Campus Crusade for Christ. It was a weeklong evangelistic training for youth from all over the world, and 100,000 people were gathered there. I was one of them. I was fifteen years old, and I went with two other kids from my high school. Every day we would go out and be trained, witnessing and sharing our faith, and then every evening we would go to the Cotton Bowl in Dallas for big rallies. Dr. Graham was the speaker on the final night, a Friday. The next day there was a big outdoor rally with a quarter of a million people in attendance, and he spoke there as well.

Even though I was young, I already knew about Billy Graham. I'd watched the crusades on television and seen many film clips of him preaching. I admired him not only because he spoke with authority and compassion, but because I never sensed that he was trying to impress me with how smart he was. He just wanted to introduce me to the Christ he knew. He spoke with such clarity that even as a boy I could understand every single thing he was saying. He didn't try to lead me into some theological thicket. He just focused on the simplicity of the Gospel and its availability to me.

So on that Friday night, it was especially thrilling for me to be in a stadium where Billy Graham would be preaching. Since I came from a little bitty town (Hope, Arkansas, population 8,000), I had never thought I would be able to see him in person.

As we entered the Cotton Bowl that night, we were all given a small candle and told to hold on to it. When Billy Graham spoke, he told us about how one person can make an impact and that every life matters. Right at the end of his message he spoke of the power of the Gospel, saying that if you let your light shine, and shared it with someone else, that power would be extraordinary.

All the lights in the Cotton Bowl were turned off, so it was dark. Then Billy Graham lit his candle on the stage. A few moments later he lit the candle of Dr. Bill Bright, head of Campus Crusade, and then they both turned and lit the candles of two other people, so the two became four. The four in turn lit four more candles, and so there were eight. And this went on, multiplying all the time. Within a very brief period of time, as people lit the candles of the people next to them, it was as if a fire had started moving around the Cotton Bowl. It was astonishing how fast this happened because the amount of light was doubling every couple of seconds. Within a matter of minutes, you could see an orange glow emanating from the Cotton Bowl. It was so overwhelming that people living in the neighborhood called the Dallas Fire Department and told them the Cotton Bowl was on fire. And it really was, but not in the way they had supposed.

What made this such a powerful moment was not just the 100,000 candles and how quickly they were illuminated. I was seated quite a distance from the stage, and what stunned me was that in this total darkness, once the lights were turned down, even the one little flame from the stage penetrated the darkness all the way to where I sat. Important and powerful as it was to see 100,000 candles, it was the power of that one candle at the beginning to penetrate all that darkness that was such a revelation to me. It was a visual affirmation of Billy Graham's message that the darker things are, the more even a small light will stand out and make a difference.

It wasn't difficult for anyone to understand that Billy Graham, the most influential Christian, probably, since the apostle Paul, could stand on that stage and have an impact on people. That was easy to see, but what I learned was that even my tiny little insignificant light could still make a difference. That was what made it so powerful. And that's why I'll never forget that night at the Cotton Bowl. It was one of those incredible, life-changing moments.

Since then, in talking to people, I've often used this story as an illustration. I tell them, you may consider yourself insignificant, that you're not a very bright light, that you don't have great training or theological degrees, or wonderful human gifts, but if you will be faithful in the life you have, you will stand out, and it will have an impact.

In a dark world, like the one we are living in now, that is something worth remembering. And I am grateful to Billy Graham for first showing it to me, all those years ago, when I was a fifteen-year-old kid at the Cotton Bowl.

·47·

KAREN HUGHES

Worldwide Vice Chair at Burson-Marsteller,
former Counselor to President George W. Bush and
Under Secretary of State for Public Diplomacy and Public Affairs

I was fortunate to grow up in a Christian home, with parents who had me baptized and took me to church and Sunday school. I remember pastors and Sunday school teachers who had an important impact on my life, and I attended confirmation classes to become a member of my church.

Nonetheless, attending the Billy Graham Crusade with my high school youth group in the early '70s at Texas Stadium in Irving, Texas, was a major turning point in my life. I vividly recall the moment when Reverend Graham invited us to walk down to the floor of the stadium, step forward and publicly accept Jesus Christ as our Lord and Savior. I remember feeling that I wanted to stand up and be counted among those who came forward, and then realizing, perhaps for the first time, the deep meaning of a public response to God's saving grace. I wanted to walk down that aisle, in front of friends and others who knew me, and make my life a visible response and commitment to God.

The Texas crusade may have been the first time I felt the need to express my faith so publicly outside of church, but many other such moments have followed. Faith is not something that we are supposed to reserve for Sunday mornings or keep hidden inside. If you truly believe that God sent His Son to willingly bear the penalty for our sins, to reconcile us to Him, that amazing gift requires a response that should shape our entire lives—the way we treat people, act, make decisions—the way we do everything. Over the course of my life, I have often felt the need to speak out about the way I approach my life and decisions because of my faith, and I trace much of that back to that moment of realization at Texas Stadium.

Many years later, I read Billy Graham's book, *The Journey: How to Live by Faith in an Uncertain World*, in which he explains that becoming a Christian takes only a single step, but *being* a Christian means walking with Christ the rest of your life. That insight speaks to me every day, because I believe being a Christian is a daily process of trying to walk with Christ, recognizing our failure to do so, then asking Him to help forgive and restore us.

The Journey also includes a powerful reminder from Reverend Graham that we should never let anything or anyone rob us of our confidence in Christ. Reverend Graham emphasizes the important truth that our salvation depends on what God has done for us, not on what we do or try to do for Him. It isn't our hold on God that saves us; it's His hold on us. And I cling to that hope, summed up in one of my favorite New Testament verses when Jesus says, "I know my sheep, and my sheep know me... no one can snatch them out of my hand" (John 10:27). I've always been a stubborn sheep, so Reverend Graham's reminder that even my strong will is not stronger than God's hold on me resonates deeply.

I had the privilege and opportunity to meet Reverend Graham in person when he was speaking at a public event in San Antonio, Texas, during the time when my boss, former President George

W. Bush, was Governor of Texas. Governor Bush graciously invited me backstage with him to say hello to his friend, Reverend Graham. Many times during my work with President Bush over the years, in the Texas Governor's office, during his campaigns, as Counselor to the President and as Under Secretary of State, I heard him speak fondly of Billy Graham's visit to his parents' house in Kennebunkport, Maine, and the meaningful and loving conversation that ultimately became the inspiration for his decision to quit drinking.

I heard Reverend Graham speak in person again at the National Cathedral on September 14, 2001, at the national prayer service following the terrorist attacks of 9/11. Watching him deliver a powerful sermon from that podium, it struck me that in so many ways Reverend Graham is really our nation's pastor. He was realistic about the shock and horror of 9/11, yet optimistic and confident about the future. He acknowledged the revulsion we felt, but ended his message with hope because he knew that beneath the rubble was a foundation that could never be destroyed, and that foundation was our trust in God. At that moment, he gave voice to the grief and hope of a nation.

Billy Graham has a way of speaking so clearly about God and God's love. I remember him telling people that God wants to be our friend, to walk with us. He radiates the invitation of God's love in a way that truly calls us to respond as I did, by stepping forward and walking down. Reverend Graham's message is so powerful, yet he is always gentle and respectful. That struck me again during the 9/11 service, where he spoke as the Christian he is, but also reached out with respect to those of different faiths.

Billy Graham is both compelling and humble, as evidenced in his address at that 9/11 national prayer service. He shared, "I've been asked hundreds of times why God allows tragedy and suffering. I have to confess that I really do not know the answer totally, even to my own satisfaction. I have to accept by faith that God is sovereign, and He's a God of love and mercy." For someone of his stature to acknowledge those questions was disarming. To publicly express that he didn't have all the answers, yet he had believed and lived by faith throughout his life, was an act of profound humility. When I struggle and question the many injustices we see in this world, I am reminded by Dr. Graham's example that we can't answer all of the hard questions here on earth, but we know through God's Word and Christ's sacrifice that God loves us and wants what is best for us.

In his books, Reverend Graham describes how inviting Christ was to people, and how they wanted to be around Him, to be near Him, and respond to Him. In many ways, that's how Billy Graham is, too. People want to be around him, to learn more about him and hear from him. He is a wonderful representative of the Savior.

As someone who spent my career advocating mostly for other people, specifically for President Bush, I cannot imagine a better advocate for God and the message of the saving grace of Jesus Christ than Billy Graham, not only through his words but also through the way he lives his life and embodies the invitation to God's love.

His book, *The Journey*, is a powerful summation of his ministry; he shares with us what he knows about God. I loved reading it, and return to it often. I've highlighted a number of places that are good reminders for me. For example, he writes, "Not only has God put us on our journey, not only does He want to join us on the journey, but God calls us to a new journey, to a new path."

Many evangelists talk about the moment of accepting Christ as our Lord and Savior. I think Billy Graham understands both the tremendous importance of that moment where we choose to repent of our sins and accept Christ as our Savior—*and* the truth that this moment is the beginning, not the end, of a lifelong journey in which we often fall and often fail, but trust in God to help pick us up and get us back on the path again.

We are all on a journey through this life, but it is not our final destination. We are so grateful to have had Billy Graham as a teacher and guide on our journey through his preaching, his writing and his powerful example. And we owe Reverend Graham our thanks for so powerfully and effectively sharing the invitation to the journey with the Savior that we know leads to life everlasting for all who love God and are called according to His purpose.

·48·

KATHY IRELAND

Author, philanthropist, actress, entrepreneur, model and designer;
CEO, Kathy Ireland Worldwide

I had the privilege of meeting Billy Graham at the Special Olympics. I did not know he was going to be there but when I saw him, he had this larger-than-life presence. Yet he was so gracious and so kind, and he actually took the time to meet with our family.

Meeting him was especially moving for me since he had taught me an important lesson about integrity. When I was a young woman, I read that Billy Graham was always aware that he needed to have boundaries in place to protect his relationship with God, and with his wife, family, and church. So he decided that he would keep his door open whenever he had meetings with members of the opposite sex. He didn't exclude women but insisted that multiple people be present to avoid any possible confusion.

As a young *Vogue*, *Cosmopolitan* and *Sports Illustrated* model, and even later when I left modeling to pursue a business career as a designer and CEO of an international licensing franchise, I found myself in a world that is often dominated by men, many of questionable character. But I had learned from Billy Graham's example that I had to have clear boundaries in place to avoid situations in which there might be some misinterpretation. Like him, I too needed boundaries to protect my values, my faith, and my family.

I understood that it's far easier to protect our reputations in advance than it is to do repair work. Billy Graham also showed me that the need to protect our reputations is not just for those of us in the public eye. Every one of us, whether we like it or not, are all role models, unless we're living in complete isolation. Someone is looking; they're watching; they're paying attention, and I think it's so important to make sure that the messages we're sending are in line with the ones we send through our behavior.

While I will never put any pastor on a pedestal, if someone's minister is living in hypocrisy, it can really do a particularly serious kind of damage. Even though we are all role models, the enormous impact that religious leaders can have on so many people's lives gives them a special kind of responsibility. Billy Graham has met that high standard. He is a man of integrity who set, and kept, boundaries that protected his faith and family, showing people like me that we must all try to live the message that we speak.

·49·

WYNONNA JUDD

Grammy Award-winning country music singer, bestselling author,
actress and philanthropist

I was raised in a matriarchal household and never knew my father. He died before I had a chance to meet him. I struggled for years with my identity as somebody's daughter and ever since I could remember, I've been curious about the identity of my heavenly Father. All my life I've been searching for meaning: "Why do I have the voice that I have? Why am I the way that I am?"

One of the first times I saw Billy Graham he was like an action figure and seemed bigger than life. I thought, "Who is this character on TV?" He spoke with such passion and conviction. I wondered what it would be like to be his daughter and what it would be like to have a dad like that. Early on, he became a very important person in my life.

Because of my success, on and off the road, I have met many leaders including military generals and presidents. I've always wondered what it would be like to meet this man. He is one of those people who have made such a difference in so many lives. He is one of the few people I trust and respect. My ability to believe what he says is absolute. There is no veil of secrecy. He has lived honestly and freely. It's the way I want to live. He is my fatherly example.

Billy Graham got the job that very few could handle. I know I would fall under the weight of it. I don't think I could do it. He does it with such reverence. He is a living, breathing example of Moses. I know he's not God, I know he's just a man, I know he's mortal, I know he's fallible, yet what I see is a servant of the Lord unlike anyone else.

Billy has touched every part of my life as a woman and as a mother. He has affected my parenting and my life as a believer. Because I didn't have a father, he's been a voice, sort of a whisper. They say the world yells and God whispers. He's been a whisper in my life that has caused me to think deeper. There were times when I certainly doubted, and when I challenged or questioned God. He's come to me in the strangest of times, when I was in a torment of the soul. He reached out to me from the television, or I'd see a book. I have the Billy Graham 365-day calendar here in my home. Because of Billy, I have wanted to spend more time and study in the Word. He's like Moses to me. He just exudes authenticity.

Recently, I sang in a small church. The church was off the beaten path and the people were very simple, salt of the earth types: go to work, go to church, have a family, you know, regular folk. Before I sang, one of my staff surprised me and said, "We want to get a video of you for a Billy Graham birthday tribute." They caught me at a vulnerable moment. I went up on stage and sang "How Great Thou Art" *a capella* and tried not to cry. I felt I was in a moment that was very holy. I had a vision of Billy closing his eyes and sang with a little extra passion that day. It was meant to be precisely this way, in this moment, in this time, in this heartbeat, and in this breath. This is how it was meant to go down. My hope is he was blessed by it.

I've always had people around me to remind me of what the truth is, what the Word is. It's bugged me, and at times I just wanted to do what I wanted to do. There have been so many chances I've had to do other stuff, but I was counseled not to. I was told it's probably not in my best interest. I'm sure Billy Graham has had to walk a very thin and narrow path. I can identify with him, because I'm definitely a servant. That's my job. My sermon comes through my music. I go out and teach people my story. I'm a spiritual singer with a wonderful comedy story about growing up with Ashley and Naomi Judd. Before I go on stage I pray, "Let me be an instrument of Thy peace."

I see Billy Graham as a peacemaker. I've been in churches where I've felt the sting of not measuring up, but never felt that way with Billy. I see him as being very open, very loving and very forgiving. I think we need that. I think we need somebody who shows us the grace and the mercy of the Lord.

He is a person who studies, pays attention, contemplates and waits on God. He is at peace. I see him constantly going to the Word, because that's what he knows. There's such a reverence when someone sits still and is quiet. There's a wonderful plaque that hangs over the door of a meeting I went to one time that says, "Be still and know that I am God. Be still and know. Be still. Be." That's what I think of Billy Graham, someone who knows how to be still and who knows God and who is also willing to be still.

Billy Graham has had a major impact on my life. I have made him my elder and guide. I look up to him and say, "I feel your heart and feel what it is you're trying to say."

·50·

TIM KELLER

Bestselling author and speaker; pastor of
Redeemer Presbyterian Church of Manhattan, New York, New York

In the early 1970s, before my wife Kathy and I were married, we were both students at Gordon-Conwell Seminary. Billy Graham was a trustee of Gordon-Conwell and a very dear friend of its president, Harold Ockenga. Billy Graham, Dr. Ockenga, and a couple of other people had just recently founded the seminary by merging Gordon Divinity School and Conwell School of Theology together.

One day Billy Graham came to campus to preach. At that time I would have to say that neither Kathy nor I had a high level of regard for Dr. Graham. Our impression, derived solely from television appearances, was that he was a nice but not terribly intellectual man. He wasn't a scholar and he didn't pretend to be one. At the time, that seemed very important.

As Kathy and I sat there, we were shocked at how powerful he was in person. He had an enormous authority. He didn't rant or wave his arms and yell, although he wasn't soft spoken either. His entire speech and manner conveyed the sense of *This is the truth and you need to do something about it.* It was very simple, it wasn't scholarly, but it was very powerful.

Even though my background was not Charismatic or Pentecostal I recognized it as an anointing of the spirit. I thought, *Wow, that is unbelievably powerful.* Everybody else felt it, too.

Shortly after the service in the chapel, Billy Graham and Harold Ockenga were standing outside the front door entrance. A photo shoot was in progress. People were taking pictures that would appear in the papers the next day. Then a student who didn't realize what was going on came out of the door while they were shooting and found himself in the picture. Dr. Ockenga, whom we called Doc Ock, was pretty irritated at the intrusion and said, "Did you not read the sign?" The student started to walk away sheepishly but Billy Graham said, "Wait, Harold." Then he put the young man between the two of them and said to the photographers, "Take a picture." They took several pictures, and he said to them, "Make sure this young man gets that picture."

Back then, in the early 1970s, Billy Graham was every bit as famous as he is now, but he had no airs about him. He didn't berate the hapless student. He was extremely kind. He didn't want the student to feel bad or embarrassed, so he took action in an instant and no doubt made him feel proud instead.

Kathy and I went away saying to each other, "This is crazy! What a great man — no wonder he's been so useful to God."

We were also saying, like all the other students, "Why didn't we walk through the door like that?"

As I reflected on the experience of hearing Billy Graham in person, I reassessed my idea that a good sermon had to be a very scholarly effort in which you show off your exegetical knowledge and your understanding of the philosophers of the time. Billy Graham's preaching style made me realize that a guy can really be powerful without having to show off his learning. He reminds me of smart people in business. They are brilliant, insightful, and intuitive but they are not necessarily scholarly or intellectual. Someone once said that a twelve-year-old could understand a sermon by Billy Graham, and that is true. His simplicity was part of his appeal. In that sermon at the Gordon-Conwell Seminary chapel, he spoke simply but he didn't lose my interest. His style was quite a contrast to my own preaching at that time. There was no way that a twelve-year-old could have understood me!

In addition to his simplicity, his genuineness had an impact on me. Although he does have a very ministerial style, it's a natural extension of how he usually speaks, so it wasn't like he put on a new persona when he preached.

You know how, when a tree is cut down, you can see the rings in the trunk, and that all those rings reveal the history of the tree? I think of a preacher's work in the same way. As you develop and grow over the years you come out with a fairly unique voice, but if you were to look back at all your years of preaching and depict it as a tree, you would see what went into that voice. The other preachers who influenced you are the rings in the tree, and there is no doubt that over the years Billy Graham contributed a number of rings to the tree of my preaching.

And it all began in that chapel in Gordon-Conwell, when a young man and his soon-to-be wife felt the power of a great preacher in his prime: simple, genuine, and immensely compelling.

·51·

BERNICE A. KING

Minister, lawyer and speaker, daughter of Martin Luther King, Jr.,
CEO of The King Center

Billy Graham was a weekly staple on television when I was in my teens and early twenties. I remember being amazed at how many people responded to his message. I grew up in a church of maybe 1,200 to 1,500 people, which was considered a mega-church back then, but I never saw hundreds of people come to the altar and give their life to Christ like they did for Billy Graham.

Even as a teen, I could relate to Dr. Graham's simple message. It was easy to understand, regardless of your age, your education or your pain. It appealed to all people, and it was a lesson I kept in mind as I went into ministry. When I was being trained as a theologian, I was taught to preach someone else's notions and interpretation of God. A lot of times, words and phrases were used that seemed complex for the average person to relate to and understand. I wrestled with finding balance between my theological training and exposure and the simplicity of presenting the Gospel in a manner that was easy for people to grasp—like Billy Graham.

My father, the Reverend Dr. Martin Luther King, Jr. was a trained theologian who loved using big words. He was gifted in blending the intellectual, philosophical and theoretical with the practical and emotional, and as a result, the simplest person understood him. Very few people can use big terms but still be understood. Like my father, Billy Graham helped me understand the importance of simply communicating the Gospel of Jesus Christ, so even a little child can understand. It amazed me that he talked simply about the Gospel and Who Christ was and what Christ does for your life, and then gave people the simple invitation to respond. It wasn't pounded over their heads that they'd go to hell if they don't do this or that. His message was more welcoming and inviting. It was appealing to the average person, and people from different age groups responded to his message. Now, every time I speak, my mind is on, "How can I reach the youngest person in the audience?" Thanks to my father and Billy Graham, I came to know that at the end of the day, it's in the simplicity of the message.

Yes, the way Dr. Graham presented his message fascinated me, but more importantly, he came across as genuine, authentic, and down to earth. He had a special way of presenting himself that drew people. With Billy Graham, there was no pretension. Like my father, there was congruency between the message and the messenger. That's what made the difference. It came out of his heart and spirit. He was truly a vessel for God. His message came through clearly, and people took it as the real deal.

From time to time, ministers were invited to some of my dad's marches and demonstrations. My mother told me that my father had reached out to Dr. Graham, but he felt that he could also be effective by continuing to do what he was doing—preaching about social harmony and refusing to allow his crusades to be segregated by race. He and my father were both committed to improving race relations in the South. And they did. Billy Graham's approach to ministry continues to inspire me today.

·52·

LARRY KING

Broadcast journalist and interviewer, host of CNN's nightly
Larry King Live for twenty-five years

Not long ago I received a wonderful letter from Billy. He sent
me a copy of his newest book and wrote the following:

My Dear Larry:

*I have been mulling over for a couple of weeks what to say after
hearing news reports that may or may not be true. If I heard it correctly,
you were quoted saying that your biggest fear is death because you don't
know where you're going, and that you want to be frozen when you die
to be brought back later. Of course I don't know exactly what you said
but I couldn't let it go by without writing to you at this very special time
of the year, when Hanukah begins tomorrow and Christmas this
weekend.*

*Our friendship goes back a very long way. We've enjoyed many
interesting conversations and interviews together, so I hope you will take
this with the affection with which it is intended. A card I just received
quoted Proverbs 30:4.*

Who has ascended into heaven and descended? Who has gathered the wind in his fists? Who has wrapped the waters in his garments? Who has established all the ends of the earth? What is his name, or his son's name? Surely you know.

From our conversations together you know my belief in Almighty God and His son Jesus Christ and my commitment to Him. Now that you are retired a little, I would urge you to make it a priority to ponder this important question a little more deeply.

With warmest affection,
Billy

P.S. I'm enclosing my new book, a current bestseller in The New York Times. *I tried to inscribe it to you. Please excuse the dreadful handwriting. The signature, "Love, Billy," is really scratchy!*

The letter is typical Billy. He cares about me; he's concerned about me; and he always tried to get me to share his beliefs, which I did not. But that has not affected my friendship with him or my respect for him.

As to what happens after death, and what happens to Jews like me, Billy says he doesn't judge it. He says that the person at death may find Christ, but he doesn't know what happens at death, and while he believes his route is the Route he would not make judgments on other people. This, of course, is contradictory. You're saying it's the Route but you're not making judgments about other people. So I would question him, and always with pleasure since I liked him so much. I'd say, "Billy, are you saying Jews are going to hell?" And he would reply something like, "No, I'm not saying that because I don't know what happens to them at their death."

It's an awfully difficult question for evangelists, "born agains," and true Christians to answer, so he answered it as best he could. In fact, I just don't think he knows. He believes what he believes. I firmly believe he is not afraid of death, and there's no charlatan aspect to Billy. I respect him but I don't share his beliefs.

What I like and respect about Billy are his gentleness and his intelligence and his understanding, his grasp of things. He would have been a success at anything. He could have been a very successful politician, broadcaster, storyteller. He was a great, great presenter. The purpose of a speech is either to entertain or move the audience or take them in your direction, and he certainly did that well. So I think he is an extraordinary guy.

Like some politicians and people in the entertainment world, he has a lot of charisma. He's outgoing, he relates well, he cares. People are attracted to him for those reasons. He changes a room when he walks in. His size, his voice, his warmth, they all have an effect. Some people have that quality. Bill Clinton does, for example. I've interviewed hundreds of world leaders and celebrities during my time as the host of *Larry King Live* on CNN for over twenty-five years. I've seen how some people change a room simply by being in it. Billy is one of those guys. He's a little stooped over now, not the same person he was physically, but in his prime he was a handsome man. Wonderful voice.

Charisma such as that is unexplainable. I know it when I see it. It is what it is, and you either have it or you don't. You can't give it to someone. You can't teach someone how to be charismatic. It's just one of those things that life presents you. Billy would think that it is God Who gave it to you. I have no idea about that. I just don't know.

Billy told me he thought I was very spiritual, and that while I may not think there is a God, that God really loves me and God put me on this earth to do what I did and be successful at it, and

He was an instrument in my life. It makes you think when someone says that to you, even though I don't believe it. Although I was raised in a religious home, I don't believe in God. Jews are taught to question. That's one of the things I loved about Judaism. But the more I questioned, the less I knew. I got no answers. My rabbi didn't tell me he understood why the Holocaust happened. Too many people say, "We do not question the ways of the Lord." One of the best things a rabbi said to me was "It doesn't matter if there is a God or not. Just do good in the world." To me, if you're going somewhere you're going somewhere. If you're not, you're not. The only thing I know is that I don't know.

Billy has always been kind to me. He flew here to come to my wedding, not to officiate but just to be at the ceremony. He's been on my show a multitude of times, radio and television. He never turned me down. I've never known a moment of him being ungracious.

The unhappiest and saddest moment for me was when I confronted him over the anti-Semitic conversation he had with President Nixon that was uncovered after the White House tapes were released. Nixon said, "Well, you know, the Jews…" and Billy said, "Yes…" I asked him about that, and he said that the toughest thing, if you were in a room with a president, and a president said something, is to take issue with him. So you either said yes or you nodded your head or suchlike. I didn't agree with Billy on this. For me, you don't say yes. I wouldn't have said yes. That disappointed me.

Having said that, there were many positives in his dealings with Presidents. He helped deepen the faith of George W. Bush when, many years before he became President, George had lost his way. Billy met with him and turned him around. Billy brought Nixon and John F. Kennedy together after the presidential election in 1960. Billy knew both Kennedy and Nixon pretty well. He was cautious about President Kennedy's Catholicism but after a while came round on that. He liked Jimmy Carter's faith, and he liked the Reagans very much, too.

As his recent letter shows, Billy has kept in touch with me over the years. He would always send me little remembrances; every book he wrote he sent me autographed. I would hear from him upon other occasions too—wishing me the best on my birthday or when I got an award, such as going into a hall of fame. Any good thing that happened to me along the road, I usually heard from Billy. He is very sweet, very genuine. With Billy, what you see is what you get. He walks the walk.

·53·

HENRY KISSINGER

Nobel Peace Prize winner, former Secretary of State and
National Security Advisor, bestselling author

It is hard to believe that it was nearly fifty years ago that I first began to hear about an evangelical preacher who was traveling around the country and drawing immense crowds of devotees. It seemed to me that it was merely a phenomenon similar to the hysteria that had followed Frank Sinatra in the 1940s and, later, The Beatles. I was working for Nelson Rockefeller in New York at the time, and there was a young woman in my office who was fanatical about this Billy Graham. Reverend Graham was going to be preaching in Madison Square Garden, and for days ahead she tried to convince me to go and hear him speak. I must admit I was skeptical and went primarily out of curiosity.

To my surprise, I found myself not only impressed but deeply moved by how he touched some profound spiritual yearning among the crowd. In fact, I was so surprised by my reaction that I went a second time to test whether my impression of Reverend Graham was authentic. But I still felt the same pull of his personality.

When I went to Washington in early 1969, President Nixon invited me to accompany him to a meeting with Reverend

Graham, whom he knew and admired. Again I found both the man and his moral and spiritual force powerful and compelling. Nixon introduced us, and over the years our friendship grew, and we got together many times to talk. He spread serenity wherever he went.

Virtually every President since Nixon has sought Billy Graham's friendship and advice, but he has never mixed politics with religion. Many have sought his counsel on the moral dimensions of an issue and have been rewarded by finding a wise way of thinking about a difficult problem. A man of deep faith, he has never imposed his own beliefs on another. He has tried to open wider horizons and better understanding of life's troubled passages.

I have immense regard for Billy Graham. He is a strong but humble man, with a generous and compassionate heart that is open to every human being of every religious faith and to those who profess to have none. His moral and ethical values and spiritual enlightenment that transcends doctrine have always touched me deeply. These qualities will be his lasting legacy to the world.

·54·

CHERYL LADD

Actress, author, star of Charlie's Angels *television series;*
Hubert H. Humphrey Humanitarian Award recipient

In 1988, my husband Brian and I attended the Republican National Convention in New Orleans as guests of George H. W. Bush and his wife Barbara. We'd become friends over the years and had been their guests in the White House. Needless to say, we felt very privileged to be at the convention seated in Mrs. Bush's private box. As we sat quietly, absorbing the atmosphere, waiting for the event to begin, we became aware of a powerful presence behind us. Unable to ignore the feeling, we glanced at each other and turned in unison to determine the source. We were surprised and thrilled to see Muhammad Ali smiling back at us. We managed to retain some measure of composure until we noticed the man seated on his right. It was none other than Billy Graham.

The feeling was beyond description, almost overwhelming. In that moment we found ourselves in the presence of three of the world's most powerful people. Together, these men represented the very best humanity had to offer: the commanding strength of a world leader, the almost superhuman physicality and charm of the champ, and then the spiritual grace and healing warmth of the Reverend Billy Graham. For a second we wondered if we'd been transported.

Although I had been in the presence of celebrities many times, from my years on *Charlie's Angels* to meeting and ultimately portraying Princess Grace Kelly, I was pinching myself, hardly believing the power of this special moment.

When we finally got the nerve to turn back around, Muhammad smiled at my husband and said, "Hey, ain't you that *Magnum, P.I.* guy?"

Brian responded, "No, champ. I wish I was, but no. I'm Brian Russell. My only claim to fame is my wife here. This is Cheryl Ladd." This caused the champ to howl with laughter. Billy smiled knowingly.

We all introduced ourselves, laughing and sharing in a truly delightful and unforgettable moment.

Billy Graham is a spiritual giant. A true guide to God's grace. He is tremendously tender and Muhammad is the same. I could see that they were close and enjoyed being with each other. Billy Graham beams love. I wish that everyone could have a one-on-one experience with him.

Growing up in South Dakota, I was a churchgoer, though my dad met God in the deep woods. He was an outdoorsman, and he communicated with God on the land, where he had his own way of being with the Lord. My mother went to church with my sister and me occasionally, but left attendance at Sunday school up to us. We in fact always wanted to go, so it was a large part of our life growing up. That's how Billy Graham came to play a significant role in my childhood. We faithfully watched his televised crusades, as well as films about him and his life. So, you know what I mean when I say that meeting Billy Graham was an absolute thrill.

Brian and I were awed by him. Through the grace of God, we

had come to be in the same room with three extraordinary men, showered with a multitude of unexpected blessings. George H. W. Bush, the future President, was now speaking on the stage in front of us, while these two extraordinary men sat behind us. My husband and I are both believers, and we were acutely aware of God's grace in that very special moment.

I did get to see Billy a few other times. He always remembered me and always greeted me with that same warmth and the power of the Lord's love.

Our meeting in New Orleans remains one of my most precious memories. Being with Billy Graham was a gift. What extraordinary gentleness, compassion and humility he possesses and has freely shared with the world!

I feel blessed each time I recall that day.

·55·

RICHARD LAND

President of Southern Baptist Convention's Ethics & Religious Liberty
Commission; ordained Southern Baptist pastor

Billy Graham was the hero of my boyhood. I grew up in a
Southern Baptist church, and Billy Graham was like our
pope. We never missed a crusade on television. Billy Graham
played a particularly strong role in my life because my father was
saved at a Billy Graham crusade at Rice Stadium in Houston,
Texas, in the early 1950s, when I was about seven years old. It
was about a year after I was saved, actually. As a result of the
crusade, my father was referred to our church and was baptized.
He became a devout deacon, a Sunday school superintendent,
and a counselor for the Royal Ambassadors (the Southern Baptist
equivalent of the Boy Scouts). He was a pillar of the church, and
in our family, our whole life revolved around the church. When
people ask me if Billy Graham crusade conversions last, I say, "I
know one that did—my dad's." It changed my life. I grew up in
a home with a Christian father because of the Billy Graham
Evangelistic Association.

The first time I met Billy Graham was in 1972. I had just
graduated from New Orleans Baptist Seminary, and I was
preparing to go to Oxford to do my Ph.D. During that

Philadelphia convention I was asked to give my testimony and right after that Billy Graham was scheduled to speak. We were backstage together. I introduced myself to him and told him about my father. He was very gracious, very humble, everything you would imagine he would be. I asked him to sign my Bible, and he did. I still have that Bible. I treasure it.

I've met Billy Graham a couple of times since then. When you are around him you get the impression that he really means it when he says the first thing he will ask when he gets to heaven is "Why me?" I've thought about this. There are preachers who are better preachers than Billy Graham. From a technical standpoint, he's good, but I could name you five that are better. So why Billy Graham? I think it is because he is one of the few men who has not let his popularity and fame go to his head. He is probably as admired as anybody in American history. People wanted him to run for president. And yet he's the same humble man he always was. He is just Billy Graham.

The last time I met him was in a hotel in Washington, D.C. Ruth, who by that time was confined to a wheelchair, was being brought out, and Billy was supervising this. I said, "Dr. Graham, how are you?" He replied, "Well, I'm a little tired." I said, "By the way, happy birthday!" He said with a big smile, "How did you know it was my birthday?" I told him it was because my birthday was one day before his. "You were born November 7th, and I was born November 6th." He replied, "Well, happy birthday to you. They're taking me out for my birthday and we're going to have a cake!" That big smile again. He seemed pleased as Punch. Just a genuinely nice, nice guy—who happens to be the most influential preacher probably in the history of Christendom.

No matter what Billy Graham did, he had charisma. When he was a young man selling brushes for the Fuller Brush

Company the summer before he left for college, he became the greatest salesman in all of the Carolinas that summer. He broke all the records. The man could sell snow cones in Alaska. Whatever charisma is, Dr. Graham's got it, and that's a spiritual gift. The Holy Spirit has touched him. I've talked to several close preacher friends about this. We have all admitted to one another that we couldn't have withstood the adulation. It takes an extraordinary man to have lived the life he has lived and be as humble as he is. This is a man who walks very close to God and understands he is God's instrument. Whatever success he has been given, he knows it comes from God. And he doesn't confuse the two. He understands what's Billy and what's God. People who have known him all his life say he has never changed.

One of the things I have observed over the years is that the one inerrant sign that all people have who walk close with God is humility. The closer they are to God the more humble they are. The closer to God they are the more they realize their own human frailties and weaknesses. They know that whatever gifts they have are gifts from God. Billy is about God, he's not about Billy.

He has influenced all of us in the evangelical movement. He is the father of the modern evangelical movement. Beginning way back in the 1940s, he took the fundamentalist movement and reengaged the culture. Because of this, even today, some fundamentalists don't like him. They think he compromised with liberalism. They believe they need to withdraw from the culture to remain pure, whereas Billy Graham and the evangelical movement want to engage the culture.

In order to accomplish this, and also because he just wanted to share his faith, Billy Graham was willing to work with people with whom he was not in full agreement, to serve the larger cause.

For example, he allowed people that were not conservative Christians to take part in his crusades and to sit on the committees that organized them.

In terms of Evangelical Christianity reengaging the culture, Billy Graham is the man who really did it, on a mass level. And he gave us, the Evangelicals, both the model for how to do it and the confidence with which to do it. There would not have been a modern evangelical movement without him. And I love the guy. He was a hero to me in my boyhood, and he remains a hero to me today.

·56·

GREG LAURIE

Founder of Harvest Crusades, award-winning author and pastor of
Harvest Christian Fellowship Church, Riverside, California

Years ago in Portland, Oregon, I had the opportunity to accompany Billy Graham to one of his crusades. On a night of what would be a record attendance, I drove over with him to the event. As I recall, Billy's long-time friend T.W. Wilson was driving. I sat in front, and Billy and his son Franklin were in back.

When we arrived at the stadium and Billy made his way to the platform, I was struck by the expressions of awe on people's faces. It was as if Moses were passing through their midst.

Billy, however, seemed completely unimpressed with all the adulation. He got up and delivered a powerful message, and then, when he was done, we all piled into the car to drive back to the hotel. As a fellow preacher, I felt like I should say something nice about his message that night. So I turned around in my seat, looked at him in the back seat and said, "Billy, that was a great message tonight."

"It's just Gospel," he replied.

I turned back around, thinking to myself, *I was just trying to offer him a compliment. Maybe I should say something more specific. I* turned to the back seat again and said, "I really liked the part where you said, 'He can re-sensitize your conscience.'"

He looked at me and said, "Well, He can."

I turned back around again and thought, *Okay, fine, I'm not offering him another compliment!*

How can a man be in the position he is in and not have that go to his head? It's been said that it takes a steady hand to hold a full cup, and God has trusted him with so much responsibility through the years. In all my memories of him, Billy just liked to sit around and chat and be a regular person. He would be as interested in you as you were in him, which didn't make any sense at all to me. Why would he want to ask my opinion or listen to what I had to say? If there's one word that sums him up, it would be gracious—but I would have to add humble, too. Billy has always been gracious, not just to a noted person like a president or a celebrity, but just as gracious to a person he just met in a restaurant or on the street. He always seems to take a great interest in individuals, and I think that has been one of the secrets of his success.

A person once wrote that if you ever see a turtle on a fencepost, you know someone put him there; he didn't get there by himself. I think Billy Graham has always recognized that. When it was all said and done, he was just a farmer from Charlotte. He was raised on a dairy farm, and he would say, "I'm just a country preacher." People would dismiss this as though he didn't mean it, but in reality he did. He was just a country preacher who was elevated by God to a level that very few others have ever been to, if any.

I remember spending some time with him after attending a Board of Directors meeting for the Billy Graham Evangelistic Association. It was just prior to the release of a major biography on Billy, and he was concerned about what had been written about him — as anyone would be. After all, you never know what the author will write about you, who they have talked to, or even if they're going to be completely truthful.

At one point in this discussion I said to him, "Billy, you have lived a life of integrity. You are a man of God. You have nothing to be embarrassed or concerned about. I know this biography will be fantastic, because you've lived a wonderful life as a follower of Jesus Christ." And sure enough, it was. But the fact that he'd even have this concern showed that he had his insecurities just like anyone else. Nevertheless, he had no skeletons in his closet to fear, and he has maintained a sterling reputation through all his years of ministry.

One time, after one of his crusades, we drove over to his hotel. We were sitting around, and Billy disappeared for a few moments. He came back into the room wearing his pajamas and dress shoes. (I guess he didn't bring his slippers.) Someone had given us some roast beef sandwiches to eat after the service. At that point, they were hours old and stone cold, but we took them out of the bag and just sat around munching on them, talking about this and that. I watched Billy eat his sandwich, completely content in his pajamas and dress shoes in a room with people he was comfortable with. He wasn't one of those people who would want to have a big party, a big celebration, or a fancy dinner. Billy was just happy to eat his cold sandwich and be around friends.

As I've reflected on it, I feel that he is the most Christ-like person I've ever met — though not without his human foibles and shortcomings. He would be the first to admit those.

If Billy Graham has a weakness — and of course we all do — I think it would be his excessive kindness, allowing people to exploit his goodwill to their own benefit. He is a very intelligent man, but he was sometimes so accepting and loving toward others that people would take advantage of that. But if you're going to have a human weakness, that's a pretty good one to have, all things considered.

Billy Graham preached about love, and he lived it. He loved his wife, Ruth, with all of his heart. I've never seen a husband and wife more in love than Billy and Ruth, yet they would have their little disagreements like any couple. The way they would speak to each other, however, was just utterly charming and fun to watch. Ruth was in every way his equal, with a great wit and sense of humor, and you could tell he loved to be around her.

When Ruth was very ill and dying, I remember being in their home. Ruth was in a wheelchair, and Billy was seated next to her. A friend of ours, Dennis Agajanian, an amazing guitarist who appeared at many of Billy's crusades, came by to visit, and was asked to play the Hallelujah chorus from Handel's *Messiah*. As he played, I found myself watching Billy and Ruth. Ruth's face was radiating light, and Billy was just looking at her, smiling. They didn't say anything. But after it was done, Ruth said, "That was a song they played on our first date." As it turned out, on their first date they saw Handel's *Messiah*.

That was a special moment I'll always remember between two people who were completely in love with each other.

·57·

JOHN LEWIS

U.S. Representative (Georgia), civil rights leader and
Presidential Medal of Freedom recipient

I grew up in Alabama in a very religious Baptist family. We attended Sunday school and went to church every Sunday. I went to college in Nashville, Tennessee, and studied for the ministry there. This was between 1957 and 1963, and it was during this time that I first saw Billy Graham in person. He was conducting a crusade in Nashville, and I was able to speak briefly with him. It wasn't the first time I had encountered his message. I had watched him on television and heard him on the radio, and I readily identified with him. He was so inspiring and uplifting as he preached his message of hope. I saw him as a man of God, a teacher, and a preacher of the Word. He was very convincing.

Many years later, in 1992, I again met Billy Graham briefly. This was in Atlanta, Georgia, and the Reverend Graham had been invited to the dedication of the Georgia Dome. He talked about the Dome as being one of the wonders of the world. Afterward, I had an opportunity to chat with him. I told him how much I admired his work and all of the good things he had done.

I didn't know it at the time, of course, but that was not to be the last time I would meet Dr. Graham. And it was the third time that was the real treat.

Three years ago I was invited to Montreat, North Carolina, to speak to a group of Presbyterian college students from all over the Southeast. A member of Billy Graham's staff saw me there and asked if I would like to meet Billy Graham. Naturally, since my previous meetings with him had been so brief, I said yes, and so arrangements were made for me to visit him at his home in North Carolina.

When he greeted me at his house he still had a solid voice and was very deliberate, hopeful, and optimistic. I felt like I had gone to heaven to be in his presence. He knew everything about me. I kept thanking him for the contribution he had made to create a better society, a better world, and for his sense of faith and hope and for preaching the good news. He kept saying to me, "Thank you, and thank you for all you've done."

We sat in his living room and talked and talked. It's a beautiful place with a beautiful view of the mountains. He told me everything about the house and how long he had lived there. It was very inspiring. I had met the Pope and the Dalai Lama, but to meet Billy Graham and to talk with him was even more of a blessing because I felt a deeply personal spiritual connection. You see, Billy Graham and I grew up in the same region of the country. We come from the same material, the same part of the world. We saw people divided by race and color, and we lived to see unbelievable changes.

I remember saying to him at our meeting, "Dr. Graham, pray for me, pray for our nation, pray for the people, and pray for the world. We all need you. We need you now." It's his faith in God Almighty that is his strength. We all have to respond to the trumpet call. That's what Billy Graham did. He responded to a calling.

Sometimes I see old newsreels of Billy Graham preaching during those unbelievable crusades. I'm always struck by how he had the capacity to bring human beings together. Almost every American president in the post-World War II era has sought his message, his prayers. What made him so great and so powerful is his belief in the future.

When I came down from being up on that mountain at his home, I felt elevated. I felt deeply moved and deeply inspired. Billy Graham is a man who stood up and spoke out about some of the great concerns of our time, and he lives the life that he preached. He is at home with himself. He is anchored in his faith. He is the embodiment, the essence, and the personification of the best of the human spirit.

·58·

ANNE GRAHAM LOTZ

*Daughter of Mr. Graham, international speaker, award-winning
author and president of AnGeL Ministries*

The week following my seventeenth birthday, my high school
held the Baccalaureate, a Sunday service for members of the
senior class, their families and friends. I knew it would be a
memorable day for several reasons, one of them being that my
father was guest speaker.

As I ran out the door of my parents' home, I told them I
would meet them at the auditorium where the Baccalaureate was
to be held. I then jumped into my mother's little Volkswagen and
floored the accelerator as I dashed down the winding mountain
road that led from the house. I knew I was running late, but I had
promised to pick up some of my friends, giving them a ride to the
service. As I rounded one hairpin curve, I came face to face with
a great big, white Buick Riviera coming up the mountain. It was
too late to avoid a collision so I slammed on my brakes and
jerked hard to the right. The VW went up a steep embankment,
but not before that big Buick had crashed into the side of my
mother's VW. I can still hear the crunch of the metal and the
breaking of the glass. As the rear wheels still spun in the dirt, I
tried to get out, but the door was smashed so I had to climb over

the stick shift and exit from the passenger side. The lady who had driven the white Buick was standing beside her car, with a stunned expression on her face. I recognized her as our neighbor who was coming up to stay at our house while we were all at the Baccalaureate. I immediately apologized and asked her help in pulling the fender off the wheel so I could continue my journey. Before I pulled away, I pleaded, "Remember, don't say anything to my parents."

Driving very slowly, I picked up my friends, arriving late to the Baccalaureate. I parked the VW with the smashed side against some bushes in case somebody walked by, and then asked my mother, "What happened to your car?" I ran to take my place in the line of seniors that were already marching into the auditorium. As I took my place on the sixth row from the front, with hair disheveled and mascara streaks on my face, I sought to look very generic in my cap and gown.

I don't remember much about the service except that my father marched across the platform, looked straight at me and then said to everybody that I had never caused him any problems and that I had been a joy to my mother and him. I prayed I would die! As I bolted for the door when the service concluded, somebody grabbed me on the shoulder and said, "Anne, your father wants to see you...." Sure that judgment was about to be rendered, I went out to the front of the building where he was. He was surrounded by newsmen and cameras, all wanting to take a picture of my father and me on this wonderful and special day. (The next day the Asheville *Citizen-Times* ran a front-page picture of my father adjusting my cap, while the mascara streaks down my face seemed to indicate that I was just emotionally overcome on this wonderful day!)

Finally, I slipped away, returned my friends to their homes, and went very slowly back up the mountain road to our home. I prayed as I drove, "Dear God, please have my daddy anywhere—he can be on the phone, he can be in his study, he can be taking a walk—just please don't have him where I will have to see him right now, because I just have to think this through. I promise I'm going to tell him—just not now."

I pulled into the driveway, parking the car so the bashed-in side was away from the kitchen door. I tiptoed up to the door and opened the screen door very carefully so it wouldn't squeak. I slipped inside poised to run up the stairs to my room. When I turned around, my father was standing right inside with his piercing blue eyes directed straight towards me. I paused for a moment, then ran to my father and threw my arms around his neck! As I clung to him, I sobbed, "Daddy, I'm so sorry. If you just knew what I'd done, you never would have said all those nice things about me." I told him about my wreck—how I'd driven way too fast and smashed into Mrs. Pickering's car. I told him it wasn't her fault, it was all mine. As I clung to him and wept on his shoulder, he said four things to me that taught me a life's lesson about my relationship with my heavenly Father:

1. "Anne, I knew all along about your wreck. Mrs. Pickering came right up the mountain and told me—I was just waiting for you to tell me."
2. "I love you."
3. "We can fix the car."
4. "You are going to be a better driver because of this."

I've never forgotten—and the life's lesson is this: Sooner or later, all of us are involved in a "wreck" where we get hurt or someone else does. It can be a physical wreck, or an emotional or financial or relational wreck. The wreck may be your fault or someone else's fault.

When involved in a "wreck" it's vitally important to not run away from our heavenly Father, or try to hide from Him, or avoid Him, or deny our responsibility, or rationalize our behavior. We need to run to Him, throw our arms of faith around Him, and confess our sin. Just pour out our hearts and tell Him about the trouble we are in and the mess we've made.

If you listen carefully, you will hear your heavenly Father whispering to your heart: "I knew all along about your sin. I was watching you when it happened. I was just waiting for you to come tell Me. I love you. I can fix the mess you've made and turn the consequences into a blessing if you will submit them to Me. And in the long run, you will be a better person because of this—more compassionate towards others and more trusting of Me."

·59·

MIKE MACINTOSH

Pastor of Horizon Christian Fellowship in San Diego, California;
founder of Horizon College

On September 9, 1983, in the midst of the heavy demands of the Sacramento crusade, Billy Graham met with me privately for about two hours. Spending that amount of time with me was most unusual, especially when he was so busy and tired, yet throughout the interview he remained totally present. He had no "edginess" about him, and I had no sense that he was thinking about other meetings he had to attend. He confided, "I have many friends and family, many meetings and many people who want to meet with me, but Mike, I enjoy every meeting." He was utterly at peace, unrushed and unworried. I found out afterwards that he had been with Ronald Reagan before me that morning. Here was a guy who went from a President down to this kid who was just trying to figure out his way in evangelism. That's his spiritual spectrum. He was as gracious to me as he was to the most important people. His heart was fully open to everyone.

I try to do this myself, and it takes a lot of dying to self, giving up your selfish needs for spiritual ones, to be in that place. Billy isn't just an evangelist who goes out and preaches and becomes famous. He's a man who knows the Lord. I don't think I have ever met another man, even in latter days, who is so open to being a vessel of the Holy Spirit. He is a man who knows his calling and why he is here, a man of love.

I came to the meeting curious to know whether Billy Graham was as real as I had heard. My first impression was that spiritually, he was almost transparent; he was so real it caught me off guard. Relaxed, calm and soft-spoken, he was a totally gracious host. As we began to talk, he seemed much like a father or grandfather to me, and when he spoke, he showed genuine concern for me. After a short time, I told him that I wasn't really there for an interview, but because my heart was seeking God and I wanted to hear from him.

When Billy recognized why I had come, that I loved evangelism and was trying to find my way, he really loosened up. Among many other gifts, he advised me not to condemn, complain or criticize, and then said; "Only he who can see the invisible can do the impossible."

At one point, I told him: "I would like to give you my allegiance in evangelism."

He immediately snapped back: "Don't give me your allegiance. Give your allegiance to Jesus Christ."

Three or four of my questions seemed to embarrass him. When I asked him what it felt like to be one of the most famous men in the world, he actually hung his head. He didn't like talking about himself at all, but he knew that I needed to learn this, and he explained, "Mike, do you know why Queen Elizabeth has me to the palace, or any of these famous people have me at their homes or whatever?"

I replied, "Well, of course, Mr. Graham, it's because you're a celebrity like they are. I've always seen you listed as number one or two of the world's most admired men. That's why they have you."

"No, not at all," he clarified. "They only have me because of Jesus. You see, people in these positions have so many burdens and they can't talk even to their own pastor if they have one, so they need a friend who is discreet, who they know they can trust, and that's a great responsibility I have. Mike, I am nothing but a North Carolina farm boy, and the day that I forget that, the Lord will stop using me."

I asked Billy about his prayer life and I have used the reply he gave me ever since. He revealed that he had been sitting there and praying for me throughout our meeting, asking the Lord what he could do to help further His goals for my life. Billy shared, "I don't necessarily always have long bouts of prayer, but I learned over the years, because of my schedule, to pray from the moment I get up, until the moment I go to bed. I try to pray for every meeting and everyone I'm sitting with. If I'm home, Ruth and I kneel down beside the bed and pray for every one of our children and their needs, and for every grandchild by name. Then Ruth lays her hands on me and prays for me, and I do the same for her. We pray again at night like that when I'm home. When I'm out of town, we talk on the phone every day. We do the same devotional so it allows us to share spiritual things that we learned from the Lord that day."

I was amazed at his humility, so I asked him what his personal relationship with God was like. He described it as internal. He felt God speaking to him as a sense of peace that guided him. When he lacked that feeling of peace, he knew that it was the Lord's will for him not to do something. He had the greatest trouble feeling God's guidance about where he should speak. He had so many invitations—sometimes 200 for a crusade—that he had to be very careful about only accepting the speaking engagements that the Lord gave him. He couldn't listen to his staff, wife or friends' advice about this. He just waited for that inner peace, which was how God communicated with him. He trusted the Lord for everything.

Ruth had supported him to go and preach in the early days while she took care of their home and children. I had a chance to talk with Ruth over dinner in Portland, Oregon, at the end of a crusade there, while Billy took off to meet with Gorbachev about launching the first crusade in Russia. I asked, "Mrs. Graham, what's it like to be going to your hotel while your husband departs for Moscow?"

She replied simply, "Well, it's nothing new at all. Generals don't take their wives to war, and Billy is a general. I know my role is to keep the family strong so that he can go do God's work."

Recently, I was speaking at the same conference as Billy's daughter Anne, who is my good friend. It reminded me of the time that I mentioned his claim that her mother was more spiritual. Anne denied this, offering an illuminating picture of her father. "You watch your father in the living room sitting on the couch watching the news on television. The telephone rings, and as he stands up to walk across the room to answer the call, he is praying, asking God for the words he needs to say for whoever is on that line. How can you be more spiritual than that?"

·60·

RICK MARSHALL

Former Crusade Director and key associate for Mr. Graham;
current pastor in the suburbs of Philadelphia, Pennsylvania

I started working in crusade evangelism with the Billy Graham Team in August, 1980. My first assignment was in Calgary, Alberta, Canada where I coordinated the youth outreach and counseling and follow-up. In 1986 I became a Crusade Director, and continued in that position until July 2003.

Because of my work, from 1980 until 1992 my family moved every year. My four children were all preschoolers when we started. We moved from Michigan to Calgary, Alberta, Canada; to Spokane and Tacoma, Washington; to Anchorage, Alaska; to Hartford, Connecticut; to Paris, France; to Fargo, North Dakota; to Rochester, New York; to Montreal, Canada and then to Glasgow, Scotland. Shaped by the "crusade culture" of moving, my children learned fast how to adapt and especially how to make friends.

Our last move was from Glasgow, Scotland, to Philadelphia, Pennsylvania where I was going to direct Billy's June 1992 crusade. My children were then ages seventeen, fifteen, thirteen, and eleven. We called them "crusade brats." The week of public crusade meeting was an exciting time for them. They would have full run of the big stadiums at an event that everyone in the community was talking about. This was their week to be cool and to be seen.

About a month before the crusade in Philadelphia, over dinner one night, I said to my kids, "Who are you going to invite to the crusade this week?" There was dead silence. Nobody was saying anything. I pushed them. "What's wrong?" I said. "Why aren't you going to invite your friends to the crusade like you always do?" It was fifteen-year-old Jessica who blurted out, "Dad, we don't want to go. It's so old and there's nothing there for us or for our friends."

You know how you can live in something and not see it? I was stunned. But then I began to reflect, and I realized that at that time Billy was seventy-four years old, Bev Shea was eighty-four, and Cliff Barrows was sixty-nine. What had we been thinking? Sure, we had youth nights, but in Anchorage, for example, the youth night featured Norma Zimmer of Lawrence Welk fame, who was in her sixties, and Johnny Zell, who played the trumpet!

I looked at some crusade attendance statistics, and what I discovered was very alarming. Fewer young people were attending our crusades, and this trend was reflected in the nation as a whole. The younger generation, the baby boomers and later the millennials, were outside the grasp of the church. And this trend was accelerating.

I didn't know what to do about that. Church attendance across the nation was down and in 1992 Billy Graham was not the household name he had been from the 1940s to the 1970s. So as a director I began to ask myself, *What can we do to reach the next generation?*

In the fall of 1993, I went to Cleveland, Ohio, to prepare for the June 1994 crusade. The organizing Executive Committee was co-chaired by two very unlikely leaders. One was André Thornton, the former Major League Baseball star with the Cleveland Indians and Baltimore Orioles, and Gordon Heffern, then Chairman and CEO of Society Corporation, the largest financial institution in Ohio.

When I met them their first question to me was, "What are you going to do to help us reach the next generation?"

At the time, I had nothing to offer. I said to myself, *There's no way we can get teens and college students to come to our meeting.* But the zeal and the convictions expressed by Thornton and Heffern got me thinking about what changes to our preparation and programming it would take to provide an opportunity for Billy to speak to the next generation. Would Billy and the Team be willing to take some risks, with new approaches in advertising, training, and programming to reach the thirteen to twenty-five age group?

To make it work the Cleveland leadership suggested six key ideas: First, we needed thousands of kids praying for their friends. Second, a communication strategy that would let the youth pastors and their kids know that this special youth night was not for their parents, it was for them! Third, an advertising strategy that targeted the MTV generation by means of radio, TV, and movie theaters. Our first slogan was "Introducing the First Concert to Benefit Its Own Audience." Fourth, video presentations during the program, knowing that if it doesn't move, it doesn't communicate. Fifth, music louder than the parents were going to like. And finally, straight talk from a caring adult. That was Billy. He was someone known across the culture for his integrity. Even though the kids didn't know who he was, nobody spoke negatively about him. He would be like a grandfather, communicating the authority of the Bible with love and simplicity.

But how could I get permission to make this experiment? First I presented my ideas to the program director Cliff Barrows. He was supportive but would not sign off: "You have to run this idea by Bill!" he said. That I was eager to do. Finally I was able to get Billy on the phone to present these new ideas. He listened patiently, and then to my great surprise said: "That's nothing. That's not a youth night. Let me tell you what we used to do!" Billy then told me about the early days (after World War II) of the Youth for Christ rallies, where no stunt was too outrageous if it would draw a crowd for the Gospel's sake. At Chicago's Soldier Field, for example, eighty grand pianos were placed on the grass for a great musical extravaganza. Toilet seats were placed on the stage, and kids were invited to come and sit on them during portions of the program. They even had a "talking horse" brought onto the stage. The trainer would ask the horse Bible questions. "Did Noah build a great ark?" The reply would be one hoof prancing for "yes" and twice for "no."

As Billy went on with his stories I became sick with discouragement, thinking he wasn't understanding me at all, until it dawned on me that his willingness to take risks had a long history! "Billy," I said. "We don't need talking horses or toilet seats in the 90s. But we need the same willingness to adapt and change our approach today to reach this generation that you were willing to take fifty years ago." There was a long silence, and then Billy said, "Let's do it!"

On that first Youth Night six months later, at Memorial Stadium in Cleveland, Ohio, on June 11, 1994, 65,000 students showed up! In fact, at 3:00 p.m. for the 7:00 p.m. start, over 30,000 students were waiting for the doors to open. That night the program featured a special Christian rock music video by Michael W. Smith and student testimonials on big-screen

Jumbotrons. There were only seven Jumbotrons in America in 1994, and we rented two of them for that event at the old Cleveland stadium.

Michael W. Smith and dc Talk started out with a concert that was followed by a personal faith testimony from Mark Price, the point guard for the Cleveland Cavs, who that year was the three-point shoot-out champ at the NBA All-Star game. And the last part of the program was a message from Billy—the straight talk. He raised three questions that night: Who Am I? Why Am I Here? What Is Life All About? The response at the invitation to follow Jesus Christ as Lord and Savior was overwhelming with over 6,500 responding. We ran out of counselors and materials, and not a blade of grass was visible because so many responded. That warm spring night, at the age of seventy-six, Billy became the oldest youth evangelist in America.

What we had come up with in effect changed the last quarter, if you will, of Billy's ministry. Later we called them Concerts for the Next Generation. From that night going forward, twenty-two concert events were held (Cleveland, June 1994 to Oklahoma City, June 2003), in places like the Metrodome in Minneapolis, the Erickson Stadium in Charlotte, North Carolina, and the Alamo Dome in San Antonio, Texas. In total, 1,286,500 people attended, with 96,651 responding. Of the twenty-two events, twelve broke the all-time stadium records.

But this success was not without some early controversy within the Billy Graham organization. One afternoon in March 1995, while we were in Puerto Rico for Global Mission, Billy asked to see me. The Youth Nights were creating a stir on the team, with many detractors. Following the Cleveland Crusade, the Youth Night in Atlanta's Georgia Dome that fall had broken the stadium records as well as several eardrums, according to some! With plans underway for similar events in Toronto in

June and Sacramento in October, Billy was in the hot seat, with pressure on him to stop these events and return to the old ways.

Upon arrival at his villa west of San Juan, I was greeted by Billy and Ruth, who were both eager to encourage me to continue with the youth events. Ruth told me about the criticism they experienced in the early days of Youth for Christ. She called these folks "old fuddy duddies." She said that as a young couple, when she and Billy had spoken of their future, they agreed they never wanted to be like that. Billy then related to me a prayer commitment he had made many years ago and had renewed as a result of the new controversy. He read to me Psalm 71:17-18: "Since my youth, O God, You have taught me, and to this day I declare Your marvelous deeds. Even when I am old and gray, do not forsake me, O God, till I declare Your power to the next generation, Your might to all who are to come."

This was the earnest expression of a deep conviction. For Billy, the youth event was not something new, something just to attract a crowd, but the outworking of a passion rooted in a lifetime of obedience to God and His Word. I asked him, "Then despite the opposition, do you want me to continue to develop the Youth Night strategy in Toronto and Sacramento?" His reply was simple: "Let's do it!"

When the heart is soft, the mind is open to change at any age. Billy has the youngest heart of any older man I have ever known. And in the crusades of the 1990s and beyond, that old man with the young heart touched millions of kids who came to hear the message of God's love. I will always love Billy for that.

·61·

WILLIAM MARTIN

Senior Fellow, Religion and Public Policy,
Rice University's Baker Institute;
author of A Prophet with Honor: The Billy Graham Story

In 1979, *Texas Monthly* published an article I wrote about Billy Graham, whom I had met briefly at a crusade in 1975. Apparently, he thought the article was compelling because in 1985 he invited me to write the story of his ministry. He sent me a note saying that it was time for someone outside his organization who had appropriate academic credentials to look at his work and assess its place in history, if any.

Over the years, the assignment turned into a full-fledged biography, which surprised me. In fact, I am still on the case, over twenty-seven years later. I spent five and a half years on the first version of the book, but I have nearly finished an updated version with four new chapters.

Billy was remarkable throughout the entire time when I was doing research for the book. He was always open. He told me to look at his organization and be critical. He gives people a lot of room to do their job. He hires people he trusts, and tells them, "Just do what you do." He's like a master painter who comes in and says, "Here is the easel and the frame. Now paint something really good." Then he brags about them a lot. He never tries to take credit for what others are doing.

Billy assured me that his organization had a lot of money, and the costs of writing the book, which he expected to be significant, could be covered. I responded, "I appreciate that, but I don't think I'll have trouble getting a sufficient advance to write the book, and I would rather not take any money from you to do this." He replied, "That's great. I don't want this to be a kept book. I want it to be your book. I don't even have to read it."

As part of my research for the book, I spent time with Billy and immersed myself in his organization. Shortly after I attended his eight-day crusade in Washington in the spring of 1986, I had the opportunity to be present at a ten-day International Conference for Itinerant Evangelists in Amsterdam that summer. The gathering was Billy's long-term dream, designed to share simple, practical knowledge that he felt would help men and women go about the task that had occupied his life: helping people answer the question, "What must I do to be saved?" The event was not designed for prominent church leaders, but for everyday, mostly unknown preachers.

The conference would not have been possible without Billy Graham. His organization recruited and vetted the participants. They put it together, raised the money, and paid for it. They invited some 8,200 itinerant evangelists from 173 nations, seventy-five percent from Third World countries. Some of the participants overcame great obstacles to be there. A Sri Lankan evangelist spent forty hours dodging gunfire and bombs and picking his way around landmines as he crossed sixty miles of civil war zone on his way to the airport in Colombo. Others bore the scars of persecution inflicted by people hostile to them and the Gospel they preached. Billy said that when he met men who had gone to prison, who had been beaten and reviled for trying to do what he had been able to do with great reward and honor, "I felt like a worm."

Those ten days of instruction and stirring messages from leading luminaries of evangelical Christianity enabled the participants to go back to their countries and preach the Gospel more effectively than ever before. Billy actually spoke only a couple of times, but his final words galvanized the conference. "You are witnesses to that light. Go preach the Good News to your nations. You are His messengers. The Glory of the Lord is upon you, for the Lord has turned our darkness into light that we may proclaim the salvation of our God through all the nations. Do the work of an evangelist."

Billy had a realistic sense of human nature. The scandal surrounding the television evangelists, Jim and Tammy Bakker, hit the news when I was interviewing him in Asheville in 1987. Since I had written a lot about televangelists, reporters barraged me with phone calls. In between calls, Billy called unexpectedly and asked for my help in talking to the media. He explained, "You know, of course, that we made rules for our organization years ago that have protected us from much of this. However, if I say that, I sound like I'm being self-righteous, and I can't be sure that I won't fall sometime in the future myself."

I conducted in-depth research on the way President Nixon's administration used Billy Graham. I found evidence that clearly revealed their intent to manipulate him, including notes on the precise things they wanted him to say or write. He was not aware of any of this, and the information stunned him when I shared it. After our conversation, he stretched out his long arms, put his hands on the back of the couch and stated, "I knew what I had said to the President, and I knew what he had said to me, but when I saw all those memos that circulated in the background, I felt like a sheep led to the slaughter."

Integrity was the quality that meant most to him. People would say, "You can split him all the way down, and he's going to be the same." Thus, when he realized that Nixon and his aides had manipulated him, he found it very difficult. It was especially hard for him to believe that Nixon himself would do this. He must have had a much more optimistic view of Nixon's religiosity than most people who knew him.

One day, after I had spent several hours interviewing Billy and visiting with Ruth, I was being driven down a steep, icy road by a handyman who acted as caretaker for the Grahams' property and whose wife helped Ruth with the cooking and housework. As he maneuvered the four-wheel-drive Jeep down the narrow, treacherous road, he volunteered, "You've been visiting with some mighty good people today. My wife and I have been knowing Mister and Miz Graham for fifteen years, and I'm telling you they are the same inside the house as they are outside."

Everyone recognizes Billy's humility, but he also had ambition and he sometimes experienced a tension between the two. Sometimes, he would say, "I wish I would never see my name up in lights again." At other times, he would point out that he didn't see enough signs announcing his mission. The dean at his college confided that Billy always wanted to do something big for God.

Billy Graham's photographer, Russ Busby, who may have known him better than anyone, once commented that Billy's biggest asset was his humility, but that he also had an ego like the rest of us. However, when his ego asserted itself, Russ explained, Billy always brought it back under control quickly. "Billy Graham is human, but he works on it," Russ told me. "It takes a big ego to be a big preacher, but the difference between Billy and the others is that when God wants to speak to him, at least He can get his attention."

·62·

JOHN MAXWELL

Author, speaker, leadership expert; founder of EQUIP Leadership,
The John Maxwell Company and The John Maxwell Team

A couple of years ago Billy Graham invited me to his home in North Carolina to spend an afternoon with him. I had known Billy for twenty-five years but I hadn't seen him for a while. He sounded very excited about it.

Because I love leadership and love to talk about leaders, I thought I would ask him questions about leaders that he had met around the world and who he considered to be the great leaders. I hoped he'd give me a very full, mature perspective on what good leadership is all about.

So I developed a list of maybe fifteen to twenty questions I wanted to ask him during our time together. We began a wonderful conversation, catching up on news because we hadn't been together for a couple of years. After about ten or fifteen minutes I thought, *Okay, let's dive into this, John. Let's find out who he thinks the great world leaders are and hear some of his stories about them.*

So I asked him the first leadership question. He replied, "John, really, I brought you up here today to talk about your ministry, what you're doing." And I said, "Well, I'm just trying to train leaders internationally like I have been." I kind of sloughed it off and dove back into my idea of talking with him about his experiences and the leaders he had met.

And so I dove back in with my list of questions. He said, "Well, tell me about Equip. What's happening in Equip right now?" Equip is my nonprofit organization that has trained five million leaders in 175 countries.

"Okay, I'll give you a quick update," I replied. I was planning just to go through it as quickly as I could—just a basic, off-the-top, *Reader's Digest* version so I could get back to where I wanted to go with our discussion.

So I told him the basics and thought he would be satisfied with that and that we could then talk a little bit about his experiences with leadership. Then he said, "Well, tell me, what is your most pressing challenge right now?"

The whole afternoon I tried to get him to talk about himself, his ministry, the leaders he knew, but he just wouldn't go there. He was about ninety years old at the time, but he still wanted to learn. He still wanted to find out what was happening. He still wanted to grow and know how to pray for me. "What are your challenges, and what can I do for you?" he said.

And he talked a lot about the fact that his ministry was evangelistic, trying to help people find God, and in our nonprofit ministry we develop that relationship with God. We try to train people to be leaders. "We're on the front end, and you're on the back end," he said. "And this is a great combination."

He went over to his desk and picked up my book, *21 Laws of Leadership*. He wanted to talk about some of the laws. The whole day, he just absolutely refused to talk about himself.

I knew this about Billy Graham before I got there, but I was reminded of it in our meeting. This is a man who is really humble, and the definition of humility is that humble people don't think less of themselves. They think less *about* themselves. That's Billy Graham. That's the way he's always been.

I learned so many lessons that day. I learned again that he wanted to keep learning and growing. It was again very clear to me his ministry was so successful because it was always about others, not about himself.

Billy Graham could have told stories all day. That's what I wanted him to do. That's what I was hoping for, but I know well why it didn't happen. A friend of mine once defined charisma as not about personality; the reason people are drawn to charismatic people is because they're other-people-minded. This fits Billy Graham exactly.

When we finished our conversation that afternoon, Billy looked at me and said, "Now, I want to pray with you." And so I went over to where he was sitting, and again it was all about my ministry and where I was going and what I was trying to accomplish. When he had finished, I kissed him on the cheek and left the room. I thought to myself, *Well, I didn't get any answers to the questions I had, but I just spent an afternoon in the presence of a great man.*

Greatness is hard to define, but you know it when you see it. And everybody else knows it, too. And one of the things about being around great people like Billy is that, you don't look at them and think, "Oh, they're great, and wow, I'm so small" because they so much believe in you and focus on you that you walk out and feel a greater spirit yourself.

I've always said that pseudo-great people, after you have met them, leave you thinking about how great they are and how small you are. There's a huge gap, and you also have this feeling that you never can close that gap. There's always going to be a distance between their greatness and your smallness.

But with Billy you're in the midst of unbelievable greatness, and yet somehow you're empowered and encouraged and uplifted by it, and when you walk away you feel like that spirit—the mantle that he has—has been placed on you, at least for a short while.

When I've been with Billy, I have found he's always uncomfortable talking about his accomplishments or what he's done. He wants to get off the subject quickly. The only time I have ever found him to be comfortable talking about his ministry is when he talks about what God has done. It's as if he is saying, "I'm really comfortable with what God has done for me and my ministry, but I'm not at all comfortable about what I myself have done for my ministry." I think that is the secret of his power. He understands that he isn't the source. He may be a vehicle, but he's not the source. I've never seen him get the two confused.

He is a perfect example of how God can bless a person and choose him because He knows He can trust him. Billy wasn't going to steal any of God's thunder, that's for sure. His life is a beautiful example of how God will use a person if that person will let Him have the credit. I've never, ever seen Billy try to steal any of the applause. In fact, if anything, he runs and hides from it. That's another quality of greatness. He has been and is a great messenger of God. A great person.

·63·

TOBY MCKEEHAN (TOBYMAC)

Pioneering Christian hip-hop/pop recording artist and producer,
Grammy Award and Gospel Music Award winner, author

When the Billy Graham organization first asked our rock trio dc Talk to perform at his June 1994, crusade in Cleveland, Ohio, we weren't sure if it was a joke. We associated Billy Graham with the great Gospel singer Bev Shea, who had performed at his crusades since the beginning. His music was beautiful, but totally conservative and traditional, so we never thought Billy Graham would use rock and roll and hip-hop.

Around that time, Billy Graham felt it was vital to connect with more young people to share the message of God's love and forgiveness. Some of the members of his organization thought that the kind of high-energy music we offered could be a powerful vehicle for that. They were essentially turning the traditional crusade model into what they eventually called a "Concert for the Next Generation." Though about half of the organization's board members were unsure about this approach, the others wanted it. Like Billy, they were strongly inspired to reach out.

A couple of guys from the mission team came to watch our

show. To their credit, they didn't just want a rock group; they wanted performers with integrity and heart. They met us after the show and told us, "This is real. Dr. Graham would love to have you in Cleveland."

Next, we were asked to meet with Dr. Graham and his wife Ruth at their small home in the North Carolina mountains. I think they wanted to get to know our hearts. When we arrived, we were invited to sit down and we all started talking. Then something happened that I'll never forget. Dr. Graham asked us if we wanted something to drink. He actually went to the kitchen and brought us two Cokes and a glass of water on a tray. That servant's heart at work even in his home impressed me deeply.

Billy told us that we were his translators for the next generation, helping put the Gospel message into a language they could understand. I saw that he cared enough for the world's youth to risk the possibility that half his people might not like us joining him on stage. However, for Billy Graham, reaching young people was worth the risk. To me, that showed who he was.

When we appeared with Billy Graham at the Cleveland Stadium, we had already performed at large arenas, but nothing the size of that stadium. I remember walking across the field to the stage in this massive, empty stadium for a sound check. It felt unbelievable. We later found out that about 65,000 people attended.

When we went up to pray with Billy at the Cleveland Stadium, I told Mrs. Graham, "We're so honored that you would invite us here, and we can't believe this place is full." She returned, "Well, that's what was supposed to happen. dc Talk stocked the pond so Billy could go fishing." Ruth was always funny and great with words. "I don't think that's true because we don't play stadiums," I responded. "We didn't stock this pond, but I appreciate the humility."

That appearance started us on an amazing run of at least a dozen concerts for the next generation. The crusade team scheduled the youth-oriented programs for Saturday nights and that's when we played. The audience was quite different from the typical one you would find at a Billy Graham event. There was much celebration, and it felt like a real concert with all the lights and big sound that came with it. The crowds were huge — 60,000, 90,000 people. We sang before Billy Graham spoke, and then introduced him. When people ask me what my best show or most memorable moments were, I always point to those evenings with Billy Graham.

We usually sat behind him on the platform, and I had repeatedly watched a river of people coming down from the stadium stands onto the field to make a commitment to faith. It was always an emotional, tear-filled experience. One evening, he spoke about whether God was real. We can't see Him, so how do we know He is real? Dr. Graham explained that we can't see the wind, but we see the trees blowing. After the sermon, I grabbed a pen and paper and started writing as I walked out of the stadium. Billy Graham's message had birthed the song, "Mind's Eye":

In my mind, I can see Your face
As Your love pours down in a shower of grace
Some people tell me that You're just a dream
My faith is the evidence of things unseen

At the Georgia crusade, something he said grabbed my attention, because it sounded so familiar. I suddenly realized that he was reading a lyric to a song I had written called "The Hard Way." You can't imagine how choked up I got. That was definitely one of the highlights of my life. I felt completely humbled.

Reverend Graham is unfailingly gentle and kind. Especially

coming from the world of rock and hip-hop, his gentle spirit and his meekness stand out for me. They honestly made me want to be like that. He took a genuine interest in all three of us in dc Talk. He always wanted to meet with us before we did something together, and he would pray for and with us. He was always extremely thankful that we would come. We felt like it was the opportunity of a lifetime, while he acted as if we were doing him a favor. I was always aware of him: he personified everything right about Christianity.

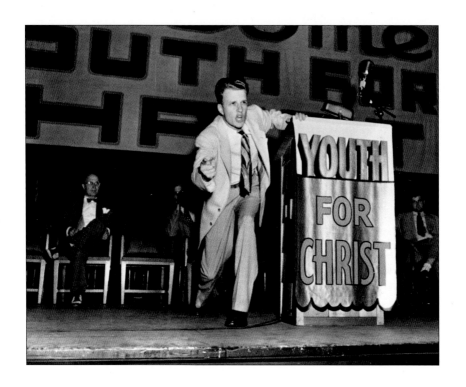

Billy Graham preaching during the Youth for Christ days.

*World War II hero
and Olympic athlete
Louis Zamperini,
with Billy Graham
in 1949.*

*A lasting friendship: Louis Zamperini and Billy Graham,
at Billy Graham's home in 2011.*

Billy Graham with Martin Luther King, Jr. in 1957.

Times Square during the 1957 New York Crusade.

Yankee Stadium during the 1957 New York Crusade.

*Billy Graham's family with Franklin, Bunny, Anne,
Gigi and Ruth holding Ned in 1958.*

Billy and Ruth Graham's home in Montreat, North Carolina.

Los Angeles Coliseum during the 1963 Billy Graham Crusade.

Charlotte, North Carolina during the 1966 Billy Graham Crusade.

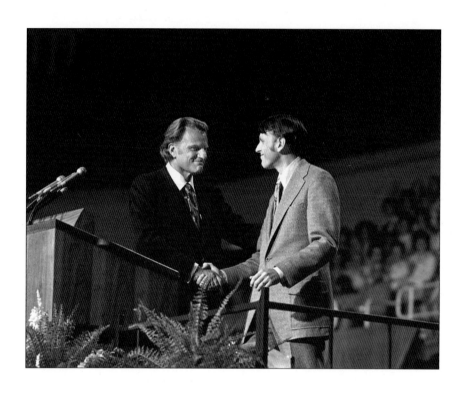

Billy Graham with associate and brother-in-law Leighton Ford during the 1972 Charlotte, North Carolina Billy Graham Crusade.

Press conference for the Georgia Prayer Breakfast,
with then-Governor Jimmy Carter, 1972.

Seoul, South Korea 1973 Billy Graham Crusade:
1.1 million in attendance.

Billy Graham with Henry Kissinger in 1973.

Receiving the Presidential Medal of Freedom Award from President Ronald Reagan in 1983.

National Prayer Breakfast with President Ronald Reagan.

Packed streets greet Billy Graham during his 1985 visit to Timisoara, Romania.

Billy Graham visiting Queen Elizabeth II in 1989.

Billy and Ruth Graham at home in Montreat, North Carolina in 1990.

Billy Graham in his office, with longtime friend and music director, Cliff Barrows, in 1992.

Billy Graham with Pope John Paul II in 1993.

Billy and Ruth Graham's 50th anniversary with their children in 1993.

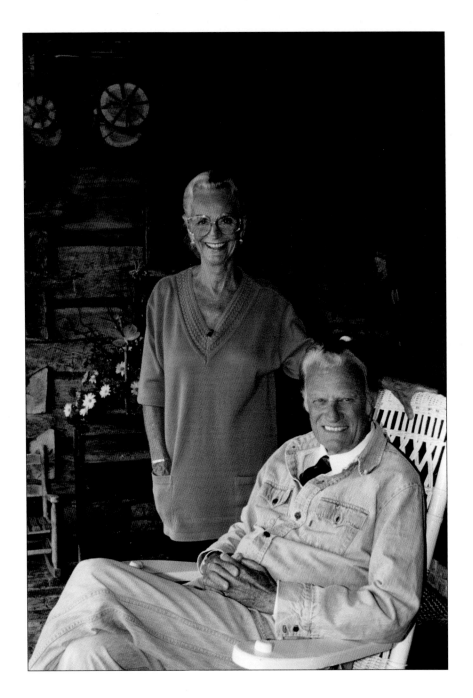

Billy and Ruth Graham at home in Montreat, North Carolina in 1993.

Interview on CNN's Larry King Live, 1994.

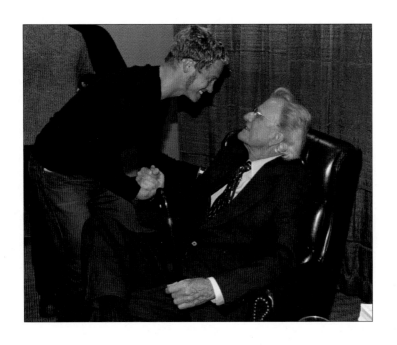

Christian hip-hop artist Toby McKeehan (tobyMac)
visits Billy Graham at the 1998 Tampa, Florida Crusade.

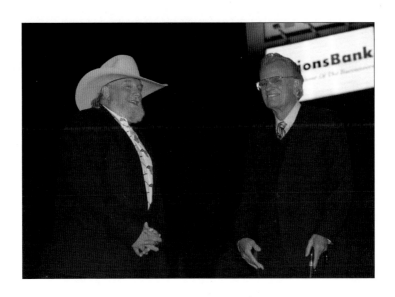

Performer Charlie Daniels with Billy Graham
at the 1998 Tampa, Florida Crusade.

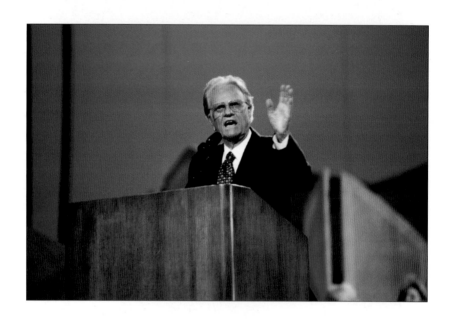

*Billy Graham preaching during the 2000 Nashville
Billy Graham Crusade.*

*Ricky Skaggs, with his Gospel Music Association Award,
visits with Billy Graham during the 2001 Louisville, Kentucky
Billy Graham Crusade.*

*Gospel singer Bill Gaither visits with Billy Graham during the
2001 Louisville, Kentucky Billy Graham Crusade.*

Billy Graham with President Bill Clinton in the Oval Office in 2001.

Billy Graham preaching during the 2002 Dallas, Texas Billy Graham Crusade.

Michael Tait, of the Christian rock band Newsboys, visits with Billy Graham during the 2003 Oklahoma City Billy Graham Crusade.

J.C. Watts, former congressman, greets Billy Graham during the 2003 Oklahoma City Billy Graham Crusade.

*Billy Graham with BGEA associate Rick Marshall during the
2003 San Diego, California Billy Graham Crusade.*

The Graham family at the 2007 Billy Graham Library dedication.

Presidents George H. W. Bush, Jimmy Carter and Bill Clinton at the Billy Graham Library dedication in 2007.

Larry Ross, Director of Media / Public Relations for Billy Graham, consults with him at home in Montreat, 2007.

*Interview with Greta Van Susteren at BGEA headquarters
in North Carolina, 2010.*

President Barack Obama visits Billy Graham at his home
in Montreat, North Carolina, 2010.

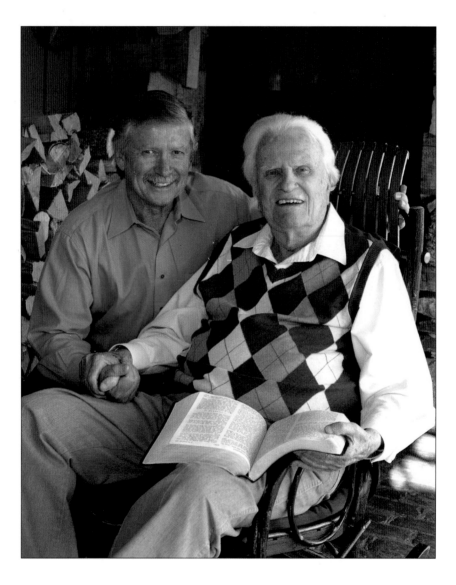

*With his personal pastor Don Wilton at home
in Montreat, North Carolina, 2010.*

·64·

MILES MCPHERSON

Pastor of the Rock Church Academy in San Diego, California;
motivational speaker and author, president of Miles Ahead Ministries

My very first exposure to Billy Graham occurred many years ago. I was about ten years old, and I happened to see part of a Billy Graham crusade at New York's Yankee Stadium on a black and white television. I remember thinking, *Who does he think he is? What is that all about?*

But now I get it. Billy Graham stuck to his task. And watching those old tapes now, I see that he was on fire. He was fighting a battle, speaking forcefully, jabbing his finger. I get fired up now just looking at it.

Billy Graham became an example to me as an evangelist. He didn't go off on tangents and get involved in things that weren't focused simply on the Gospel.

I do altar calls very regularly, and they don't change. The essence of them hasn't changed in 2,000 years, and seeing Billy Graham be faithful to that same simple message has been an encouragement to me to stay focused as well.

I met Billy Graham in 2003, at the crusade in San Diego. I was the chair of the group working with young people, so I was involved in organizing the youth night and I was there every day. He was such a down-to-earth, straightforward guy.

I realize now that there are certain people throughout history who have been called to perform certain tasks, and all the stars aligned to make them bigger than life. Like Martin Luther King, Jr. and the civil rights movement, for example. People like that come at very specific times when the culture needs them or wants whatever they have to offer. Billy Graham is one of those people. God used him in a very specific way, and at a time when our society was ready to have crusades night after night, filling stadiums.

It was a different time then. God needed a guy who was willing to make personal sacrifices. The crusades were long, and Billy Graham was gone from home for long periods at a time, yet he gave his life to that enterprise. He showed his commitment to the Gospel.

We are in a different era now. I could sit in my home and type something on my computer and reach the world. People don't go to crusades as much as they used to. They don't have to, as evangelists have other means to reach them. So it's a very different era.

Back in those days, when there were huge crusades, Billy Graham knew exactly how to speak to a vast crowd. The spirit of God speaks to everybody individually, and so did Billy Graham. He knew that a crowd is just a collection of individuals. All he had to do was talk. He just spoke the Gospel, and people were drawn to it. They were just waiting for the altar call. Some were already convinced they were going to get saved, and others had a revelation when they were there. When he spoke at those crusades, the Holy Spirit grabbed people's hearts and prepared them to make that decision. I believe that the preparation had actually started months and years before they even got there. So

Billy Graham just had to speak and give the altar call, confident that God had prepared him to deliver the message. He was just there to do his part.

God uses people in certain ways. A lot of times we may think, in explaining someone's success or the direction they took in life, well, this person had the personality; this person had the sense of humor, and so forth. Sometimes people say, "I have a big church because I was a professional NFL football player," but that is an insult to God. It's really the work of the Spirit of God and is the province of God.

So too with Billy Graham. The power he had in his preaching days was God-given, whether it was his personality, his humble spirit, his tone of voice, or other personal qualities. It is all God-given. What counts is how the spirit of God flows through each particular personality, and how faithful the person is to the mission.

Billy Graham was devoted to his mission. Golf pros will tell you that you can't win a golf tournament on the first day of the four-day tournament, but you can definitely lose it on the first day. So too, there are things that a minister can do to disqualify himself, even near the end of his earthly ministry. A lack of devotion can quickly destroy a lifetime of work. It's devotion that has kept Billy Graham in the game for all these decades. He must at some point have had some disappointments, like we all do, but he just stuck to it. I so admire that. His devotion is amazing, and for me, he will always remain an example of a true evangelist.

·65·

BARBARA MINTY MCQUEEN

Photographer, widow of actor Steve McQueen;
author of Steve McQueen: The Last Mile

Steve McQueen and I had only been together for four years and married for one when he died at age fifty. He had been extremely ill for some time. He suffered from a form of cancer called mesothelioma, caused by exposure to asbestos, and it had widely metastasized. Being one of the biggest movie stars of the time, the glare of the press was nearly constant.

Steve had been using some non-traditional approaches to treating cancer available in Mexico and he had decided to go there for an operation that was essentially a last-ditch effort to save his life. The minister of our evangelical church in Ventura knew Billy Graham, and Steve asked the minister if they could meet before the surgery. They really wanted to see each other, and it just happened that Billy Graham had a break in his schedule that allowed him to come.

When he arrived, Billy sat with Steve for a long time. Nobody was at their meeting except the two of them, so no one else will ever hear what they discussed, though I know that Steve told

Billy that he had found Christ and they talked about it. I love that Steve got to have this meeting with Billy and didn't have to share it with his fans. Even I wasn't allowed to hear about what transpired, but I can imagine some of it. I think it was like Steve's last hurrah.

Steve was always curious about life, and I think he wanted to meet Billy Graham so he could get some guidance, some answers. He probably perceived Billy Graham as someone with the wisdom and experience to guide him to the unknown. He seemed relieved and happy when the meeting was arranged. I didn't get to talk to Steve about his impressions of the meeting because he went right to Mexico, but I knew it had given him serenity. I drove instead of flying, but Steve's right-hand man, Grady Ragsdale, traveled with him and told me that Steve was at peace after his time with Billy, that he was good with everything. I am so grateful for his time with Billy Graham.

When Steve arrived in Juarez, he settled into the clinic and the rest of our small group settled into a funky, little hotel. We knew that his heart might not be strong enough to survive the procedure, but if successful, it could have given him a few years. He had the operation the next day, but his heart failed and he passed that night.

When I got the phone call at four in the morning, I was in shock. The first person I called was Billy Graham. He spoke with me for quite a while. He was strong, yet kind, and somehow he made everything okay. He helped me understand Steve's death as a loss of one type, but a gain for Steve. I'm not a traditionally religious person, and I hadn't followed Billy Graham before that time, but I am very spiritual. I took what he told me and put it into my own terms and I work with it. The kindness he showed and the words he shared remain with me to this day.

After some confusion, we got Steve home and gave him the

most glorious sendoff. I feel him with me in spirit every single day. I especially felt his presence taking care of me for the years it took me to get my feet on the ground and know I was truly okay.

Those events provided the biggest lesson of my life and I see it all as a gift that keeps on giving. Life throws all sorts of curve balls at you to see which way you're going to hit them. It makes you strong, so you can be healthy and go on with it. Each day I learn a little something, and I think about things that Steve might have done or said or how he would have handled a situation. I start complaining about stupid things and then I remember that I am blessed just to be alive. It's as if Steve is trying to straighten me out and kick me in the behind, saying, "Hey, you're there; I'm here," wherever "here" is. "Put a smile on your face and enjoy yourself."

When Steve took that flight to El Paso on his way to Mexico, Billy accompanied him to the airport and was with him when he boarded the plane. Right before he left, he gave Steve a Bible. It looks like a personal travel Bible that had accompanied him on a world tour. It says "Billy Graham" on the front of it, and is extremely well worn, complete with what look like coffee stains. It contains verses, notes to President Nixon, and notes for big speeches, as well as for presidents of foreign countries and other people with whose names I'm familiar. It's spectacular.

When the clinic where Steve passed made it possible for us to see him, Grady found the Bible on Steve's chest. He graciously gave it to me, and I still treasure it to this day.

·66·

MIKE NAWROCKI

Voice actor, writer and director;
co-creator of the popular children's animated series VeggieTales

Billy Graham has touched my life in big ways. To tell my story, I must go back to the mid to late '70s. My dad was in the Air Force, so I grew up in a military family. We moved around a lot, and at the time, my dad was transferred from Denver to Washington, D.C. When we had difficulty selling our house, he went to D.C. ahead of us and ended up moving in temporarily with his commanding officer.

We had grown up going to church but my dad was strict and oftentimes distant, and by the time we joined him in Washington, he had changed considerably. His commanding officer was a believer, a Christian, and my dad had come to know Christ as a result of just spending time with him and then living in his home.

So for us as a family, experiencing this brand-new dad upon moving to Washington, D.C. was just amazing, and we started going to a church in town. It was a Christian and Missionary Alliance denomination, and I started to become involved with the youth group there. I saw kids there who really loved God and I saw how that affected their lives.

So I was well prepared for what I call my Billy Graham

moment, which came in 1977. I was eleven years old. I remember that I was sitting down watching TV, and it just caught my eye—there was a Billy Graham crusade on. I forget where he was, but I do remember being drawn into it. I was at a point in my life where I was ready to hear the message. I remember very vividly Billy Graham preaching the Gospel message and the biblical verse he would frequently quote near the end of his message: "Behold, I stand at the door and knock; if anyone hears My voice and opens the door, I will come in…" (Revelation 3:20).

In that moment, just sitting there and watching Billy Graham on TV, I came to know Christ. Basically, I just invited Christ into my heart, saying, "Yes, I'm a sinner; I've been separated from God. I would love just to know Christ as my Savior." I had already known the effect such a statement had had on my parents, and at the church I'd seen how God has an effect on people's lives and can make a real change. Now Billy Graham was there to make everything very clear to me and just say, "Okay, this is how we are separated from God, and this is what Christ offers us." And by that He meant Christ's sacrifice and the promise that He has for us, giving us the ability to have communion with Him, to know Him, and to be redeemed.

I don't remember having seen other preachers on TV, but I remember the clarity and the tenderness with which Billy Graham spoke, and I felt very drawn to him as a speaker. The Gospel made so much sense to me, having him explain it. I don't know why.

I just remember feeling happy at the time. We were going through tough times in our family but I was seeing how God was changing my dad, and how He was working in the lives of my mom and brothers. It was all very real to me. It made perfect sense. I'd seen the before and after.

So that was my Billy Graham moment. That one decision set the path for the rest of my life.

A couple of years later I felt like God was calling me to the ministry. I went to Crown College, a small Christian college in the Minneapolis area, where I took a number of Bible and theology classes. That was where I met Phil Vischer, on a student ministry doing puppetry. He and I became great friends, and I soon found myself making children's movies and television shows. That led to *VeggieTales*, which Phil and I created together.

I am still a Christian believer, and that is a huge part of what we do with *VeggieTales*. We create shows that remind kids that God made them special and He loves them very much. Our motivation is to bring kids closer to God and to tell stories that parents can use as a resource to share biblical values with their kids. That's born out of my decision to accept Christ into my heart, and my belief that God loves us and wants a relationship with us.

I continue to study the Bible every day, for work and for personal understanding. I consider what I do in *VeggieTales* to be a ministry because we're teaching kids Bible lessons and biblical values, all based on a biblical worldview, which comes from studying Scripture.

And in so many ways all this started with Billy Graham and his ministry. It was through Billy Graham that I made that decision for Christ when I was an eleven-year-old kid watching him preach. With the simple clarity of his message, Billy Graham touched my heart and changed my life. As someone who has been devoted to ministering to children, it would not surprise me to learn that in many ways, Billy Graham's influence is having a similar impact on eleven-year-old kids today.

·67·

SAM NUNN

Former U.S. Senator (Georgia); co-chair and
CEO of the Nuclear Threat Initiative

The first time I remember being with Billy, I was ten years old. It was 1948, and I lived in a little town called Perry, Georgia, 110 miles south of Atlanta. Our Methodist Youth Fellowship went to Atlanta to the home of the Atlanta Crackers, which was an AAA minor league baseball club, and Billy had a rally held there in the baseball stadium. They held the rally outdoors, and I remember he was a wonderful preacher. Of course, I was one of a huge number of people out there so I did not meet him personally, but he had an effect on everyone in our young crowd that night. He had a terrific message. Of course, he was a young man then, too. He's twenty years older than me, so he would have been about thirty.

When I served in the U.S. Senate, I attended what we called Senate Prayer Group luncheons, on Wednesdays. We had a group of five or six of us — two Republicans and two Democrats: Mark Hatfield and Pete Domenici, and Lawton Chiles from Florida, and myself. Doug Coe, the evangelical minister, and Dick Halverson, who was chaplain of the Senate, joined us every week. Then we gave a standing invitation to two other people. One was

Arthur Burns, who was Jewish, a wonderful man, and head of the Federal Reserve for years. And the second one was Billy Graham, who would come whenever he was in Washington.

In this group, we were very open with each other about our problems, our families, our faith, the challenges of political life, and the challenges of personal life. And Billy, when he joined our group, was as vulnerable as the rest of us. He didn't come in to preach. He came in as a fellow human being and a friend who had his own challenges and doubts, his own sense of the need for fellowship and the need for friendship and sharing. He was real.

Billy reached out to all people and all religions, and he did it in the spirit of Jesus. He felt there was too much emphasis on religious organizations and not nearly enough focus on Jesus and His life, on His example and His lessons. Of course, he spoke to millions and millions of people about this, but he also talked about this during private conversations.

I always recall how he would reach out to people all over the world, to those with different faiths, and to many people with no faith at all. And he led by example, such as standing up for civil rights in the 1950s when it was very important. He tore down the racial barriers between congregations. He told organizers to remove the ropes that were supposed to separate people by race during his crusades. He really did carry the spirit and the message of Jesus, not only with his words, but with his life and his example.

I gave him a small Bible once. It was very small, one you could put in your pocket. I saw him many years later toward the end of his career of actively holding crusades around the country. It was during a crusade at the big Coliseum in Atlanta, and I was up on the stage with him and six or eight other people. I said "hello" but hadn't yet had a chance to talk to him. But he pulled that Bible out in front of thousands and thousands of people and said that he had gotten it as a gift from me, and he'd had it with him in his pocket ever since. That was an amazing memory, especially since I'd given him the Bible at least five or six years before. His authenticity and sincerity shines through. People realize it instinctively. That distinguished him from any preacher I know of in that generation who was in the public limelight.

There are a lot of preachers who are sincere, yet they aren't world famous. But Billy Graham is, and yet you couldn't have lunch with him and sit there for an hour without knowing that this man is genuine and his faith is real. His purpose was not self-centered. It wasn't about being famous. For so many years, people have understood that, and the reason they believe he is authentic and telling the truth from his perspective is because that's the way he really is.

I spend most of my time now working with the Nuclear Threat Initiative, trying to reduce nuclear dangers, including catastrophic terrorism and getting nuclear materials under control. In 2005, I read an article which reported that Billy had made a statement about nuclear terrorism and the need for prayer. So I wrote Billy a letter and sent him some information on projects that we were working on. I told him not to write back because he was about to have a rally in New York City, and I knew he had too much to do. But he replied with a very nice letter, adding a handwritten note at the bottom that said, "I'm praying for the people of New Orleans." This was just after the devastation of Hurricane Katrina. Well into his eighties, he was still keeping up with everything, and praying for everyone.

The last time I saw Billy, he gave the prayer at a dedication event where I was speaking at the Mayo Clinic. He still had a commanding presence and a commanding voice and commanding credibility with the audience. He was certainly not as physically rigorous as he had been when I'd seen him before, but he still had all the Billy Graham strengths. Watching him speak, it occurred to me that back when I was ten years old watching him preach, I had never dreamed that I would personally get to know him when I grew up. Seeing him again reminded me of what a real blessing it has been, having a friendship with Billy.

·68·

BARACK OBAMA

44th President of the United States

At a National Prayer Breakfast in Washington, D.C., Senator Mark Pryor read a letter written by Billy Graham:

I want to convey my personal greetings to each of you assembled this morning for the National Prayer Breakfast. I miss being with you all, having been a part of this annual event sponsored by the House and Senate prayer group since the very beginning, often as a speaker. Though age and health prevent me from being there in person, I am with you in spirit and you are in my heart. I want to say a special word of encouragement to the many friends meeting today from across the country and across the world, especially President Obama and his wife Michelle and Vice President Joseph Biden and his wife Jill for whom I pray every day as the Scriptures command us to do. The National Prayer Breakfast is one of the most amazing gatherings as people from most of the nations of the world, representing every race, color, creed, religion and political affiliation, or none, come together in the name of Jesus to focus on his teachings and follow his example of how to live and love each other. Throughout my ministry spanning more than 60 years, I have tried to lift up the name of Jesus to audiences and individuals in many of the countries you represent today against the backdrop of polarization in our nation this election year and the tensions across the globe due to war, disease, poverty and other problems. I pray that foundation of unity you embody around the person of Jesus may be an example to the world and a catalyst for peace, freedom and reconciliation as each of us discovers in our own hearts the love and forgiveness He offers to those who seek and turn to him in repentance and faith. May God richly bless your time of fellowship and inspiration this morning. And may the Lord give each of you a special sense of the Spirit as you pray together and pray in Jesus' name.

President Barack Obama then delivered his own reflections on what was read to the group:

Mark read a letter from Billy Graham, and it took me back to one of the great honors of my life, which was visiting Reverend Graham at his mountaintop retreat in North Carolina, when I was on vacation with my family at a hotel not far away.

And I can still remember winding up the path up a mountain to his home. Ninety-one years old at the time, facing various health challenges, he welcomed me as he would welcome a family member or a close friend. This man who had prayed great prayers that inspired a nation, this man who seemed larger than life, greeted me and was as kind and as gentle as could be.

And we had a wonderful conversation. Before I left, Reverend Graham started praying for me, as he had prayed for so many presidents before me. And when he finished praying, I felt the urge to pray for him. I didn't really know what to say. What do you pray for when it comes to the man who has prayed for so many? But like that verse in Romans, the Holy Spirit interceded when I didn't know quite what to say.

And so I prayed—briefly, but I prayed from the heart. I don't have the intellectual capacity or the lung capacity of some of my great preacher friends here that have prayed for a long time. But I prayed. And we ended with an embrace and a warm goodbye.

And I thought about that moment all the way down the mountain, and I've thought about it in the many days since. Because I thought about my own spiritual journey—growing up in a household that wasn't particularly religious; going through my own period of doubt and confusion; finding Christ when I wasn't even looking for him so many years ago; possessing so many shortcomings that have been overcome by the simple grace of God. And the fact that I would ever be on top of a mountain, saying a prayer for Billy Graham—a man whose faith had changed the world and that had sustained him through triumphs and tragedies, and movements and milestones—that simple fact humbled me to my core.

I have fallen on my knees with great regularity since that moment—asking God for guidance not just in my personal life and my Christian walk, but also in the life of this nation and in the values that hold us together and keep us strong. I know that He will guide us.

He always has, and He always will. And I pray his richest blessings on each of you in the days ahead.

·69·

BILL O'REILLY

Bestselling author, commentator and host of Fox News Channel's
The O'Reilly Factor

I've been aware of the Reverend Billy Graham and his work almost all my life. When I was a little kid my parents would watch him on television when he was preaching at his crusades. Then we saw him with Bob Hope and then again when he was engaged in other church activities. When I was older I noticed that he was very often with U.S. Presidents.

He came across to me as a very decent man. Although I'm a Roman Catholic, and he is a Protestant preacher, I just thought the message was very simple. He seemed to be a guy who loved his country and just wanted people to practice the basic tenets of the Christian religion, such as loving your neighbor as yourself. I admired him for that simple message.

When you are brought up in a religious home like I was, and go to Catholic school, you learn certain things—a basic philosophy about how you should act, what behaviors you should exhibit. Then later, when you notice that somebody is on the same wavelength as you are and puts things in terms that are very easy to understand, you have a positive feeling toward that person. That was how I felt about Billy Graham.

My upbringing in suburban New York City was very different from Reverend Graham's. We came from two very different parts of the United States. But I did admire the fact that he was trying to do good, and had the respect of so many U.S. Presidents.

I always noticed that he wasn't a negative guy. Some of the preachers can get a little negative, but he was basically trying to convince people that the kinder you are, the better. He just wanted people to understand that. As for me, I'm a simple guy. I like simple messages. I like consistency. I like very clear-cut topics of discussion, and he provided that.

Billy Graham's son Franklin told me one time when he was on *The O'Reilly Factor* that his father watched my program every night. I was surprised. "Why does he take the time to do that?" I asked. And Franklin Graham replied, "He likes the simplicity of the message." So what I admired about the Reverend Graham, he apparently liked about my show.

I can't say that I followed or participated in all his crusades, but it was obvious that people trusted him both personally and in the message he was delivering. That sense of trust is a very special thing. Being a commentator on political and social affairs, I have noticed that in the higher echelons of power, people only gravitate to those whom they trust, so it was apparent that all of those U.S. Presidents who confided in Billy Graham trusted him. Maybe some of them had their own political motives for forming a relationship with him. Perhaps they wanted to be seen with him because he had a big constituency in the country and they thought this might give them some political advantage. Who knows what their reasons were? But they certainly trusted him, and I think that for the most part there was something much more than political calculation at work. There must have been something special, even unique about the Reverend Graham and the fellowship he offered that made these U.S. Presidents go out of their way to be with him, to call him for advice, to be seen with him and photographed with him.

Given the fact that these powerful men would take the time to seek his counsel, I think that over his lifetime he has had just as much influence in the world through such private, one-on-one meetings as he did in the public sphere, preaching to large audiences.

There aren't too many people who rise to that level of acceptance in the corridors of power, especially the highest political office in the land, over such a long period of time, in so many different situations. In fact, I can't think of anyone who had more access to so many people in powerful positions in so many administrations as Billy Graham did. There had to be a reason, and I think it lies in his decency, his goodness, his simplicity. These are very transparent virtues. They cannot be faked, and by all accounts Billy Graham has them in full measure.

All these things register with me as someone who observes and watches and tries to be fair in evaluating Americans and how they are contributing to their country. Billy Graham's contribution has been a great one indeed. We are all in his debt, and the simple virtues he preaches never go out of fashion.

·70·

JOEL OSTEEN

Bestselling author, broadcast minister and
senior pastor of Lakewood Church in Houston, Texas

I grew up as a preacher's kid. My father was a Baptist minister for over nineteen years before he and my mother founded Lakewood Church in 1959, the church my father would lead for another forty years, and the one which I lead today. In addition to my own father, John Osteen, I grew up around many great ministers of the Gospel. They were revered in our family, and we were taught that there was no greater thing one could do than to bring the good news of Jesus Christ to the world. But of all the many ministers and evangelists we met and listened to over the years, there were none more admired and respected by my family than the Reverend Billy Graham. As a result, I saw him as a living legend.

Given this, one might be able to imagine how I felt when — about six years ago — I was given the opportunity to meet this great hero of the faith for the first time. Through a series of connections, I was invited to visit Reverend Graham at his home in Montreat, North Carolina. When I told my wife Victoria of the news, she became as excited as I was. From the moment we left for the airport in Houston, I was filled with anticipation. I remember telling Victoria that I felt like I was on my way to meet Moses or Elijah.

When we arrived in Montreat, we were met by Dr. David Bruce, Billy Graham's long-time executive assistant. Our first stop was the train station in Asheville where so many times Reverend Graham had begun his worldwide journeys. I remember feeling like I was in a movie—like we had stepped back in time. I could imagine this great man along with his team checking their luggage with the porter, waiting on the platform, and finally, boarding the train that would launch them on their great mission. I remember thinking how travel for him was more difficult in his early days and how easy we have it today. It was a dimension of his ministry that I had not considered before.

Next, we traveled to the house where Billy Graham's father-in-law, Dr. Nelson Bell, lived. We then drove up this steep and winding road to a place where Billy Graham used to run for exercise. I thought, *It's such a steep hill. He must have been in really good shape.* From there we drove through a gated entrance and soon came to a log cabin, the home of Billy and Ruth Graham. Dr. Bruce escorted us through the back door and into the cabin. It was very warm and inviting and reminded me of my grandmother's house back in Texas. As we admired the many mementos decorating Billy and Ruth's family room, Dr. Bruce told us to make ourselves at home and then excused himself to inform Dr. Graham that we had arrived.

After a few minutes, Billy Graham appeared wearing a flannel shirt and house slippers.

At that moment, I didn't even notice what he was wearing; I felt like Moses had just entered the room. Though he was slightly frail, in my eyes, he stood ten feet tall. With all my strength, I struggled to contain my emotions, though I truly felt overwhelmed by them. Victoria began to cry. He greeted us so graciously, telling us how happy he was that we had come. We embraced for a moment and then we were seated.

After all the anticipation and excitement that led up to this moment, I sat there not knowing what to say. I had been ministering to people since 1999 and had gained some notoriety over the last couple of years, but this was all new and different. I was now sitting with one of the greatest men I would ever meet, one who had devoted an entire lifetime to a great cause. What does one say to a man like this? All I could think of was to tell him what an honor it was for us to be there.

His reply was one I will never forget. He said, "You know, Joel, I feel very honored that you would come to see me today. Thank you, Joel." And then he followed up with, "I can't believe you are here."

I was amazed. I thought, *How can you not believe I am here? Who am I compared to you?* I told him once again, "No, Dr. Graham, Victoria and I are the ones who are honored."

He interrupted me and repeated, "I can't believe you came to see me." Then he asked earnestly, "What are you doing in town? Do you have a meeting?"

I said, "No, Dr. Graham, we flew here to see you."

He was genuinely surprised and again said, "I can't believe you came just to see me."

It was immediately clear to me that I was witnessing the very essence of Billy Graham—his humility.

We spoke a while longer—about half an hour—when I asked him if he could give me any advice. He simply said, "I don't know anything I would tell you, Joel, except keep doing what you're doing." Then he added, "Don't let people change you; stay true to what God has called you to do."

I have thought often of that advice and taken it to heart. But what really struck me was that here was a man who has impacted the world. I'm sure he could have gone on for hours and told me a hundred things that he had learned and experienced over his long and distinguished life. But he didn't. He was too gracious and too humble a man.

"I want you to come meet Ruth. I want you to come see Ruth," Dr. Graham repeated eagerly as he rose from his chair. He became visibly excited. Ruth was in the back bedroom lying in bed. She had not been well for some time.

"Ruth," he said, "Joel's here. Joel and Victoria are here."

As Victoria and I spent time with the Grahams, I watched him as he tenderly talked to her, caressed her hand and looked at her with such love and conviction. I was certain that Victoria was going to cry again. Then he rose from her side and walked a few steps until he stood beside an aquarium filled with various kinds of fish.

"I bought her this aquarium," he said. "She looks at life and movement in these fish."

This man, who had spent his entire life in service to God and men, was now spending his last years serving the woman he loved. Victoria and I were deeply moved. The three of us prayed with her before we left the room. That was the last time Victoria and I saw Ruth Graham. She went to be with the Lord a few months later.

We then spent a while longer with Dr. Graham, sitting in rocking chairs on the porch overlooking the magnificent Blue Ridge Mountains. There we were able to visit with two of Billy and Ruth's grown children, Franklin and Anne. They were very gracious, and we enjoyed sharing childhood stories.

After we prayed with Dr. Graham, we embraced and he kissed Victoria goodbye. Again he told us how honored he was that we came all that way to see him. As we drove away, I mentioned to

Dr. Bruce how humble and sincere I had found Dr. Graham to be.

"Well, that's the way Billy Graham is," he said. "He sees everything as the best. He'll have a piece of apple pie and say it was the best apple pie he's ever eaten."

I have had the privilege of visiting Dr. Graham on several occasions since that day, and while I am always impressed by his humility, one conversation remains etched in my mind. As we sat on his porch, he said to me, "Joel, I watch you on television three times a week and can't believe how you get up there and speak in that big stadium."

When he said that, I thought, *Dr. Graham, you've spoken in stadiums your whole life.* And then I replied, "Dr. Graham, I've learned from the best. I've learned from you."

He just laughed, looked at me and said, "I don't know what you could have learned from me."

·71·

LUIS PALAU

*Longtime associate of Mr. Graham, author, founder of the Luis Palau
Association; has preached to millions of people worldwide*

Billy Graham opened more doors for me than anybody in the
world. I met him when I was twenty-six years old. There was
a crusade in Fresno, California. My wife and I were missionaries
with Overseas Crusades (now OC International), although we
hadn't yet gone into the mission field to preach.

I volunteered as a Spanish translator for Mr. Graham
throughout the San Joaquin Valley. When Mr. Graham came to
town for the Fresno crusade, I sat across from him at the team
breakfast meeting. He didn't know me at that point, so he started
up a conversation. He said, "What are you planning to do?" I
said, "Well, I hope to have crusades. I've been learning about
how you do citywide evangelism and I want to do the same in
Latin America." He gave me simple advice that I never forgot.
"Go to the big cities," he said. "The biggest cities you can afford.
The cities are like mountains. When a man is in the mountain,
his voice echoes all around. Big cities bless the small towns. Go
to the big cities." I followed his advice.

Because of Mr. Graham, I was invited to the first World
Congress on Evangelism in Berlin in 1966, and to the second one

in Lausanne in 1974. It was there where I was asked to give a major address on mass evangelism. Billy Graham always stayed in touch, writing me letters, affirming me, encouraging me, and giving me opportunities to preach. He gave me another open door at the Congress on Evangelism in Amsterdam in 1983. On the second evening I had the privilege of giving the main address, speaking about the personal life of the evangelist, holiness, and integrity.

And he didn't stop there. Mr. Graham did it again in 1986, also in Amsterdam, inviting me to speak at the International Conference for Itinerant Evangelists. There were nearly 10,000 evangelists from all over the world. It was a time of recommitment to the Great Commission, and the event built confidence for our team to go all over the world. People trusted Mr. Graham, and Mr. Graham trusted us. What a life-long blessing that has been!

Through the years Mr. Graham would often say, "What can I do for you?" I always told him, "Please, speak well of me." That was worth gold to me. And he did. He was a man of his word. Many times he invited me to give my testimony at his crusades or he opened doors for me in other cities. He was a blessing in our lives.

When I was in his presence, I could feel how he honored Jesus Christ. I remember when I was praying with him, he would often flip open his New Testament. He always carried it in his inner pocket, and he always had something fresh, very Christ-centered, to say. You could tell he was close to the Lord on a daily basis, not just formally or once a week.

He is very knowledgeable about the Bible. He is such a deep-thinking man, not only about Scripture but also about life, about history, and even political news as it relates to the Bible. He has such a profound knowledge of God and of the world. He has always kept himself well informed, reading and absorbing all sorts of information.

One day I had the privilege of meeting his mother. She told me that when Billy was a teenager, especially after he was converted, he would take the *Encyclopedia Britannica* and lie on the floor in the living room of their house in North Carolina for hours, reading through the encyclopedia.

Although Billy Graham was extremely knowledgeable, he never took any credit for it. He would insist on saying, "To God be all the glory. To God alone the glory." I remember one incident in particular that is a marvelous illustration of Mr. Graham's humble spirit in that respect.

We were in Essen, Germany, for a youth congress. He and I were both speakers. One day we were in his hotel room, and T.W. Wilson, his assistant for many years, came in and said, "Billy, a young German evangelist wants to see you." Mr. Graham said, "Okay, bring him in."

A tall, handsome, well-dressed young evangelist entered the room. He said, "Mr. Graham, I was converted under your ministry. I want to be an evangelist like you. I studied theology at the university. I've formed a team." I think he said seventeen people. "I have money," he continued, "but I get no invitations. What can I do?"

I felt so sorry for the young lad, and Mr. Graham did as well. Mr. Graham was nonplussed. He had never had the problem of no invitations. He looked at T.W. and me as if he were saying, "I have no idea what you do to get invitations."

Mr. Graham talked to the young man for fifteen minutes or so. His advice was to "pray about it, and befriend the other clergy and ask them of the possibility to do some kind of evangelistic event. Start small. Don't think that overnight you can have a citywide campaign."

As their time together was coming to an end, the young man said to him, "Mr. Graham, would you bless me?" Mr. Graham was again a little surprised and taken aback, but he said, "Let's pray." And he began to pray for this young fellow. It was very touching. He was such a big man, and he was pouring out his heart to God for a young guy he'd never met before and would probably never see again. He was crying out to the Lord, "Lord, give him campaigns," he prayed. "Give him his heart's desire."

I was brought up among the Anglicans and I always close my eyes when I pray. And I heard Billy Graham's voice sound sort of muffled. It didn't sound as if he was speaking out loud or with his head up. So I opened my eyes to see what was going on. Mr. Graham was literally lying flat on the ground, spread-eagled with his face on the carpet in the hotel room. Just spread out flat. It was so touching. The greatest evangelist in the world—one of God's greatest servants—and here he was, on the floor, passionately praying for a young fellow he'd just met.

We got up and said goodbye to the young man. I was so moved by what had happened, I just blurted out, "Why were you on the ground?" He replied, "Well, Luis, the Bible says to Humble yourselves before the mighty hand of God that in due time He may exalt you." He continued, "I don't care how theologians explain that. I think that we who are in the public eye, and who people call by nice names, need to proactively humble ourselves before the mighty hand of God so that in due time He may exalt us if He chooses to exalt us."

When I was young, I often wondered why Mr. Graham insisted on repeating that phrase, "To God be all the glory." I later realized that when you are famous and people write books about you, there is a temptation to think highly of yourself. You've got to put the ego down. And I think he did that. Mr. Graham's love was not for himself but for God and the church.

He loved the church broadly. Interdenominationalism was one of the great lessons I learned from him: to love all people even when you disagree with them on doctrine. T.W. had a saying, "We are broad in our relationships but narrow in our message." In other words, the message of the Gospel, the pure Good News, is very narrow. Not in a negative sense, but very clear. Very pointed. Actually, T.W. got that saying from Mr. Graham. We copied him shamelessly in the early years. I copied almost everything he ever did! I once told him that I had preached his sermons many times, which was true. Now my son Andrew preaches my sermons, and they're Mr. Graham's, too.

I remember Mr. Graham speaking many times at the annual National Prayer Breakfast in Washington, D.C. He knew how to pick the right stories and use history and even politics appropriately. He seldom made a mistake. Many a time the Prayer Breakfast was pretty bland. Sometimes the speaker would not be very clear. But when Mr. Graham would get up to give the benediction, his prayer was like a little sermon. He would say something like, "Because of Jesus Christ, His shed blood on the cross, and His resurrection, if you confess your sins now and receive Jesus Christ by faith as your Lord and Savior, then you can have eternal life." He would enhance that breakfast because he always made sure to honor God. One of the things that Mr. Graham taught us, by his life and his actions, was 1 Samuel 2:30, in which God says, "Those who honor Me I will honor and those who despise Me shall be lightly esteemed." I think Mr. Graham honored God every time. He honored the Lord, and the Lord honored him. I would put that fabulous verse under his picture: Billy Graham. "Those who honor Me, I will honor."

·72·

KYRA PHILLIPS

CNN's HLN News anchor and
winner of two Edward R. Murrow Awards

It was 2005 and Billy Graham was about to launch his final crusade in New York. Because this man has had such an amazing influence in America and in the world, my producer and I approached CNN about doing an hour-long special on his life. "This is a huge deal," we explained. "We'll look at his politics, his faith, his background, and his relationship with his family. He is such a pillar, it will be powerful!" CNN said, "It's a go!"

My producer and I worked on the Billy Graham special for months. She made the arrangements and I interviewed his family and his friends. Two of his closest friends in the ministry, Cliff Barrows and Bev Shea, have known him for more than sixty years. Cliff directed the choir and Bev was a standout soloist during Reverend Graham's crusades. Their stories about him revealed fabulous insights into the man. Moreover, we traveled around the country, got to know his hometown and his farm. It was an extraordinary journey. My producer and I both grew up in Christian environments, and the values we possess led to the strong respect we have for Reverend Graham.

Weeks and weeks went by, and it was now just a few days

before the last crusade. I was in New York with my producer. Both of us agreed it would be a remarkable opportunity if we were granted a final interview with Reverend Graham. The people who represented him told us he was not feeling well and, more than likely, would not be able to speak with us. I told the representative I understood but assured him that I would be quick and as unobtrusive as possible.

A day or two before the crusade my producer woke me with an early morning phone call. She couldn't contain her shock and dismay. "You are not going to believe this!" she screamed into the phone. "Reverend Graham's people granted an interview to one of our co-workers!" As you can imagine, I jumped out of bed, completely blown away. "What are you talking about? We've been working on this special, we've been interviewing the entire family, we've gone to his hometown, and we've been tracing his roots! What do you mean a co-worker got the interview?" I got off the phone with my producer and immediately called Billy Graham's representative. "What is going on?" I bellowed (as respectfully as possible). "We've been working on this special and you know how important this is to us. We assumed if Billy Graham was well enough to talk, he'd talk to us." I didn't hold back. I really let him know how disappointed I was and how hurt I was. To be quite honest, I was devastated. I hung up the phone, upset and frustrated. About half an hour later, I got a call from the representative. This time he said, "You've got forty-five minutes to get to the hotel in New York City. You have the final interview with him."

Immediately, I went into action—jumping in the shower, throwing stuff together, calling my producer, and at the same time jotting down every essential question about America's pastor that I, and our viewers, wanted answered. I wanted to ask him about his amazing marriage to Ruth, about his discipline, about forgiveness, and about praying with our Presidents.

In less than half an hour I leaped into my car and headed to Reverend Graham's hotel. I called my producer en route and with mixed emotions I blurted, "I can't believe it's going down this way! I just want to make sure I get everything right." Then I started sobbing. I was excited and wanted the interview to be a home run. I was also feeling betrayed. All these emotions were going through my head. I said to my producer, "I've got to calm down. I've got to get it together. I need you to do me a big favor and pray with me right now." She said, "Okay, here we go." After leading us in prayer, I gratefully said, "Thank you!" In tears she said, "You bet."

I arrived at the hotel with so much on my heart. With my notebook in hand and lugging my suitcase behind me, I tried to find Reverend Graham. Finally, I located the conference room and knocked on the door. It opened to reveal Reverend Graham in the middle of a room that was beautifully lit. He was in a big chair with his hands on his knees looking calm and peaceful. He looked over at me and smiled.

I took a breath and said, "Hello everyone. It's nice to meet you." I introduced myself and got my notebook. I said, "Reverend Graham, it's great to meet you." He said, "It's very nice to meet you." I shook his hand, sat down, nearly overwrought with anxiety. My mind was spinning. I only had ten minutes for the interview, and it could be the last interview he was ever going to give. Suddenly it dawned on me—I was sitting there with the Reverend Billy Graham, the most powerful man of prayer in our country and, ironically, my journey to get to that point had left me completely stressed out. I decided to ask him to pray with me. I looked at the camera crew and asked, "Guys, could you do me a favor and shut the cameras off for a minute?" They powered everything down. I made sure the red lights were off.

I looked at this legendary man of unwavering faith and said, "Reverend Graham, I'm a little overwhelmed right now. It took so much to get here. I didn't think you would grant me this interview. I was told it wasn't going to happen. Then, I was told it was on. I'm not quite sure which way is up and which way is down at the moment. Could we just pray?" He looked at me like a caring father. This man, who over six decades counseled presidents and gave millions of Americans hope for a better life through faith, smiled at me and simply said, "Well, of course." Then he held my hand and we bowed our heads. We prayed for a few minutes, then opened our eyes. I sat back. I felt so at peace, so calm, and so relaxed. I never once looked down at my notes. We had an amazing conversation, one of the most memorable and beautiful moments I have had in my career.

·73·

GARY PLAYER

Grand Slam Champion golfer, member of the
World Golf Hall of Fame and founder of The Player Foundation

Billy Graham is one of the all-time great American heroes. And I don't say that lightly. When you win enough major golf championships, you get to travel and meet people from all around the world. I have been doing this for over sixty years and I have never met anyone who did not love him.

When he came to South Africa he filled the stadiums. He gave people a lot of encouragement, and he always gave such a well-balanced talk. He dedicated our youngest daughter to Christ during that crusade, and wow, she is a true daughter of Christ! She's something special. She has seven children and still finds time to teach all the neighborhood children every morning.

I first met Billy Graham in about 1960. Arnold Palmer and I were playing an exhibition game in Asheville, North Carolina, and he played with us. He played very well, too. But the most amazing thing for me was that the following year he invited me to his house. I spent two days there.

On one of those days, we were in the swimming pool together and Billy said, "You know, you've been playing so well this year." This was true. I was the leading money-winner and had won several tournaments leading up to the Masters. Billy went on to give me some great thoughts to use and carry with me when I was playing. He understood the pressure of the game and what it took to win the Masters, and he gave me some great tips that helped me tremendously over the years.

"Keep relaxed, keep cool, but stay keyed up at the same time," was one piece of advice I remember him telling me. I didn't have any trouble with the second part of that because I was always very pumped and focused. But it helped to have the idea of also remaining calm, no matter what was going on in the heat of competition.

Billy also said, "You are going to have adversity in a tournament, whether you like it or not. When you have a bad hole you have to look up and say thank you very much for that bad hole, and I'll show you what I'm made of now and how I'll come back."

So at the Masters that year I realized before I teed off that it didn't matter how well I played—I was going to face adversity. And that's exactly what happened. At one stage I was leading Arnold Palmer by about four shots. But then I got a 7 at number 13 and a 6 at number 15. They were both par 5s where normally I'd get 4s. Suddenly, I was facing possible defeat. But I was determined, just as Billy told me, to stay cool and come back from an adverse position. When I came to the last two holes, numbers 17 and 18, I made miraculous pars. It was a very strong finish, and I won by one shot.

Over a decade after that memorable visit, Billy visited my home in South Africa. It was a thatched roof house on a big piece of ground. We invited about two hundred people to come along and meet him, and he gave us a wonderful sermon right on our lawn. I remember our Golden Retriever running through his legs while he was talking, and people sitting on the grass. It was a wonderful occasion. I get quite tearful thinking about it. I have a picture of him from that visit thirty-nine years ago that hangs in my ranch in South Africa.

Billy is a man who is so full of love. The last time I saw him was when I was flown in a helicopter from our home at The Cliffs in South Carolina to his home in North Carolina. His wife was near the end of her life and I felt sad. They had such a great marriage and he loved her so much.

Sometimes I wish he was nearby so I could just visit him and ask him about life. I think we all go through phases in which we worry about various things. You worry about your grandchildren, you worry about death, or if your wife dies. I suppose it's just natural. Of course, I know the general theme of what he would say about "going to a better place," but I would love to hear his exact response because he always had such a well-balanced, well-thought-out answer.

Talking to Billy Graham always reminds me that everything we have is a gift from above. It doesn't matter what our achievements are, because in a sense they are not really ours at all. Take my own situation, for example. I'm the only man on the planet who has won the Grand Slam—that's the four biggest tournaments in the world—on the regular tour and the senior tour. People say, what an effort, but I say, no, it wasn't me; it was purely a gift, a gift from above. I would be very conceited if I took all the credit or honor for myself.

I have that sense every day of my life as a gift, that there is something bigger than me at work, and I am always thankful for what that larger presence brings me. I never forget to say thank you when a plane lands, and when I leave a hotel room I say thank you for having had a bed to sleep in. All these things are gifts from God.

I try to explain this to children when I speak to them. They think I'm from another planet when I start by asking them, "Do you have a bed? A toilet? A bath? Soap? Clothing? Do you have a car to take you to school, and a TV?" When they answer yes to all these questions, I tell them that most of the children in the world don't have any of those things. They are shocked. They are not used to thinking of these things as precious gifts.

It's that attitude of honoring the gift that God gave and continues to give that marks Billy Graham's life and work. People always respond to what he says because he embodies the spirit that the Lord gave him, and he also earned that spirit. He was able to impart his spirit and his feelings to people, and that has been a special gift that he has shared with everyone. He is a great contributor to mankind worldwide, and what greater compliment can you give a man than that? Everyone wants to leave here knowing they have contributed to this planet.

I think back again to the time of our first meeting. It was wonderful playing golf with him right in his home state. He played so well, and he was happy, and happiness is contagious. Billy is the kind of man who would never put energy into criticizing people. He always uses that energy for something constructive. He is always interested in what others are doing. He once said to me, "Never forget to enjoy the success of others because when you do well you would like them to enjoy your success." And you can't get better advice than that.

·74·

SALLY QUINN

Bestselling author and journalist; founder and editor-in-chief of
The Washington Post website's "On Faith"

When I was little I remember thinking that Billy Graham was the President. I assumed he was President for life, and that all the people he was seen with in the White House were coming to visit him! In my mind he was a benign father figure. When I would see him on television in the early days I remember thinking that he was going to sprout wings and suddenly fly away.

It didn't occur to me until I was about ten that he wasn't the President. The tip-off came when General Dwight Eisenhower ran for president. My father was in the military and was very close to Eisenhower. I remember asking him how Eisenhower and Billy Graham could be President at the same time. My father explained that Billy Graham was always there to advise the President.

But as far as what Billy Graham represented, I was conflicted, even at an early age, because of the existence of evil in the world. My father's regiment liberated the Nazi concentration camp at Dachau in World War II and he had his staff photographer take pictures of all the corpses and emaciated bodies, so when he came home he had scrapbooks of what had happened there. I remember looking at the scrapbooks when I was five or six and thinking that there could not be a God. How could there possibly be a God? No God would ever allow this to happen. I would go down on my knees every night, saying my prayers, "Now I lay me down to sleep, I pray the Lord my soul to keep," and I would say, God bless this person and that person, and then I thought, *Why am I saying this? All those people in the prison camps must have been praying to God, too, and God didn't save them.*

I remember telling my father that I didn't want to go to Sunday school anymore, but my parents made me go, which really annoyed me. When I was thirteen I learned there were atheists, and I called myself an atheist for most of my life, until I started the religion website On Faith, for *The Washington Post*, which is now in its sixth year and thriving.

What changed my mind was a conversation I had over lunch with Jon Meacham, then editor of *Newsweek*, who has written books about religion. He talked me out of being an atheist. He said, "You are not really an atheist and the reason you are not is because you are not a negative person. Being an atheist is being negative because you are against something." He also said that I didn't know anything about religion, even though I had been rejecting it.

He was right. I had been so hostile to religion. My attitude was that most of the evil in the world had been done in the name of religion. Jon Meacham told me I needed to study the subject before I reached a conclusion. So I did. I learned that there is an enormous amount of good in religion, and I also realized that religion was a huge issue from a journalistic standpoint. It was a story that we weren't covering, even though religion plays a huge role in politics and foreign policy. It's a big story all the time. I tried unsuccessfully to persuade the editor at the *Post* to step up the coverage. Eventually the publisher suggested I set up a website that focused on religion.

I asked Jon Meacham if he would be my co-editor, since I had no credentials in the field. Soon we got some big names in religion on board, including scholars and writers such as Martin E. Marty, Elaine Pagels, and Karen Armstrong, as well as Archbishop Desmond Tutu. And Billy Graham's written for us, too.

Billy Graham is of course a key religious person, both in the United States and around the world. People have said, after the pope, there is Billy Graham. I was just rereading an old article by Martin Marty about him in *Christianity Today* ("Reflections on Graham by a Former Grump"). Marty presents Billy Graham as the "non-mean" man in whom the "fruit of the spirit" is evident, as described in Galatians 5:22-23: "love, joy, peace, forbearance, kindness, goodness, faithfulness, gentleness and self-control." If you want to describe Billy Graham, that's it.

Billy Graham himself has talked about three areas that were a concern to him in his personal life: finances, morals, and pride. For the first two, he set up ways to prevent even the appearance of impropriety. For his Evangelistic Association, for example, he set up a board that allocated his salary and handled all the financial affairs. This meant that he could never be accused of using his success for personal financial gain. Second, he would never ride in a car, or be alone in any other circumstances, with an unaccompanied woman. That way nobody could accuse him of wrongdoing.

As for the third item on that list, pride, one very important thing about Billy Graham is that it has never been about him. I recall the great opening line of Rick Warren's book *The Purpose Driven Life*: "It's not about you." A man like Billy Graham, who had incredible success, who could have been a zillionaire, could have done so many things that he chose not to do. He could have had a cathedral built for him and lived the high life. There could have been Billy Graham airports, statues, and monuments, and all that kind of thing. But he eschewed all that, remaining instead normal and humble. This is extraordinary to me. His life simply was not about accumulating all those things. It was about the message of healing and helping other people.

But for me the most important thing about Billy Graham is how he has changed over the decades. He has grown. He once said, "You can't help but grow and become more tolerant." And he has. Often people will become more hardline as they get older. It is easy to get locked into your own views and become rigid, in terms of who you are and what you believe in. But then there is no acceptance. For Billy Graham, I think it has been exactly the opposite. He has become much more accepting, more tolerant, more pluralistic, more open, and he has literally followed the Word of Christ. That's what I admire about him the most. In the "fruits of the spirit," Billy Graham has only grown.

·75·

THOM RAINER

*Award-winning author, researcher, speaker, and president
and CEO of LifeWay Christian Resources*

For me, Billy Graham has always been a model of evangelism.
When I think about his influence on my life, I look back to
the personal encounters that left such a lasting impression on
me.

One of these occasions was at the Louisville Crusade in 2001.
At the time I was the dean of a new graduate school called the
Billy Graham School of Missions, Evangelism and Church
Growth at Southern Seminary. Dr. Graham came to the
dedication of that school and of course had a vital interest in its
health and its future.

Shortly before he preached at Cardinal Stadium, I went to
speak with him in the green room. One of his daughters was
there and she introduced me: "Dad, this is Thom Rainer. He's
the dean of the Graham School."

His response just floored me. "I am so honored to meet you
finally," he said.

I thought, *This is crazy. This is absolutely wacky. In terms of
historical importance, I'm nothing, and this man is everything, and he's
saying, "I'm so honored to meet you!"*

He was not being disingenuous. He really meant it. His humility made me look at my own lack of it, and it served as a constant reminder to me, like that in Philippians 2:3: "Do nothing out of selfish ambition or vain conceit. Rather, in humility value others above yourselves, not looking to your own interests but each of you to the interests of the others." Dr. Graham was a man who lived by those words.

Although that meeting in Louisville was an inspiration, probably the most meaningful encounter I had with Dr. Graham was shortly after he turned ninety years old. I was in North Carolina and asked if I could visit him at his home, and he kindly agreed. So my wife Nellie Jo and I made a visit to the cabin up on the mountain near Montreat and got to spend some great time with him.

He was, as I knew he would be, very gracious. He asked about my family and about mutual acquaintances, and as usual we talked for a while about various topics. But on this particular occasion, there were also two things I wanted to ask him.

"Dr. Graham, do you mind if I ask you a couple of questions?" I asked. "I have been wanting to ask you these questions for years, and I've never gotten around to it."

"Certainly," he said.

"What would be the single greatest advice that you could give me? I know that's a big, big thing, to ask, but here I am talking to one of the greatest leaders and Christians of our era, and I want to know what's the single greatest advice you can give me." I didn't know what to expect in reply.

He simply said, "Don't turn ninety. It's a bad age."

I thought that was absolutely hilarious.

One thing I learned from Dr. Graham was to keep a sense of humor.

We were in his bedroom during our talk, and he was sitting

up in his bed. At the foot of his bed was a picture of his late wife, Ruth, and he pointed to her and said, "There are so many things that I want to get to heaven for, and that's close to the top." It was clear how much he missed her. I saw how he had kept a perspective, even in his old age, when his health was failing and he could no longer preach. What remained most important to him was the memory of his loving wife, his caring friends, and the love he had for his family.

My other question was much more pointed. "How do you deal with all the critics that you've had?" I asked. "So many have had accolades for you, but there have also been people who have taken pot shots at you, who have criticized you over the years."

He simply said, "I have to ignore most of them, or I don't keep a healthy perspective."

Of course, I'm not as high profile as Billy Graham, but he reminded me that although there are times when we should listen to our critics, given my position in Christian leadership I cannot live my life constantly listening to them.

I came away from that visit uplifted by Dr. Graham's simple teaching: perspective. I had been listening to a man who had counseled presidents and kings and who had lived nine decades, who is recognized as one of the most influential leaders in the world, and will be for many years to come, and yet he showed me the importance of keeping things in perspective. His wisdom was basic but profound: family is so vitally important. Critics come and go, so don't lose your focus. And there is more to life than life — there is the eternal life.

When you come to the end of life, what's really important? I saw that for Dr. Graham, it is remembering his wife, his friends, loving his children, and looking forward to eternity. This is the wisdom that he offered me that day: keep life in perspective. And have a sense of humor.

·76·

DAN RATHER

Peabody Award-winning investigative journalist;
host, Dan Rather Reports; *former anchor* CBS Evening News

In 1951 or 1952, when I was an undergraduate student at Sam Houston State Teachers College (now Sam Houston State University), in Huntsville, Texas, Billy Graham brought his crusade to nearby Houston.

My roommate and I decided to go to the Sam Houston Coliseum to hear Billy Graham. We were skeptical, even borderline cynical. We saw ourselves as intrepid investigative reporters—we were all of nineteen or twenty years old at the time—and wanted to "expose" the Billy Graham Crusade. It must surely be a moneymaking operation, we thought.

So on one of those nights at the Coliseum, my roommate and I were in the crowd. My roommate, by the way, was nicknamed The Weeper, because when he had a beer or two he would get furrow-browed and depressed.

We didn't really know much about Billy Graham at the time. Television was still new and not very many homes owned one. We had heard Billy Graham on the radio but I don't think we'd seen anything other than just a few news clips. We had no idea what we were in for.

The crusade got under way, and everyone was singing hymns. The hymns were carefully picked, each one an old standby like "The Old Rugged Cross." The music helped to create and build an atmosphere, and before we knew what was happening, The Weeper and I started to be enveloped by it. Something was definitely happening, and it was powerful. There was an aura about it.

Then Billy Graham came to the platform, and he preached a tremendous sermon that night. There was something magical about the occasion—not only the sermon but the entire evening.

By the end of the sermon, when Reverend Graham made his call to come down to the front and accept Jesus Christ into your life, it was all The Weeper and I could do to hold back from accepting the invitation! (I had "accepted the call" and was baptized at the little West 14th Street Baptist church in Houston, Texas in my youth many years earlier, and reminded myself of this that night.)

We had gone there as (in our fond imagination) zealous investigative reporters, but that had all fallen away. Now we were something else—we were actually open to Billy Graham's message. That was quite a transformation. We were looking at each other, and I don't remember who said it first, but one of us said, "I think I'm going to go down," and the other said, "Well, wait a minute, let's think about that." It was all we could do to hold each other back. Our cynicism had just melted away.

In the end, we didn't go down to the front, but we left the crusade inspired, with a whole different view of Billy Graham than we had had going in. It was quite unexpected and made a deep impression on me.

It might be hard to understand from the vantage point of today, but there was a kind of magic in a Billy Graham Crusade at that time, in the 1950s, when Graham himself was at the peak of his oratorical power. Graham was one of the two or three best preachers of his time, and one of the two or three best orators that I have ever heard. And he was able to preach in this powerful manner night after night after night. The Billy Graham Crusades were, after all, a very large undertaking. My roommate and I were there for only one night, but the crusade continued for several nights in Houston alone, and then it went to other locations concentrated in the South and Southwest. Night after night, week in week out, in venues thousands of miles apart, the Billy Graham Crusades continued, and that was pretty impressive.

Many years later, I was to learn that not only was Billy Graham a very powerful preacher, he was also a man of shrewd judgment. In the early 1980s I interviewed him, and he spoke about his desire to hold crusades in Russia. This was at a time when the Soviet Union was under atheistic communist rule, and the Cold War was at its height. I put it to him that the Soviet Union was a godless country; the godless government permeated society all the way down from top to bottom. "To whom are you going to preach?" I asked.

I had been to the Soviet Union many times, and I was trying somewhat aggressively to point out to the Reverend Graham that in the Soviet Union the only people who went to church were very old women in their late eighties or their nineties. The reason was that there were communist government apparatchiks standing in the church taking down the names of people who went, so nobody would go to church because they didn't want their names on a list.

After I made this point, Billy Graham replied, "What you don't understand is that below the surface, there are a lot of religious people, and they are afraid to come out, they won't risk coming out, but in effect, Dan, there are many, many, quiet, secret Christians, far more than you can imagine."

I didn't believe this at the time of the interview. But Billy Graham went ahead and visited Russia in 1982, and then again in 1984 and 1988, and on each occasion he preached to overflowing crowds. It turned out that he had been right all along, and I was wrong. He understood the basic religiosity of people even when their religious instincts had long been repressed.

Part of Billy Graham's power over the years is that he has stayed on message. That message hasn't varied since he started preaching in the 1940s. Decade after decade he has preached the Gospel. It's the way he has lived and is the key to his success. He has always said, in effect, *I'm Christ-centered; I want you to be Christ-centered; I want the nation to be Christ-centered.*

And you feel this when you are with him. You can't be in his presence and not notice it. Year after year, over the course of a lifetime, he has not wavered. Who among us can say we have done that? It's a rare person who can look back on a long life, and particularly a life in the limelight, and say that. To use the current political vernacular, there has never been any flip-flop with Billy Graham.

He knows what he is about. He felt called to the ministry many decades ago, and look at the changes that have taken place since then. Changes not only in politics and society but in the rise of the televangelist phenomenon, in which new evangelists would rise up and attain celebrity and then fade away. Yet Billy Graham has been constant. He was the first televangelist, the first man to harness the power of television for the Word of Christ. Not only did he do it first, the record shows he did it best over an extended period of time.

It is truly remarkable. This man is inspiring. I think that even if a person has no interest in the message Billy Graham preaches, or is an atheist or of a different religion, he or she would still find him inspiring because he has been steadfast, knowing who he is, believing strongly that he is fulfilling his destiny. Someone who is that dedicated to sustaining a mission outside himself and keeping his commitment to it for a lifetime is both humbling and inspiring.

·77·

MICHAEL REAGAN

Bestselling author of Twice Adopted, *motivational speaker,
political consultant; and founder of the
Michael Reagan Center for Advocacy and Research*

Dr. Billy Graham, "America's Pastor," has prayed with every U.S. President from Harry Truman to Barack Obama — and that includes, of course, my father, Ronald Reagan. I have known Billy Graham for many years, at least as far back as when my father was governor of California. I've known the Graham kids — Franklin, Nelson, Gigi, Anne, and Ruth — since they were children.

A few months after my father died in June 2004, the Billy Graham Evangelistic Association called and asked if I would speak at Dr. Graham's Los Angeles Crusade in November. I asked, "Are you sure you've got the right Reagan?" The representative explained that Dr. Graham had heard me eulogize my father at the funeral, and he was so moved that he wanted me to speak at the crusade.

I was awed and humbled. I have such respect for Billy Graham that I felt unworthy to share the stage with him. Yet if he wanted me there, how could I say no? "I'd be honored," I said.

As the day approached, I learned that nearly 100,000 people

were expected at the Rose Bowl. The enormity of the event began to weigh on me.

On the day of the crusade, my wife Colleen and I went early to the Rose Bowl so that event organizers could tell me where to stand and when to speak. As we were on the platform, they showed me Dr. Graham's new high-tech pulpit. Because of Dr. Graham's age and Parkinson's disease, the pulpit was designed to be electrically raised and moved into position, and there was a seat where he could sit comfortably while speaking.

After our tour of the stage, Colleen and I went back to a "green room" area. Dr. Graham came over and chatted with Colleen and me about our family and about my dad. I'm sure Dr. Graham sensed that I felt burdened by the responsibility of speaking to such a vast audience. "Michael," he said, "there are times when God gives you a task like this, and the best thing to do is to give it up to the Holy Spirit. Ask the Spirit to enter the stadium and meet the needs of everyone here."

When he said that, I felt a sense of calm and peace. I knew my job was to simply tell my story, and let the Holy Spirit do the rest.

Finally, it was time to go out on stage. After a musical program, the worship leader led the crowd in several worship songs. As the crowd sang, someone came out and removed the lectern I was to speak from. I thought, *Hey! They took my lectern!* The crusade representative next to me leaned over and said, "Change of plans—you'll be speaking from Billy Graham's pulpit."

I looked at him incredulously and said, "Have you cleared this with God? Are you sure He would approve?" The man assured me it would be all right.

As I got up to be introduced, I remembered Billy Graham's advice. "Holy Spirit," I prayed, "I give myself completely to You.

Give me the words to speak. Enter this stadium and meet the needs of everyone here."

I walked up to Billy Graham's pulpit, looked out over the crowd, and felt a prompting within: "Michael, leave the preaching to Billy Graham. Just tell them a story about a man who was lost and now is found."

So I told my story. It was the story of being molested by a day camp counselor as a child, of growing up with incredible guilt and fear. From childhood into adulthood, I hated myself, and I believed God hated me, too. I thought I was doomed to hell, beyond the reach of God's grace and forgiveness. When my wife, Colleen, led me to a relationship with Jesus Christ, I found forgiveness and a release from guilt and fear.

I told how God had healed my wounded relationships, including my relationship with my father. Because of Christ, Dad and I began to say "I love you" and hug each other every time we were together. This bond of father-son love continued even after Dad fell under the shadow of Alzheimer's disease. Even when he could no longer say my name, he would always put his arms out for a hug.

That was the story the Holy Spirit prompted me to tell that night at the Billy Graham Crusade. I concluded my story with these words, "As you listen to Dr. Graham tonight, I want you to think of our Lord and Savior Jesus Christ. He's standing at the doorway of your life with His arms wide open, waiting to give you a hug."

As I came away from the podium, Billy Graham stopped me, shook my hand, and said, "Michael, you should have stayed out there and kept speaking!" What an honor it was to hear those words from Billy Graham himself.

As I sat down and listened to that great twentieth century apostle preach one of the last sermons of his long career, it struck me that Billy Graham and Ronald Reagan were very much alike. They were both great men who deeply impacted their times. Both represented ideas much larger than themselves. Billy Graham represented the Gospel of Jesus Christ; Ronald Reagan represented the office of the President. Neither man was caught up in who he was; each was caught up in what he represented.

It has been a rare privilege to have known Dr. Graham and his family for so many years, and to speak at one of his final crusades. That night, Billy Graham, well into his eighties, walked slowly, needing help from a walker, needing a special pulpit to accommodate his infirmities—but to me, he looked like a runner taking a victory lap. His mind, soul, and spirit were as strong as ever.

I watched him do what he counseled me to do. He gave himself over to God and allowed the Holy Spirit to enter that stadium, to speak through him, and to meet the needs of everyone there.

·78·

CATHERINE B. REYNOLDS

Business leader and philanthropist, chairman
and CEO, The Catherine B. Reynolds Foundation

As a young girl, I watched the Billy Graham Crusades on television with my father, who was an enthusiastic follower of Billy and his message of salvation through Jesus Christ. As a result, I had a strong love for Billy long before I actually met him. Our first meeting was arranged many years ago by Mike Deaver, an advisor to President and Mrs. Ronald Reagan. Mike was close to Billy, and credited Billy with helping him through his darkest hours with alcoholism. Mike knew how much I admired the reverend.

On the appointed day, Mike, my husband Wayne and I flew down to have lunch with Billy. I was so excited to meet Billy; you feel like you have known him forever. He has the ability to make you feel as if you are the only person in the room when he talks with you.

That lunch was the beginning of a long and rich friendship that has evolved and flourished over the years. Wayne and I attended crusades, visited him when he came to Washington,

D.C., and connected with him in many other settings, cultivating a friendship that has been one of my life's greatest blessings.

In 2005, during George W. Bush's presidency, Billy called to say he was in town, and invited Wayne and me to visit him in his suite at the Mayflower Hotel in downtown Washington, D.C. This was at the time when Billy was becoming physically frail. When our lovely visit ended, Wayne and I started to leave and we all hugged each other. He told us that he loved us, and I responded, "Now, Billy, you take care of yourself." He looked at me, and said, "You know, I'm not going to be around much longer." I was speechless. Then I hugged him and insisted that this was not so, and we would see him again soon. "Well, I just hope the Lord has His arms wide open at the gates of heaven," he replied. My husband reacted quickly to Billy's words, "If you're worried, how do you think I feel?" It never dawned on Billy that if the gates of heaven would be wide open for anyone, it would clearly be him. This underscores his deep humility.

Billy is a blessing to someone every day. The fact that he continues to strive to become more Christ-like, godly and righteous in his thoughts and actions is a lesson for all of us who struggle with our own human nature. The number of people that Billy has touched is extraordinary. He transcends political parties, geography, gender and culture. Sixty years later, his crusades continue to play on TV. He was one of the first to use television as a medium to bring the Word and introduce vast numbers to Christianity.

As someone who tries to make a difference through philanthropy, I have known any number of special individuals, but no one quite like Billy. He is a unique human being, with a special ability to reach people. His influence is felt not only when you meet him in person, but also when you see him on television, hear him on the radio, or when you read his books. It's probably due at least in part to his authenticity and consistency. He is who he is. He is the same today as he was yesterday and I'm sure will be tomorrow.

Billy is a true trailblazer as well—he achieved and set the standard for what today we refer to as television evangelists. He achieved many things that were not easy. In many ways, he is a social entrepreneur, creating crusades around the world and using the medium of television to reach millions of people. His God-given talents gave him both the vision and ability to build a global mission. At the same time, he continues to live a personal life that people genuinely admire, which increases the effectiveness of his message exponentially.

I was brought up Catholic and attended Catholic school, but I found Billy's way of preaching and delivering the Word much more powerful and meaningful than what I experienced growing up. Billy has also greatly influenced my husband, who is Jewish, and has a friendship and relationship with Billy that is as strong as mine. This reflects who Billy is at heart. He genuinely loves and embraces everyone. Most people tend to gravitate to others who are like them. Generally speaking, it is difficult to connect and appreciate others who are different from you. It is hard either for lack of understanding or lack of interest. It is close to impossible to influence dissimilar people in a positive way. However, whether consciously or not, these are the folks Billy touches. It is a natural outgrowth of his unconditional love for people.

Billy Graham's footprint in the lives of countless individuals across the world is enormous. It cannot be overstated. I doubt that anyone can step into his shoes. He has been a gift in my life and countless others.

·79·

PAT ROBERTSON

Founder of the Christian Broadcast Network
and television host of The 700 Club

My first encounter with the full Billy Graham experience was in the summer of 1957 at the crusade Billy Graham held in New York City. I was a theological student at the time, and I was one of the counselors at the crusade. I was overwhelmed by the experience in Madison Square Garden. The Garden holds 20,000 people, and it was filled every night from May to September.

New York is a very sophisticated, blasé city, but that summer it was just turned on its ear. Billy Graham spoke not only at Madison Square Garden but also on Wall Street, near the U.S. Treasury building. There was a huge crowd there, a couple of hundred thousand people. Imagine it—hardened stock and bond traders came during their lunchtime to hear this preacher from North Carolina talking about Jesus!

Billy Graham also spoke in Times Square, and the crowd there was just as huge. The city turned itself inside out to welcome him. It was extraordinary how this one man did something that the business leaders on his team thought was impossible. Here was a man from North Carolina preaching the simple Gospel of Jesus

Christ, and New Yorkers were falling over themselves in amazement.

This wasn't the first time I had heard Billy Graham. My father, who was in the U.S. Senate, had helped him when he came to Washington some years before that, and my mother and father had made contributions to his ministry. They thought the world of him, and I had met him myself in Washington. But this New York crusade was a bigger experience altogether.

It was a normal New York summer, with the typical heat in the city, the crowds, and the hustle and bustle of commercial life. And yet it was as if the city just slowed down to listen to this message. Suddenly these cynical New Yorkers were turning to faith in Jesus. It was astounding.

I think it was word of mouth that helped to produce the huge crowds. The news spread through all the churches. The air was electric that summer. When Billy prayed for the anointing of God it was powerful. The people in Madison Square Garden were just transfixed. They were on the edge of their seats listening to what he had to say. And there I was, a young theological student, amazed at what God was doing.

I was there many nights at the Garden because I was one of the counselors for the crusade. I happened to be in charge of the college follow-up in Queens, New York, as well. When people would come forward at the meetings, a counselor would go along with them, talk to them, and invite them to go to the counseling room on a lower floor. The circus had been there before us and had put the elephants in the room where we were now doing the counseling. It was still a little pungent, so you had to overcome some of the animal odors during the counseling!

What was it about this man Billy Graham that was so compelling? Billy Graham once said, "If God would ever take His hand off of me, my lips would turn to clay." He knows where the power comes from. It's God's spirit. Jesus said, "If I be lifted up, I will draw all men to myself." Billy never drew people to himself. He always pointed them to Jesus. He said constantly, "Don't look at me, look at Jesus." I think it was Jesus who was drawing the crowds to the New York Crusade, and Billy was the messenger. He was very handsome, very dynamic, and he lived a life of great integrity. People saw that. There was nothing false about him.

And that's what people wanted, then and now. New York can be a cold and impersonal place. I lived there for a number of years. You find yourself in these big canyons of buildings, and the subways are jam-packed with people. There are always crowds, and everything is hustle and bustle. You have to fight for a parking place and for whatever you do. In New York, your life seems tenuous because you're not out in a field or a farm or some natural setting like that—you're up a high-rise building and if the power gets cut off or some other essential service is interrupted, you don't have anything. People in New York have that feeling of insecurity. But Billy Graham brought the message of certainty.

In Madison Square Garden, above the podium where he was speaking, there was a large banner that proclaimed the words of Jesus: "I am the way, the truth, and the life." This was the certainty that people sought, and they responded. It was astounding. Every night Billy Graham would give an invitation. He would stand there with his head bowed, his arms across his chest, and wait for them to come. And they came by the thousands. Some people were weeping. Their lives had been transformed, and you could sense they were so happy they had made this decision. They welcomed those of us who were counseling who wanted to say more to them. We answered their questions and prayed with them, and they were so grateful for people who loved them. People are looking for love, and the people at those crusades sensed its presence there.

Billy Graham was the man anointed by God who made all that happen in New York City that summer in 1957. God's anointing, by which we become aware of the presence of God, is available for all Christians, but some do have more of it than others. Billy is a specially chosen instrument to bring the Lord's message around the world. He is unique.

At the New York crusade, all the theological students, me included, stood in awe of him. He had tremendous humility, and he always remained an extremely humble man, even though, as the years went by, he had a claim that few human beings have ever had. He walked with U.S. Presidents, he knew world leaders, and yet he always remained a very godly man, a man of prayer.

I've been with him on a group prayer retreat. He's just a humble man under God. He puts on no airs or pretense, none of the "flash and dash." He lives very simply. He once told me he had been offered an airplane—someone wanted to give him one, but he wouldn't accept it. He felt that he should not have luxury for himself. People in his kind of position are offered everything, and he said no.

It was that simplicity and humility that characterized his ministry. It was apparent at that crusade in New York in 1957, and all the time I have known him. He loves the Bible, he loves Jesus, he has tremendous faith. And that's the thing that touches us all. When you see a great man as humble as he is, it has a profound impact on you.

I learned a great deal from him. We've been friends now for so many years, and I love and appreciate him. I was with him for his ninetieth birthday party in West Virginia a few years ago. The biggest things I learned from Billy Graham are self-control—living simply, not indulging your appetites—humility, dedication to the

Lord, and boldness in proclaiming the Gospel. That's who he is, it's what he is known for, and it will be his legacy.

·80·

JAMES ROBISON

Founder and president of the relief organization LIFE Outreach
International, television host of LIFE Today, author

From the moment I began preaching in Texas, when I was
nineteen, the response was staggering. People would crowd the
churches where I spoke, and within a year, I was conducting a
citywide crusade in Houston that lasted fourteen days. Hundreds
of people were being saved, and that caught Billy Graham's
attention. He sent me encouragement and assistance, and told
me that I was very blessed. He said that I would need a non-profit
organization, and then proceeded to set it up, with the help of a
law firm that donated their time to me at his request. Our
friendship thus began with the tremendous gesture of kindness
so typical of Billy. It has lasted fifty years, during which his
wisdom and generosity have continued to enrich my life and my
mission greatly.

Billy kept track of me during my twenties because our crusades
were breaking attendance records in large venues all over the
country. During one of his annual times set aside for prayer and
spiritual refreshing Billy said he was led by God to share that he
was impressed by my teaching and that I should be doing it
regularly on television. This was a time when many people,

including executives at Walter Bennett Communications, were urging Billy to consider producing his own weekly TV program. However, he felt God had told him I was the one who needed to be on television on a regular basis, while he continued to air his crusade television specials on prime time.

At first, I resisted the idea because I liked to see the people I was speaking to. However, Billy asked me to pray about it, since he believed he had heard the Lord. I got the message, and suddenly, at the age of twenty-five, I began airing a nationally televised Sunday program because of Billy Graham's prayerful encouragement.

Billy is so humble. I don't know how you could wrap more humility in a single package. He used to tell me, "I don't know why so many people come to hear me. Why do they come?" I would respond, "Billy, you're anointed. It's God!" And he would insist, "Man, I'm not even a very good preacher. You're a good preacher, and there are so many others much better than me." Even when Betty and I visited him in his home in his early nineties, he was still questioning why people wanted to hear him.

In my early twenties, while attending East Texas Baptist College, Billy commissioned me to try to witness to his son, Franklin. He was rebellious and having problems in school and life in general. Billy felt that Franklin had never really trusted Christ, and since Franklin and I both loved the outdoors, I could connect with him. I made all kinds of appointments with Franklin, including invitations to go fishing or hunting, but he broke every one of them.

Some years later, when Billy was in the Dallas/Fort Worth area doing preparatory work for a crusade, he called to ask me to play golf with him and his close associate T.W. Wilson. We had a great time. As we were riding down the ninth fairway toward the clubhouse, he inquired, "Did you hear about my boy? Did you hear about Franklin?" I told him no, and so he said, "Let's go in and get a sandwich. I want to tell you about it. Then we'll play the back nine."

We sat down at a table and Billy revealed that Franklin had given his life to Christ. God had supernaturally converted Franklin in a hotel room while he was overseas. His eyes filled with tears as he told me how it happened, though he is not usually an emotionally expressive person. As we talked, he began to explain how God had done deep work in Franklin's life, and then he shared, "You know, James, probably some of the greatest advice I ever got concerning Franklin—because it was really tough for Ruth and me—was from a Christian counselor. He explained that though I could not condone or approve where Franklin went or what he did, I should let him know that the door at home was always open. I should be sure he knew that."

Though I was only in my thirties and Billy was thirty years older, we had prayed together and loved Franklin together as a kind of agreement in prayer. It was extraordinarily moving to see Billy's prayers for Franklin play out in front of me. After that conversation, we went back and played the back nine.

Billy and I became good friends. We talked a good bit, always openly and honestly. Sometimes we would share concerns about the crusades and discuss why some were more effective than others, including why the people in some areas of the country were harder to reach than others. It seemed tougher in the Bible Belt. Sometimes we would call each other about things that concerned or disheartened us, such as difficulties with ministers who would not cooperate with each other in evangelistic outreaches.

When it came to theology, I was always confrontational. Jerry Falwell used to say that I made even conservative Baptists look like a bunch of liberals. He once commented that I even made Bob Jones and Rush Limbaugh look like liberals. And I was often too harsh and angry. I was abrasive and seemed to lack compassion. I later realized that Billy recognized that characteristic, but he would never confront me about it. He was such a gentleman and so kind. I would persist, however, by challenging and asking him, "How can you associate with all these different people who, in my opinion, have some theological beliefs that are just plain wrong?" There I was, challenging a true giant in the faith, saying things that were so immature, and yet Billy responded with such gracious encouragement. He never confronted me directly about my attitude, but one day a simple conversation with Billy transformed my life. He asked me if I knew the people I was telling him to stay away from. When I replied that I did not, he simply said, "I suggest you get to know people you've been taught to avoid."

I then understood how wrong I was, how we can take our differences to such extremes. We don't have to compromise our beliefs, yet sometimes in defense of our faith, we compromise God's love. In the simplest way, Billy drove home the point that Jesus taught everything in the context of love—for everyone. Through the outreach this lesson inspired, it not only changed my life, but also the lives of many religious leaders who have differing theological positions but have now joined together, seeking common ground to discuss our common concerns. They are also joining together in soul-winning and mission outreaches. I would never have ever been able to speak to them about spiritual harmony and unity without Billy's example and influence.

I once told Billy that it was his inspiration that allowed God to use me to help bring so many different leaders together who would otherwise have never met. My life has been transformed in many ways by his advice—encouraging me to get to know the people we have been taught to avoid.

Through the years, I've learned many things from Billy Graham, but no greater lesson than to do what he has done, which is to speak the truth, and always do it with love.

·81·

RICKY SKAGGS

*Fourteen-time Grammy Award-winning country
and bluegrass singer, musician, producer and composer*

The first time that I met Dr. Graham was during one of his crusades in the 1980s when I was asked to play a few songs and share my testimony before Dr. Graham began preaching. It was pouring rain. I was on a covered stage, but the audience was sitting in the rain and getting wet. I did one song and was setting up my second song when Dr. Graham came onto the stage. The rain stopped, just as if you had a garden hose and turned it off. I thought, man, this is Old Testament stuff right here. I was really moved by that experience. It was awesome.

Another time, I did a crusade with Dr. Graham and his son, Franklin. Afterwards, Franklin said, "Hey, you want to come up to the room later, and we'll order some room service?" So I went to my room, and put away my guitar and stuff, and headed up to Franklin's room. I knocked on the door and walked in, and there's Dr. Graham sitting with Franklin. Someone said, "What do you want to eat?" Dr. Graham said, "I want a cheeseburger." Franklin looked at me and said, "You want a cheeseburger, too?" I said, "Yes, sir, I'll have a cheeseburger with you." I thought, man, having a cheeseburger with Billy Graham has got to be the coolest thing in the whole wide world.

I once went over to Dr. Graham's house to sing a few songs for him. I had committed to do a spiritual forty-day fast, drinking water and hot tea and a little coffee. The body is an amazing thing, and you can actually get along without food for quite a while. I've had friends that have done two fasts a year for nearly thirteen years. You don't just jump into something like that without really feeling God inviting you to a fast. It's a spiritual thing. Fasting was something that was very common in the days when Jesus was walking the earth. But we've gotten away from that lifestyle. In other religions it still happens quite a bit, but it seems like in the Christian religion it's a bygone thing. I got to Dr. Graham's house around lunchtime. I walked in and of course we hugged and said our hellos. He sat down at his table and said, "Would you have a hot dog with me?" The first thing I thought to myself was, *Oh, you're fasting. You can't do that.* But I really felt like I heard the Lord say, *Yes, you will have a hot dog with him. Don't let the fasting be an offense to him because that nullifies the whole fast if you do that.* So, I didn't tell Dr. Graham anything about the fast because I did not want to make him feel bad that he was eating in front of me, and tempting me. Instead, I said, "Yes, sir, I'd love to have a hot dog with you." And that was the best hot dog I've ever had.

My ministry is totally different from Dr. Graham's, but he knows that what I do is for Christ. I go to the bars and the clubs and the casinos where I play my music, and I take the church and the Gospel to those places where Dr. Graham may not be as welcome. If he walked into a casino or a bar or a club, the people might not listen. But because of the music that God has put in my heart, I can go in there and play bluegrass for fifteen or twenty minutes and they let me speak about what's on my mind.

If I walked in there and immediately started talking about the Gospel and preaching to them, they just wouldn't listen.

There's a great story I heard Johnny Cash tell one time. Johnny and Dr. Graham were like best friends. He loved Johnny Cash, and John loved Dr. Graham and Ruth. They'd go on vacations together or down to Jamaica with John and his wife, June Carter Cash. It was a great relationship. Dr. Graham was never ashamed to be around Johnny Cash and the country music crowd. Johnny told me about one of the first times that he was with Dr. Graham. They were walking into an arena, and all these young people started hollering, "Johnny, hey man, we love you!" Dr. Graham said, "Wow, those are your people." John said, "Yeah, I've got a few people here tonight." And Dr. Graham was excited to preach to individuals who might otherwise not attend.

I have pictures up in my studio of prophets, pickers and preachers. I've got Bill Monroe and Flatt & Scruggs and The Stanley Brothers and people like that who are my musical heroes, but I've also got this awesome picture of Dr. Graham, the Youth for Christ picture where he's standing straight up and is holding his Bible over his head as high as he can reach. The way the picture was shot, he looks like he's eight feet tall, bigger than life. Everybody that comes into my studio sees that picture. I think they're touched by the power of Dr. Graham's life, especially seeing him as a young preacher in his twenties and then seeing him in his nineties, still desiring to see souls saved for the kingdom.

One time, I went to see Dr. Graham at a crusade, and as soon as I walked into the room, I started crying and could not stop. When I think about it now, I still start to well up. He was sitting in a little place they had partitioned off back there in the arena. There were curtains up around him. I just walked in and, bam, I started bawling. It was the humility and the brokenness and the fragrance of Christ that I could really sense in the room. There was a spirit of the Lord that was so on him at that moment. He hugged me and said, "Bless your heart," and kissed me.

That moment reminded me of the biblical story about the prostitute who took her costly alabaster jar of fragrant oil and broke it so she could anoint Jesus with its perfume. The jar of oil was really for a dowry, an expensive gift to be saved for a wedding. It was as if she was getting married to Christ because of the forgiveness He gave to her. Everyone else was ready to stone her, but she came to Christ, humbly and broken. When she broke the jar, the fragrance filled the room. I think when our lives are broken, our souls are broken in humility because of the love that we have for Christ. I think that when people are around those who preach and sing the Gospel, they can sense the fragrance of forgiveness. That's how it was when I went to see Dr. Graham and began to weep, feeling the humility, the shared brokenness, and the fragrance of Christ that had filled his room. It was more than just an ordinary visit. Something deeper was going on.

There have been other times I've seen Dr. Graham and I've always teared up because I'm always wondering if it is the last time I'll get to see him on this side of heaven. I love him dearly. Every time I'm around him, I get inspired.

When he's in the arena, in the pulpit, there's a switch that gets turned on somehow. He turns into Billy Graham the evangelist. There's no doubt about it. Most of the time I've been around him was at a crusade. But there have been times that I've been around him where he was just talking about stuff, like his family and his kids. And he loves baseball. He's just a common man who serves an uncommon God.

I've heard the phrase so many times, "You're just too heavenly minded to be any earthly good." Well, I don't agree with that. I think Dr. Graham is definitely heavenly minded, but he is definitely earthly good, too.

Not long ago, I visited with Dr. Graham. I walked in and saw him sitting at his desk, and he looked at me. "I'm asking God for one thing," he said. "Dr. Graham, what is it?" I asked. He answered, "I'm asking God for one more time to preach. If even one more person would come, it would be worth it." That broke my heart, to see him in his nineties, with his heart and marrow still boiling for souls. I thought, *Dr. Graham has probably led more people to Christ than any one person that ever lived. Yet his heart's desire is to see one more come.* It blew my mind. I looked at Dr. Graham and asked, "If you could preach one more time, what would you say?" Before I could get all the words out of my mouth, he said, "Oh, I'd tell them about the cross. I'd tell them that there is no heaven without the cross." He just went on and on, like he was preaching to me right there in the living room. He just could not stop speaking about God's love for us.

·82·

KEVIN SORBO

Actor, producer and director; star of Hercules: The Legendary Journeys; *spokesman for A World Fit For Kids!*

In a movie called *The Persecuted*, I played a Billy Graham-type character. The movie takes a dim view of governments that restrict religious freedom. There's a senator who is trying to pass a bill for a one-religion state, and I'm the biggest thorn in his side. My character says, "You can't dumb down my religion, and you must allow everybody—Buddhists, Muslims, Lutherans, whatever—let them have the speech they want to have within their own religion. That's part of freedom of speech." He won't budge, and he won't back down, and he has the great power that speaking the truth gives him. Like Billy Graham, whose convictions gave him an incredible intensity that I first experienced in real life when I attended one of Billy Graham's revivals back in 1973.

It was in St. Paul, Minnesota. I'm from the Minneapolis area, and I went with a big church group, including my friend Jeff. I was about thirteen years old. I had always considered myself a Christian, but I was absolutely blown away by what Billy Graham was saying. It was a hot, humid August night, the sky was so dark, and the stars were so bright. That evening is something that has stuck with me all my life.

There were 60,000-70,000 people there. Billy Graham asked people to come up at the end if they wanted to give their lives over to Christ. Jeff and I walked up and met one of Billy Graham's associates. We sat and prayed and talked for a really long time. That was a very special night for me.

Before I went to that revival, the only preacher I'd heard was our pastor. He was a Bible-banger, spouting horrible warnings about hellfire and damnation; even breathing seemed to be a sin. I was already starting to get rebellious about church, but it wasn't like I was barking against God; I just didn't like the way my pastor was preaching.

I remember saying to my mom, driving home one day, "You know, I don't think God's that angry at us." I think inherently we all know what's right and what's wrong. If we do something wrong, we know it.

That night in St. Paul, I discovered what an amazing orator Billy Graham is. I remember looking around at the faces, watching the tens of thousands of people listening with rapt attention to what this man had to say.

That was during the Vietnam War, and I remember that at dinner we would watch the war and all the protests on TV. There was so much hate and anger. And yet to hear this man Billy Graham speak, with tens of thousands of people around, and see people be so positive, showed me what a great speaker could offer the world.

I still remember Billy Graham that night, saying, in effect, "Look in the mirror, and push yourself past whatever you think are the problems out there, and stop blaming the world." His message was a strong one for parents, schools and communities about responsibility. It was very inspiring.

A World Fit For Kids! is an after-school program I've been the spokesperson for over the last fifteen years. We serve 12,000 children in poor communities, from first grade to twelfth. We teach them healthy choices and job preparedness, but most importantly, we teach them personal responsibility. I tell these kids not to start blaming everybody else but to learn to make a better life for themselves, to "look in the mirror," as Graham would say, and believe in themselves.

Billy Graham played a big part in making me who I am today. It began on that one night in 1973 when there was something in me, even at such a young age, that was ready to accept his words.

·83·

DANIEL SOUTHERN

Author, corporate trainer, leadership coach
and former Crusade Director for Mr. Graham

The first time I saw Billy Graham after I was hired, I was only twenty-three and still wet behind the ears. I was being trained for a role in organizing his crusades. At the first crusade I attended, I held his overcoat and hat for him while he preached. When he had finished and was leaving the platform he looked right through me with his piercing blue eyes. We connected in that instant. He said simply, "Thank you. God bless you," and I knew that he meant it and that he cared about me. I wasn't just the young man standing there holding his coat and hat. This was the beginning of my admiration for the man behind the ministry. He always had that gift of connecting with people quickly and in a very personal way.

Billy was known for giving people meaningful gifts, not just chocolates or trinkets but something that would really impact them. I was involved in the Billy Graham Evangelistic Association for nearly twenty years, and over those years I personally received many devotional books that he and Ruth had signed to mark a special occasion in my life, such as upon my ordination or my marriage engagement. They were always signed personally in their own hand by him and by Ruth—there were clearly two different signatures in these books.

I remember two specific incidents that show how Mr. Graham's giving of gifts—in each case a Bible—profoundly impacted the recipients; one a politician and the other a celebrity.

The first incident involved U.S. Senator Sam Nunn, who shares his own feelings about Mr. Graham in this book. In the context of my work for Mr. Graham as a crusade organizer, my staff and I would put on events in the major cities of the world. When Mr. Graham was in town to preach I would often meet the famous people who would come to these meetings as guests. In Atlanta in 1994 I had the pleasure of meeting and hosting Senator Nunn, a Democrat from Georgia, who by that time had spent over two decades in the Senate.

As I briefly visited with Senator Nunn, he reached into his pocket and pulled out a very small New Testament. It was covered in brown leather and well worn from use. Its dimensions could not have exceeded about 3 x 4 inches. As he held it up to show me, the senator told me that Mr. Graham had given him this Testament many years ago. Mr. Graham had signed it personally to him, and Senator Nunn showed me the inscription. "I carry this everywhere I go," he said. "It's my constant companion. Whenever I have some spare time I can just read some Scripture and be encouraged by it." I thought how awesome it was that Billy's unsung influence was felt in the halls of our nation's congress and that this well-known politician was a sincere follower of Christ.

The second incident, which stands out in my thinking, took place some years earlier in the late 1970s. I was working in a church in Ventura, California, and heard the story of how Steve McQueen had recently become a Christian. I learned that Steve regularly attended services in the very church where I was working and where he had become a believer. I greatly admired Mr. McQueen, one of Hollywood's most popular actors, and thought it was wonderful that he had become a Christian. I wanted to meet him, so one Sunday I positioned myself in the balcony of this little missionary church because I had heard that Steve liked to sit there for the service. Sure enough Steve McQueen took his usual seat in the front row just ahead of me. He was paying rapt attention to everything the minister was saying, and had *The Living Bible* open in his lap. The easy-to-read Bible written in everyday English was still fairly new, having first been published in 1971. I was familiar with this paraphrase of the Bible because I had known a girl in college whose father was the author and I used it often for my own reading.

I watched Steve intently throughout the service and when it was over I introduced myself as someone who worked with Billy Graham. He said, "Oh, really, you know Billy Graham?" I confirmed that I did and he said, "You mean you *really* know him *personally?*" Again I confirmed it, and he said, "Well, do you think if I gave you my phone number you could get that to him?" I said, "Sure, I would be pleased to do that." So he scratched down his phone number and said, "I'd like to see him some time. If he could meet with me, I'd love to buy him a Twinkie and a Pepsi." Then he added, "By the way, you need to go back to bed and get some more rest so you can grow up a little bit." I smiled at the tough-guy actor for the joke he had made; you see I'm six foot six and not a "little guy." Before we parted, he said with some urgency, "I've got some questions that I would like to talk to Mr. Graham about if he could spare the time."

As soon as possible I contacted Mrs. Graham and gave her Steve's phone number because she was very savvy and I knew she would make a point of ensuring that Mr. Graham got this important message.

As Steve's wife Barbara tells us in this book, when he passed away from cancer, he was found in his bed with a Bible lying on his chest. It had been Billy Graham's personal Bible, which he had given to Steve as a gift.

Mr. Graham was always very careful about how people perceived their need of Christ. On one occasion he was holding a crusade in Las Vegas and the pastors there wanted him to preach strongly against gambling and condemn those who worked in Sin City's huge casinos. Billy refused because, he reasoned, if you're not involved in gambling you may be misled into thinking you're fine with God. "Everyone is a sinner whether they gamble or not. It doesn't matter what kind of sin you might be involved in. All sin separates us from God and we are all sinners who need Christ as our Savior. I'll speak against sin, but I'm not going to speak specifically against gambling." He even held special services at unusually late hours so casino workers could attend. As a result, he had thousands of people who were working in the casinos, or had come to Vegas to gamble, coming to his meetings and many of them found a relationship with Jesus Christ. Billy understood how to make his point without unnecessarily alienating those who needed his life-changing message.

These are just a few out of many possible examples of how Billy's wisdom, generosity, thoughtfulness, and kindness deeply touched people's lives, not just in single moments but on multiple occasions over the course of his entire life and ministry.

Billy Graham was the real deal both in public and in private. He was always a gentleman and never bombastic. Whether someone was involved in questionable activities, a famous actor, a powerful senator, or just a young man holding his jacket as he preached to thousands, Billy learned early in his ministry that you don't categorize people because of appearances or judge them by the label they wear.

Because he looked beyond the external, in some ways, Billy didn't seem to fully grasp how famous and influential he himself was. He didn't have a desire to be honored as a celebrity or to make any profit from what he was doing. Remaining humble, generous with his time and his gifts, he saw himself as just another man, but a man who was on a mission. It was always his mission that was preeminent. Billy Graham was driven to share with everyone who crossed his path his understanding of why we are on this planet and how we all equally needed to come to God through Christ as our Savior.

·84·

DAVE STONE

Pastor of Southeast Christian Church in Louisville, Kentucky,
preaches to over 22,000 people weekly

Billy Graham has had an enormous influence on my life. Among other things, he has always been one of the preachers I respect most. We met when I visited the Billy Graham Center in Charlotte. I got to shake his hand and talk to him. He has been a great role model for all of us, and I have been continuously impressed with his unwavering faith and commitment to God's Word. He has withstood the pressures of ministry and the challenges of being away from his family for long stretches of time, and he has remained faithful to God and to his family.

Billy Graham has strongly influenced three generations of my family, beginning with my father. In 1952, my dad was sixteen, in high school in Albuquerque, New Mexico, and uncertain about what he was going to do with his life, when Billy Graham came for a major crusade. It was the biggest event in Albuquerque in some time and they actually built a special area for the crusade. My dad, who was working for the school newspaper, got up his courage and requested an interview with Billy Graham for the paper. Much to his surprise, the crusade organizers said, "Sure!"

Dad reported that from the moment Billy arrived at the

interview, Dad was impressed. Billy was sincere, thoughtful, warm and friendly. The photographer who accompanied my dad was Jewish, and he, too, was impressed with Billy Graham's candor and kindness, and snapped pictures all the way through.

Dad asked him: "What do you think is the biggest challenge facing young people?"

Billy answered, "Deciding what you're going to build your life on." Then he talked about the importance of making Jesus the foundation of your life.

Dad asked many more questions and Billy remained gracious with his time. When they got up to leave, Dad inquired, "Is there anything else you'd like me to tell the students?"

Billy Graham responded, "Just tell them that the Christian life is the greatest life of all."

That was sixty-one years ago and my dad still treasures the photo taken of the two of them. He decided to enter the ministry the next year. The advice that Billy Graham shared was pivotal in Dad's decision and was probably the same advice he would give students today.

My father, brother and I are all preachers, so I know that preachers tend to look to different people when they are formulating their own style, and they always have certain people to whom they enjoy listening. I always liked listening to Billy Graham on television because he was engaging, brief, bold and biblical. In my mind, those are the marks of a great preacher.

I preach to more than 20,000 people each week at our church in Louisville, Kentucky, and a preacher has to try and connect with everyone in his audience. Billy did his homework and captured the culture of his audience. His illustrations were always relevant. Whether they were believers or unchurched, he had a way of engaging them. He never spoke too long, and thus never wore out his welcome, something particularly important in a culture with such a short attention span. Regarding his boldness,

Billy was uncompromising about what he shared, which made me want to be bolder in my own preaching.

Billy was truly biblical. In his autobiography, and in other teachings and writings, he tells about a crisis of faith he underwent in 1949 about the authenticity of Scripture that determined whether he would continue his Christian mission. It took place in Forest Camp in the San Bernardino Mountains, just before a citywide evangelist mission in Los Angeles. He was suffering some frightening doubts about whether the Lord really wanted him to go to Los Angeles. As he described it, Billy set his Bible down on a tree stump out in the woods and began to pray, telling the Lord that if he could not trust the Bible, he could not go on. Then, in a kind of epiphany, he decided to accept by faith that the words of the Bible were the Lord's, saying something like, "Lord, I don't always understand everything in my intellect, but I'm going to accept by faith that this is Your Word and that it is true." That was his turning point. The Los Angeles Crusade extended way beyond the three weeks originally planned and his prominence rose to a whole new level.

I think God raises up prophets at different seasons in the nation's history and the world's history, and I think that God knew that Billy Graham was a person who would be an open, receptive vessel. He knew Billy was someone who would use the talents with which the Lord had blessed him to proclaim the Gospel, which is exactly what Billy Graham has done for more than seventy-five years.

When Billy came to Louisville in 2001 for a crusade, I went every night. It felt so surreal to have him in our city when we had watched him so often on television in other places. Around 30,000 people attended and they filled the football stadium. The experience goes to a whole new level when it's live and not halfway around the world. Now, whenever I hear the song "Just

As I Am" I still see the people pouring down front in response to the invitation to publicly declare themselves for Christ.

When I met Billy Graham in Charlotte, I also toured the Billy Graham Library along with several other preachers, including Ed Young, Sr., Jack Graham, and Mark Driscoll. As we moved from room to room, we found ourselves getting emotional. In the last room, which is like an IMAX theater, we sat down to listen to Billy Graham share the Gospel. When the lights went out and the film started, we saw Billy at a crusade and we heard his voice. It felt like we were transported there. Here I was in a room full of preachers and leaders, and everyone's heart felt a tug. We were all wiping tears away as we walked out.

The whole thing was done with such excellence. When we left the room, prayer volunteers were waiting for us in case we needed to talk with someone about a decision, or if any of us wanted to pray with someone. There we were, many of us preachers ourselves, and our hearts were being moved so deeply as we watched Billy preach. I felt like every one of us, before we left that room, had renewed our decision for Christ. It was very personal for me, a real "ta da" moment.

When I returned from my visit to the Billy Graham Library and told my high-school-age son about my meeting with Billy Graham, I watched his eyes light up. My own dad had entered the ministry after meeting Billy Graham, and then in turn, he passed his inspiration on to my brother and me. It's cool to think about how God can use my teenager, and that what's going through my son's mind might be very similar to what went through my dad's mind when he was sixteen. I can't wait to take my son to Charlotte so he too can experience the words and images of Billy Graham that still move even the most seasoned of preachers, and which will continue to inspire new ones.

·85·

JOE STOWELL

*Host, Strength for the Journey ministry
and president of Cornerstone University*

I have been blessed to serve on the board of the Billy Graham
Evangelistic Association for over a decade. In our board
meetings, Billy was always focused on Christ and the Gospel. He
consistently reminded us to uphold the name of Christ in all that
we said and all that we did as an organization. He encouraged us
to function with integrity and do nothing to damage the
reputation of the Christ that we represent. Reaching the lost of
this world was an unquenchable passion and foremost in his
ministry. He not only had a great sense of his calling but was also
a man of impeccable character.

He was driven by the need to rescue as many people for
heaven as possible. In the early 1980s, he went to Russia and
spoke in the major church in Moscow. Some people believed this
was just a showcase church that was a front for the communist
regime to cover their clamping down on religious freedom
everywhere else. Hence, Billy was criticized for going to the Soviet
Union at a time when the government persecuted and jailed
Christians. But you have to understand Billy. It was an
opportunity for the Gospel. For him to freely speak the Gospel

to the Russian culture was a prevailing and compelling opportunity. He had a great love for the persecuted church, but he wasn't deterred by the fact that the Soviet government was hostile to Christianity. If he had an opportunity to proclaim the Gospel in the heart of Moscow, he was not going to turn it down, even if others questioned the wisdom of his trip.

Sitting on Billy Graham's board gave me many occasions to get to know him personally. I remember our first one-on-one talk. It was a striking moment for me. I was aware that I was sitting next to a world-famous, highly respected religious icon whom I had admired my whole life. So, I was fishing for something to say that would be of interest and came up with this question: "What have you enjoyed the most about your ministry?" His answer was so spontaneous. I will never forget it. He simply said, "By far and away, the best thing in my life has been my fellowship with Jesus, walking with Him, relying on His wisdom, and sensing His presence with me." It was a stunning response. It was from the core of Billy. This was a man who has known presidents and frequented the White House, interacted with world leaders and been welcomed in all nations as a hero of the Church. But what has mattered most to him is his fellowship with Jesus. Just in case I had missed the point, he repeated to me what he said, almost word for word. It was a wonderful moment for me. I felt both challenged and convicted at the same time. Convicted, because I'm not sure that would have been my first response, and challenged, because I would love for that to be my first response.

His answer to that question showed me something that I have always noticed about him. Billy is not taken with himself. He's almost embarrassed by himself. The humility of Billy Graham is striking. For a person at his level any measure of pride or arrogance would damage his work. God gave him stellar gifts and appointed him to a highly applauded position. I would like to think that God gave him the gift of humility to ensure that Billy didn't injure the message. One time, when I was chatting with Billy in his home, he said, "Joe, sometimes I feel like such a failure." I replied, "Billy, you've got to be kidding." Billy then confided, "I sometimes feel I haven't done all that I could for God, and maybe I should have done more." It was that kind of humility that protected and empowered his life and ministry.

He always treated people, no matter who they were, with dignity and respect. No one ever sensed they were insignificant or unimportant when in his presence. Once when I was at a board meeting in Charlotte, I saw my friend Sam, who happened to be in the same building, and suggested, "Maybe I can get Billy to say hi to you since you came to know the Lord under his ministry." I always wanted to be sensitive to Billy, because you can imagine how many people would love to touch even the hem of his garment. Just then, Billy happened to be walking down the hallway. I took the opportunity and said, "Hey Billy, Sam accepted Christ in your last crusade." Billy lit up and talked with Sam like he had all the time in the world.

Billy Graham was not only uniquely chosen, called and anointed, but he also filled that calling with a depth of character and a clear reflection of the person and passion of Christ. I count it an honor to have known him.

·86·

MICHAEL TAIT

Lead singer for the popular Christian rock band, Newsboys

With the other members of the band dc Talk, I first met Billy Graham when I was about twenty-five years old, in 1992 or 1993. This was after the Billy Graham Evangelistic Association decided to make Saturday evenings "youth nights" during Billy Graham's visit to a city for a crusade. We were invited to perform on those youth nights, which we did several times.

One time we did a concert at a crusade that included a song we wrote called "The Hard Way." Later, in his message, Billy used some of the words we wrote for that song. I remember sitting and watching Toby McKeehan (of dc Talk), and Toby was watching me. We both had tears coming down our cheeks because Billy Graham was using our words. We were just blown away. And people came forward that night in droves for salvation.

The Grahams must have thought that we were doing a good job, because they invited us to their home in Montreat, North Carolina. I was excited by the prospect of going to Billy Graham's house. I was counting the days.

We took a flight and then drove a long way to Asheville and then on to Montreat. I was expecting a big White House-type home, but when we got there we found it was small and unassuming, like a little bunker in the middle of the gorgeous trees and hills of North Carolina. And I thought how humble it was for this man who has touched and changed the world with the Gospel to live in such a simple way.

One night, I was sitting at the table with Billy and Ruth. Ruth looked at me and said, "Michael, honey, you guys are so special." I was thinking that her husband was the one who was special. She continued, "You guys stock the pond for Billy to go fishing." Her remark went over my head at first. Then she explained, "What I mean is that during Billy's crusades you bring the kids in, so Billy can go soul fishing." I was honored to hear her say that. She was right in that we did bring the young people in. Every time we played at a Billy Graham event we broke the stadium records for attendance.

When I spoke to Billy Graham on that first evening, I called him Dr. Graham, but the next day, he said to me, "Michael, just call me Billy." I said, "Okay, Dr. Graham."

Another time when I visited, Billy was sitting there in an easy chair, and when he saw me his eyes lit up. He looked at me and I looked at him, and I got teary-eyed. "How are the boys?" he asked. He remembered us all.

Then he said, "I have a story for you, Michael. Last night President Obama was sitting in the chair you are sitting in."

I was blown away. "What was he doing here, Billy?" I asked. (I was finally calling him Billy!)

"Well, he wanted to come and see me. He called from the Oval Office. The Secret Service was all around, you know, but he walked in by himself, sat down there, and we spent half an hour together."

"What did you talk about?"

"We talked about the country, and this, that, and the other."

"Do you think he's a believer?"

"Well, I believe the man knows the Lord. We prayed together, and before he left, he asked me if he could pray."

And Billy was impressed with the depth of the President's prayer. We talked about that and about life and about lots of things. We had a wonderful time. My experience of Billy Graham has always been that he has a powerful presence, carrying the Gospel with honor and decency. You've got to respect that. He is also so unassuming, humble, and relaxed, he just disarms you. It was disarming for me because I had built up an image in my head. He was such a powerful man of the Gospel, and he mixed with presidents, met kings and queens, spoke all over the world. Movie stars admired him. He was the go-to guy. I thought he would be living in a castle, eating from silver plates and drinking from fifteenth-century goblets that kings had used. And you walk in and it's not like that. He is so natural. And he looks good, too, still with a handsome, rugged face, and that beautiful gray hair.

Not only that, he takes a real interest in you. He understands people. I remember talking with him about how my father had been a preacher, and Billy asked the sort of questions a person asks when he really wants to know about you. He gave me his undivided attention. That's why I call him my grandpappy. Who wouldn't? He is like a second grandfather to me.

·87·

STEPHAN TCHIVIDJIAN

*Grandson of Mr. Graham, president of the Caleb Group
and a pastor at Calvary Chapel, Fort Lauderdale, Florida*

I am the first grandchild of Billy Graham. My mother, Gigi (short for Virginia), is the oldest of Billy and Ruth's five children. She married at age seventeen and I was born one year later. I'm the oldest of seven children in my family.

People sometimes ask me, given the family I was born into, if I was expected to become a preacher. My answer is no. We were taught early on that we all had a unique opportunity—everyone does—to have a personal relationship with God through Jesus. So even as I was growing up I had to wrestle with that on my own. My grandfather may have been a high-profile Christian leader, but that didn't by itself make me a Christian. We were taught that these were all personal decisions. Everyone had to make his or her own assessment. You can't just ride in on the coattails of somebody else. I learned that profound lesson very early on, and I attribute much of it to the tone set by my grandfather.

I was introduced to ideas about God and the Bible and Jesus

in a very healthy environment in which there was no hypocrisy, no difference between public persona and private person. What I saw in my family was consistent across the board. That's not to say that anyone was perfect, but it was a very healthy environment to grow up in, and it was a big influence on who I am today. I think that is true of my brothers, sisters and cousins as well.

There was a consistency and genuineness to everything my grandfather said and did, the way he lived his life. He did not regard his life as an evangelist as his claim to fame, ticket to stardom or wealth or anything like that. He was always genuine, as was my grandmother. This is why my early exposure to religion was a very positive experience for me, and it remains so today.

My grandfather never adopted the attitude that he had to keep up a public image. He never felt he had to make his family toe the line so that no one would embarrass him. He never tried to control the personal relationship we had with God.

He was really the opposite. He encouraged us to make our own decisions. His love for me was unconditional, just as I was taught that God's love is unconditional. So I never had to be someone I was not in order to be loved or accepted by him, and that was true of my parents also. I didn't grow up in a home where there were a lot of dos and don'ts. It was a home where we were taught that God loves us and sent His Son to die on the cross for our sins, but it was our decision whether to accept that or not.

In today's culture, everybody is suspicious of the integrity of others, whether it's politicians, Wall Street financiers, movie stars, or anyone of any prominence. We tend to be suspicious of their authenticity. But for me, as a kid growing up, I saw nothing but genuineness in my grandfather.

Not only that, he is probably the most humble person I know. When you sit down and talk to him he is much more interested in what you have to say than anything he has to say. That blows me away! I look at him and think, *My goodness, you have more in your pinky than I have in my whole brain, and how dare I even speak?* I think he's honestly blind to his fame. I don't think he is conscious of it. He doesn't think of himself as different from anyone else.

I remember one story in particular from my childhood that shows both the genuineness and the humility of my grandfather.

When he was doing his big crusades he decided to start taking each of his grandchildren along to "shadow" him. Since I was the oldest, I got to do it first. The crusade was in San Diego in 1976, and I was twelve or thirteen years old at the time. In those days he would travel to the city a week before the crusade to get acclimated to the community, and meet with the press and city leaders. After the four- or five-day crusade, he would remain in the city for a day or two. So I spent two weeks with him in San Diego, and I remember shadowing him wherever he went. If he went to the morning news show for a live broadcast, I went too, and I got to sit and watch and meet all the people. If he went to the "top gun" school, I went there also and met the pilots and the Navy people. If he was having an important meeting, I was invited to attend.

I shadowed everything, and I remember to this day never once being treated like a little kid. Once, after a speaking engagement, my grandfather took me and a few members of his staff back to the hotel room, and I remember him saying, "Okay, guys, let's talk. How did it go tonight — any input, any advice for me?" He even asked me what I had to say. I don't remember my response, but I do remember him listening and saying, "That's a good point, Stephan." He instilled in me early on that there was worth in who I was.

I have an incredible memory of being with him and getting that insight. At that time, had there been any skeletons in the closet, any hypocrisy or lack of integrity—if he had lost his temper with one of his staff behind the scenes or had treated a waitress badly at a restaurant—I would have seen it. But that never happened.

The experience I had as a grandchild forever helped to shape my love and respect for my grandfather, not only as a man, a husband, father, and grandfather, but also as a man of God. So many people say, *I don't have a problem with God, but I do have a problem with God's people.* Growing up, I had a different experience.

Given all this, I feel blessed by my heritage. To this day, people often come up to me and say they have their own story about how my grandfather influenced their lives. Sometimes they apologize for intruding on me, but it is always a pleasure to hear their stories. My grandfather has been so generous with his life, helping so many people, and I like hearing how he impacted someone else's life in a profound way. That's an amazing experience to have, and Daddy Bill, as we call him in my family, is an amazing grandfather.

·88·

CAL THOMAS

Author, syndicated op-ed columnist, radio commentator and panelist on Fox News Watch

I first met Billy Graham in the mid-1970s while interviewing him for my book, *Public Persons and Private Lives*. He came down a little driveway with two enormous German Shepherds. "Don't worry, they won't hurt you unless I give them the code word," he said. I laughed and replied, "Don't tell me what it is." He said, "Actually, I forgot it!" and we both laughed. He invited me in and could not have been more gracious: simple house, simple man. Amazing man, actually. I've never met anyone like him.

Over the years he has shared a number of stories with me. They all provide great lessons, and I remember them still.

He told me that in his younger days and even as he got older, he never allowed himself to be alone with a woman other than his wife, or to be picked up by a woman at the airport unless her husband accompanied her.

I always thought of that as a great preventive, and I have applied it in my own life. It is in my contract when I go and speak, as a precaution, because we are all fallen people. Given the right circumstances, even those who think they "never would" just might. Some people fall into temptation because they don't take precautions. They get on Facebook and connect with an old girlfriend or boyfriend from high school and invite trouble.

On another occasion, Billy and I were at the National Press Club. He was there to speak and we attended a reception beforehand. Someone wanted a picture taken with him, and he asked me to hold his glass. He was drinking a Coca-Cola. Later I asked him why he had done that. He said, "I find it best not to have a picture taken with a glass in my hand because people might read something into it."

In an interview in the 1970s, I asked him if he ever went though temptations of the flesh. He said, "Sure, as a young man, who wouldn't? But I asked God to strike me dead before He ever allowed me to dishonor Him in that way." Then he told me a story I think was autobiographical, although I have no way of knowing. A preacher was in Paris one night and felt tempted. He took his hotel room key, locked himself in and threw the key out the window.

You can guard your heart and your character if you care about your family and your reputation. These days we don't take our own moral character as seriously as people used to because the media encourages us to do whatever we want, pretending there are no consequences.

Temptation, of course, comes in many guises. Anyone who has watched Billy Graham on television or seen him in person in a stadium is aware of the enormous charisma of the man. He once had offers from Hollywood because of his good looks, and from political people to run for the Senate from North Carolina. These were great, worldly temptations, but he turned them all down. He said he was called to be a servant of Jesus Christ.

This is a man who knew early he was called to preach the Gospel. He tells a story that one day as a young man he was conflicted because of his inability to understand certain things in Scripture. He went out outside, put the Bible on a tree stump, got down on his knees, and said, "God, I don't understand all of it, but I understand enough of it, and I believe in You, and I will take what I don't understand and accept it as coming from You."

You can see in that story the humility of the man. Indeed, I have never known anybody who was as famous around the world as Billy, but also as humble, and genuinely so. He really doesn't think he's that great. He also had the gift of surrounding himself with people who were ready to hold him accountable and keep him humble in the midst of fame and adulation. One of his associates told me a story years ago. Billy had just concluded a huge stadium event, with many people coming forward. When he got back to the hotel his associate turned to him and said, "You're not as great as they think you are!"

Humility, kindness, and generosity are the hallmarks of Billy Graham and his family. In 1986, my wife and I were in Amsterdam for the International Conference for Itinerant Evangelists that he and his association organized. Our suitcase was broken into and some clothes and other items were stolen. Billy's wife, Ruth, lent my wife a dress until we could get some other clothes. These are people who would literally give you the clothes off their backs.

If you don't know Billy Graham it's hard to compare him to anyone. The closest would be Mother Teresa. I met her once and she was the real deal, too. There are few such people in the public arena. Billy even says things like, "When I get to heaven I'll have to ask the Lord to forgive me for all sorts of things." He is the most transparent famous person I have ever known, in the sense of being free of all pretense or deceit.

Of course, he has some regrets. He's written and spoken about them. He became too identified with Richard Nixon and politics, and in the 1950s he spent too much time pounding the pulpit against communism. Not that that wasn't a good thing to be against, but it was not his primary calling.

Some people may not know that Billy was also a friend of Dr. Martin Luther King, Jr. Billy would refuse to hold services unless they were racially integrated. He told me that King said to him, "I know you can't go out on the streets because you have a unique ministry, so you take the churches and I'll take the streets." Insisting on integrated services was a courageous stance to take in those days. There were many people in the South and elsewhere who thought that black people were inferior and that God didn't want those of us who are white to associate with them. So that was extremely brave of Billy Graham, himself a southern preacher, to take a stand when a lot of his colleagues condemned him for it.

Some people wonder what will happen when Billy passes from the scene. My answer — and I think his answer — would be that God will raise-up others. He always has. He did when He raised up Billy Graham.

·89·

THOMAS TRASK

Chair, Convoy of Hope Global Prayer Initiative;
former General Superintendent of the Assemblies of God

When I was a pastor in Detroit in the early 1980s, I served as co-chairman of the Billy Graham Crusade at the Detroit Silverdome. It was a joy to work with the Billy Graham team back in those years. The care that the Billy Graham Evangelistic Association (BGEA) put into the organization and preplanning of the crusade was remarkable. The association wanted to ensure that the churches that participated would follow up with the "inquirers" who came forward for salvation, rededication or reassurance of their faith commitment. Their names were distributed to the pastors so they could generate the follow-ups for those people and integrate them into the local churches. That spoke volumes about the care the BGEA showed for those who had come forward for salvation. It was a great testimony in itself.

There are so many people who have come to know the Lord Jesus Christ as a result of Billy Graham's crusades. It was a time in America that Billy Graham worked with God to bring the Gospel to this nation of ours and around the world. And in all those years Billy Graham's character was impeccable. He moved among presidents, government officials, and church officials, but never did you hear anyone say an unkind word about the person, the Christian Billy Graham, and that's a great, great testimony.

We have all seen men to whom God has entrusted great gifts, and who have risen to heights of popularity, but then their mistakes almost neutralize their message. Never did one hear that about Billy Graham. As a minister of the Gospel — and I served as General Superintendent of the Assemblies of God — it made me proud to identify with him and his crusades and ministry. You could speak about it in the marketplace, in the city, or wherever, and even men who had not come to know the Lord Jesus Christ had great respect and reverence for the man. I'm positive that God has been pleased, and I'm sure that's one of the reasons that Billy Graham has enjoyed a long life. He gave himself to the Gospel and its propagation, and to the joy of being part of the Church of Jesus Christ. It has been one great testimony.

He brought people together across denominations. He reached denominations of every flavor and belief. I so appreciate that cross-denominational work that brought in not only the evangelical denominations but also the Methodists, the evangelical Lutherans, and others, including Catholics. The leadership of the Catholic Church was not always involved, but in some cases it was. It was a local decision. This cross-denominational work spoke so well of the Billy Graham Association. As Jesus said in John's Gospel, "Lord, that they all may be one."

When Billy Graham preached the Gospel he did not deal with the different doctrines of the denominations, which would have been divisive. As a result, men and women could gather around the Word of God itself, and that brought harmony and unity to the Body of Christ. Billy Graham's ability to do this was born out of his relationship with the Lord Jesus Christ. The Scripture says we are ambassadors for Christ. Billy Graham was an ambassador not for any one denomination or even his organization. He was an ambassador of the Lord Jesus Christ, which meant that men and women of different denominations could identify with the simplicity of the Gospel. They were able to be a part of it. Over the many years in which he modeled this presentation of the Gospel, it brought unity. It was not divisive but was as Christ would have been, and those of like heart and like faith could rally around it. I saw this spirit at work in the Detroit crusade, and it was a joy to be a part of it. For Billy Graham to be able to fill those stadiums was in itself a testimony. God's hand of favor and blessing was upon him and the organization, which was made up of men and women of character and integrity and passion.

In his presentation of the Gospel and his messages, Billy Graham was uncompromising. He said it well, he said it clearly: there is a heaven, there is a hell, you can have eternal life, you can be lost. For some, that would be confrontational, and the Gospel *is* confrontational. But he presented it in a manner that was both passionate and compassionate, and people recognized what was at stake and that he had their eternal well-being in mind. It was truly a great testimony, carried on over many decades, without blemish.

·90·

GRETA VAN SUSTEREN

Recipient of the American Bar Association's Presidential Award
for Excellence in Journalism and host of Fox News Channel's
On the Record

The first time I met Reverend Billy Graham was at his ninetieth birthday party in 2008. It was an incredibly special occasion and I was thrilled to celebrate this birthday with the Reverend, his family and his many, many, many friends—some friends had known him fifty years!

We all hoped he would speak to the room full of birthday celebrants and he did not let us down. As you might expect, he spoke about his faith and family—but we also got a taste of his sense of humor. At one point during his speech it seemed like Reverend Graham was getting a bit sad, but then suddenly he changed gears, caught us off guard, and said he would see us at his ninety-fifth birthday. His good cheer, sharp mind and good heart were contagious. He made us all feel good—no, great.

At one point during the evening, I introduced myself to Reverend Graham. To my great surprise he told me he watches my show, *On the Record*, on the Fox News Channel. People often say they watch to be polite—but I believed him because he immediately quizzed me about a recent interview I had done with

Alaska Governor Sarah Palin. He not only watched, he paid close attention. I was beyond flattered! It was a memorable moment for me—and yes, I confess to having bragged later about the fact that Reverend Bill Graham watches *On the Record*.

Two years later, in December 2010, I had the opportunity to sit down with Reverend Graham for an interview at his library in North Carolina. It was the first interview he'd given in years, so I was honored to speak with him on-camera and share his story with our viewers.

Because of my twenty years in news, I have met exceptional people—from American Presidents to world leaders. Many have made an enormous impact on the world—but none has come near to creating the impact that Reverend Graham has made. He has made an impact on Presidents—he has met every U.S. President since World War II. But even more than the famous world leaders, he has made an impact on millions and millions of people from around the globe whose names we don't know. Everywhere I go I run into people who tell me they have heard Reverend Graham preach or read his books and each says he changed their lives.

Reverend Graham's list of accomplishments seems endless and I could have interviewed him for hours. There were so many questions to ask—including how he became the world's most well-known evangelist. How did it start?

Reverend Graham told me about his time at Bible school in Florida during the Great Depression when he was about eighteen or nineteen years old. He was overwhelmed by the magnitude of the economic struggles facing so many. Reverend Graham told me that he used to wander around the streets witnessing incredible hardship and he would ask God to give him direction and purpose in his life. One night, he told me, he was lying on the eighteenth green of a golf course near the Bible school campus, surrounded by palm trees and darkness. In that moment, Reverend Graham said he heard the Lord call on him to preach the Gospel and he never looked back.

In pursuit of this calling, Reverend Graham went on to study at Wheaton College near Chicago, where he met classmate and future wife Ruth Bell. [By the way, I would have loved to have known her!] The two would go on to have five children. As Reverend Graham recounted his story to me, I could almost feel his love and devotion to his family. He spoke fondly of the big Christmas celebrations he and Ruth would put together for the children, which consisted of Christmas morning prayers followed by opening gifts under the tree.

I know he is a humble man, but I hope Reverend Graham knows how much he helped people. I also hope he realizes that his legacy continues—with his children.

Over the years I have become close friends with his son Reverend Franklin Graham. Franklin is the president and CEO of the international relief organization Samaritan's Purse. I've traveled with the younger Reverend Graham and Samaritan's Purse to North Korea, Haiti, and the Dominican Republic and witnessed the extraordinary work Franklin and Samaritan's Purse do. They are doing relief work—saving lives—all around the globe. They also from time to time risk their lives—for instance, doing relief work in Sudan and South Sudan—just because they want to help.

The elder Reverend Graham's spirit of giving and compassion can be felt around the world and now through the work of his children and those who have been inspired by his family.

It is truly remarkable to look at the way his influence has transcended generations and borders.

·91·

JIM WALLIS

Bestselling author, speaker and preacher; founder of Sojourners which articulates the biblical call to social justice

In 1975, I was a young Christian recently out of seminary in Chicago. I was living in Washington, D.C., in the early days of creating Sojourners, our new Christian community and outreach organization. One day I received an invitation to the pre-Prayer Breakfast for evangelical Christian leaders that takes place the day before the annual National Prayer Breakfast, where the President of the United States speaks to members of Congress and the Senate, most of the Cabinet, and about 3,500 invited special guests from around the world. All the established evangelical leaders would be there. I was still in my twenties, and I had never been to a prayer breakfast.

I was quite suspicious of the invitation. Our Sojourners Community was fighting for social justice, using the Bible as a text, but we didn't have a lot of support from older, established evangelical leaders. We were the "Young Evangelicals," as a book by that title would later call us. I wondered why they wanted me to come. Was I being set up for a confrontation? I didn't know what to expect.

The next day I went to the Washington Hilton where the

pre-Prayer Breakfast was to be held. I didn't know where to park, so I arrived late, and by the time I entered, the place was full. I explained rather sheepishly who I was, and one of the staff said, "Oh yes, follow me." I wondered why I was to follow him.

I was led across this room full of evangelical leaders to a table in the far corner. Looking ahead, I saw that sitting at the table was none other than Billy Graham! I almost stopped in my tracks. I had grown up in an evangelical family and we watched all the Billy Graham crusades on television together. He was a hero to us, and now here he was in person—and I was being led to his table!

Then I saw there was an empty seat right next to him. He looked up, saw me coming, seemed to recognize me and gave me a big smile. He motioned me over to sit in the vacant seat. I couldn't believe I had been invited to this event to sit next to Billy Graham.

So I sat down, very nervous, wondering what my parents would think. Billy looked at me with those piercing eyes of his and said, "Jim, it is so good to meet you. I think that you will be one of the leaders for the next generation of young Evangelicals. I want people to know that I agree with you on more things than they would imagine, and I think we should start talking together."

Over breakfast we had a lovely conversation about the Bible and social justice. I told him about the Sojourners experiment in which we found two thousand verses in the Bible about the poor. "We took an old Bible, Billy, and we cut out of it every single reference to the poor, and our Bibles were full of holes. They were in shreds and falling apart. I used to take mine and preach and say, 'This is the American Bible, it's full of holes!'"

That wonderful pre-Prayer Breakfast conversation in Washington was the beginning of our relationship, and in the years that followed we would meet and talk in different times and places.

On one occasion, we at Sojourners were planning a series of "justice revivals" across the country. We called it Let Justice Roll. I wrote Billy saying that if he had any advice, I'd love to hear it. He wrote back, saying he would like me to meet Sterling Huston, who was the director of all Billy's crusades. So my team met with his team in Chicago, and his people spent the whole day advising us how to do our revival in cities around the country. It was wonderfully gracious of Billy to send his top leaders to give us such counsel. Huston told me, "Billy sees his ministry and mission as the proclamation of the Gospel of personal salvation, and he sees you as preaching the social implications of that personal salvation. Billy sees your roles as complementary. That's why I'm here today, because he wants to help and support you in doing that."

One day in late 1978, after Billy had been preaching behind the Iron Curtain in communist Eastern Europe, I received a letter from somebody in Austria. According to the writer, an Austrian newspaper had run a story about Billy visiting Auschwitz and saying something like "Auschwitz will be only a dress rehearsal for the Holocaust that is to come if we continue down this pathway of a nuclear arms race."

I wrote to Billy, asking him if he had indeed said that at Auschwitz. I asked if this was a change of heart for him on nuclear weapons. And if so, I asked if I could interview him in Sojourners about the change.

He wrote back and confirmed that the report was accurate, and yes, it did represent a change of heart from the more hawkish position he had taken when he was younger. He agreed to be interviewed for Sojourners, and said that would be appropriate because we had taken a lead as Christians against the nuclear arms race.

The cover of the Sojourners issue had a picture of Billy with the phrase "A Change of Heart." It was a very candid interview. What had happened was that like any good preacher, he had fallen in love with those he was preaching to. Preaching to Russians and Eastern Europeans, he realized they were the targets of American nuclear warheads, and we were the targets of theirs. And he began to think about this in new ways and came out against the arms race.

He didn't get involved in the particulars of policy choices, but made it very clear that we were going in the wrong direction. We had to reverse the arms race. We were targeting each other, God's children, with nuclear weapons, and this could become another Auschwitz.

I later learned that most of Billy's advisors had been against him doing the interview, and people on the conservative side didn't quite know how to react to it. But he did not speak as a politician. He would never have said that we should have x number of weapons. His response was not a political one but a moral, Christian one.

The last time Billy and I talked was a few years ago. I was at Harvard teaching a course at the Kennedy School of Government called Faith in Public Life, on Monday nights, and on this occasion Billy was also visiting Harvard. It was likely the last visit he would make there. On the Sunday morning before, when he preached in the Memorial Church at Harvard, many of the students had slept overnight on the sidewalk so they would be able to get in and hear him.

The following night Billy was scheduled to speak at the JFK Forum at Harvard's Kennedy School of Government, the most prestigious university forum in the world. I moved my class and told my students we would be going to hear Billy Graham.

I was kindly invited into the green room beforehand by my friend Alan Simpson, former senator from Wyoming, who was at that time director of the Institute of Politics at the Kennedy School. Billy and I found ourselves alone together in the green room for a few minutes.

Billy said, "Jim, I'm really nervous tonight."

"Why in the world would you be nervous?" I replied.

"I feel very weak physically, and am not sure if I will be effective answering questions from these Harvard students."

At that moment, I had such a feeling of great warmth for him. "Billy, they slept overnight on the sidewalk to hear you preach," I said. "The room is full. They're not here to eat your lunch. They're here because they want to tell their grandchildren they were in the same room as Billy Graham."

His vulnerability, his humanity, was so much in evidence in that moment, and I had the chance to do what many of us have known with our aging parents—to give something back to them. I said, "I'll be sitting right in the front row, and I'll be praying for you the whole time. So if you get nervous, just look down and you'll see me there praying for you. They're here to hear from you. Just speak from your heart, from your soul, and they're gonna love it."

He gave me a hug and he went up to the podium, and a couple of times as he was speaking he looked down at me, and I put my head down and prayed for him.

Of course, despite his doubts, Billy gave an incredibly brilliant, statesmanlike talk about faith and public life. After the talk, there was time for questions. Harvard's evangelical Christian triumphalists were all there, hoping to take full advantage of the fact that a man whom they regarded as one of their own was the speaker that night at Harvard.

The first questioner said, "Dr. Graham, Jesus said 'I am the way, the truth and the life and no man cometh unto the Father but by me.' Doesn't that mean that all non-Christians, including Jews, are going to hell?"

Billy replied, "God will judge us all. This is a God of love and mercy but also justice. We all will come before the judgment of God, and I am so glad that God has that job and I don't."

The questioner looked disappointed. "Could you tell us what you think God is going to say?" he asked.

Billy replied, "Well, God doesn't consult with me on things like that." The despondent questioner walked away.

The second questioner was ready to try again. "At least Jews are monotheistic," he said. "What about the Buddhists? They're not."

Billy replied, "I've been to Buddhist countries to preach the Gospel, and I've met a lot of Buddhists who, frankly, are more Christ-like than many of us as Christians are."

The questioner just hung his head and walked away.

Another questioner said, "Reverend Graham, you spoke yesterday at the Harvard Memorial Church where the minister is openly and avowedly homosexual. How do you justify that?"

"I had such wonderful hospitality yesterday from Reverend Gomes and his staff," Billy said. "It was a wonderful day for me. I'm not a member of the board of trustees of that church and I don't deal with those kinds of issues. I just had a wonderful day there."

His answers to questions were so humble and so wise, and he quietly put down the Christian triumphalists, demonstrating a grace and civility so often missing from too many Christian leaders today.

Billy was against bigotry and injustice, and this created a special bond between us. Just before he walked out to speak to that Harvard audience, we had a last moment together. He stood up tall and put his hands on my shoulders. "Some of us haven't been as courageous as you have been to speak out against things that are wrong," he said. "And that's why I've always tried to support you as best I can."

I went home that night and called my dad and mom to tell them what Billy had said to me. "And Billy Graham hugged me!" I told them.

So from the moment I met him at that prayer breakfast in the 1970s to the hug on our last meeting, he's always been so affirmative and very supportive. Billy Graham has been a wonderful mentor, encourager, supporter and friend.

·92·

RICK WARREN

Bestselling author, visionary leader and founder of The PEACE Plan
and Saddleback Church in Lake Forest, California

Billy has been, first and foremost, an *evangelist* of the Good News. But in close second place he's always been an *encourager* of Christian leaders. I think of all the international conferences he planned and paid for to encourage those in ministry. As I've traveled the globe, I've met ministers everywhere who were also *personally* encouraged by Billy Graham.

Billy has been one of my seven life mentors for nearly thirty years. His invaluable leadership advice and his personal encouragement, especially in the early years of Saddleback Church, often kept me going when I felt like giving up. I could share example after example of his encouragement, including the fact that Billy was the *first* person to endorse *The Purpose Driven Life*, even before I'd finished the manuscript. But let me share just one incident that demonstrates the encouraging heart of this spiritual giant.

For fifty years, Billy either preached or prayed at most U.S. President inaugurations. When illness prevented him from praying at President George W. Bush's first inauguration, Franklin took his place. Four years later, President Bush asked me to give the invocation at the opening celebration of his second inauguration week. It was bitterly cold, and I told myself, "If I ever do this again, I've got to get a hat to stay warm!"

Well, four years later, President Obama asked me to pray the invocation at *his* inauguration, so I promptly went out and bought a nice hat from a store in West Hollywood. But I left it in a hotel room a few days later and it was stolen. I was disappointed, but had no time to buy another.

To this day, I still don't know how Billy found out about my hat loss. But about a week later, an unexpected package arrived at my home. Inside, carefully wrapped, was a beautiful black Homburg hat from Billy Graham! It was *the hat* Billy had worn at the inaugurations where he'd prayed! Attached was this note: "It's your turn, Rick. It's your hour. This is your hat now." Tears filled my eyes. Once again I saw the greatness of my mentor, his deep love for others, and his encouraging heart. I wore Billy's hat when I prayed on the Capitol steps at that 2009 inauguration. Billy was unable to attend, but once again, his influence was present. Thank you Billy, thoughtful friend and encourager to millions!

·93·

J.C. WATTS

Former U.S. Representative (Oklahoma),
co-founder of the Coalition for AIDS Relief in Africa
and chairman, J.C. Watts Companies

As I was growing up, there were times when I could not swim in the public swimming pool or sit on the main level of the movie theater with my white friends. Instead, I was confined to the balcony. When I was in the third grade, my uncle and father protested the pool restriction and got the swimming pool opened to all people. I didn't fully comprehend at that point what they accomplished or the implications of the balcony-only policy in the movie theater. However, the older I get, the more I appreciate the stand that people like my father and uncle took and the sacrifices they made.

Reverend Graham was such a person and I therefore admire him not only as a Christian, but also from the perspective of civil rights. Billy Graham fully understood the truth of God's Word and at a difficult time in our nation's history, he insisted on applying it universally. In so doing, he gave us a tremendous picture of what living out of faith should look like.

The more I discover about Reverend Graham, the more I peel away the layers of the onion, so to speak, the more impressed I am. Reverend Graham would be the first to tell you he is not perfect, but as someone who has observed his life over many years, he has consistently walked the walk in his life and in his preaching. By consistently, I mean he never tries to change God's Word to fit the times. He remains constant on the nature of God's Word, its truth and revelation.

God loves you and He wants to have a personal, intimate relationship with you. That has been his message over and over. The simplicity of this message has been wonderful through the years and I believe the consistency of his walk has been the reason his message has resonated with and impacted so many people, leading thousands and thousands to a personal, intimate relationship with Christ.

Scripture says God gives to all of us the measure of faith. I don't think God gives Billy Graham any more faith than He gives anyone else. However, faith is like a muscle; the more we use it, the stronger it gets. Reverend Graham's faith in the truth of God's Word encouraged him to believe at all costs, even in the 1960s during the civil rights movement, when it wasn't popular in some parts of the country to point out that John 3:16 says: "For God so loved the world, that He gave His only begotten Son, that whosoever believeth in Him should not perish, but have everlasting life."

In addition to the significance of the words, "gave his only begotten Son," the word "whoever" is key. Even in the face of segregation, discrimination and Jim Crow, Reverend Graham believed "whoever" meant everyone: black, white, brown, yellow, red, rich, poor, man or woman. That has been his unchanging position.

We often exercise our faith based on how we feel or how others feel or what they say or what the news media says. Billy Graham affirms that these things don't matter. What matters is

God's Word and God's Word states that whoever believes in Him should not perish but have everlasting life. Reverend Graham has always held that this is true for people of all colors and all nations all the time.

I applaud ministries today—white, black, red, yellow and brown—that preach and teach this, but what separates Billy Graham from the pack is that he preached this even when it was most unpopular, back in the '50s and '60s. The difficulties in our lives or the difficulties that society faces don't create character; they reveal character. I did not have to face prejudice and Jim Crow the way my parents and grandmother did, but I saw enough of its ugliness to realize that anybody in Reverend Graham's position who stood up against it was surely revealing something special in his character. His spiritual strength and integrity seem even more amazing to me today than they probably would have back then.

I had the privilege of being around Reverend Graham during his visit to Oklahoma City in 2003, where he held one of his famous crusades. As a member of Congress representing Oklahoma's Fourth Congressional District, I was on the program to share a testimony. I went backstage to a room where he and others were waiting and spent about twenty or twenty-five minutes with him. If I had not known about Billy Graham or had not ever seen him before in my life, never in my wildest dreams would I have thought that this had been the face of evangelism all over the world for decades. His humility and his desire to be totally obedient to the Lord were remarkable and inspiring.

I've operated in a number of different arenas in my life. I was a youth pastor for eight years and I still preach about eight or ten times a year around the country. I was also a college quarterback and professional athlete. I have run businesses and I spent twelve years on the front line of politics including eight as a member of the United States Congress. In all these spheres, the cheer of the crowd, even the praise of the individual, can be highly seductive. People call you "The Honorable" or tell you, "Man, great game" and "Man, you were wonderful; you were fantastic," and the media says how great you are. On Sunday mornings, after you preach, people come to you and say, "Hey, a great sermon. You so touched my heart and I gave my life to Christ." In business, when you close the deal and take your company to another level as the CEO, you start to think how good you are and that whatever is happening is about you or because of you. It's easy to lose perspective and humility in any and all of these circumstances.

Billy Graham was surrounded by these kinds of situations. If ever someone in America could have lost their perspective or their humility or earned the right to use the pronoun "I," it was Billy Graham. Yet it seemed like all the attention embarrassed him. He totally refused to be a superstar.

After my personal introduction to him, I felt a great personal bond and I wanted to learn more about him. I started reading about him and I had the privilege of visiting the Billy Graham Center Museum at Wheaton College in Illinois. As I found out more about his life, I recognized the contribution his humble beginnings in North Carolina had made to his character and demeanor, though I think by and large that is just who he is.

Reverend Graham's involvement in evangelism has probably touched four or five generations of Americans, including four generations in my own family—my grandmother, my parents, my children and myself—with the steadfastness of his message. I think his family contributed to that consistency. I can't imagine a better partner, wife and friend for Reverend Graham on his journey than Ruth Graham and I know how important that is. Billy and Ruth Graham stood in the truth of God's Word and now their children are associated with the ministry. Teach your children the way they should go and they'll never depart from it.

His mission was not to impress kings, queens, heads of state, members of Congress and ambassadors, but to impress upon the hearts of the people who heard him speak that God loves them and wants to have a personal, intimate relationship with them. I'm convinced that has been his only interest and when someone speaks from the heart, people feel it. So, it's not a tall order to comprehend who Billy Graham is. Anybody prepared to look with an open mind and heart, regardless of his or her skin color, would say, "Billy Graham has a special sauce."

·94·

JUD WILHITE

Bestselling author, pastor of Central Christian Church in
Las Vegas, Nevada, one of the largest churches in the U.S.

When I first decided I was going into the ministry I had major self-confidence issues. Could I do this? Could I speak? Would anybody care? I was wrestling with these issues and even thinking that maybe I should just do something else. This was around the spring of 1991, about two years after I came to faith.

Then I heard a pastor speak about Billy Graham, and what he said has stuck with me all these years. It seems that when Billy Graham was young he had the desire to preach, but nobody would listen to him. This was exactly where I was at the time. I had the desire and the passion to preach, but I also had fear and anxiety about it.

I later learned that when Billy Graham was young he would practice preaching to trees, and while taking long walks through the countryside he'd often sense God's presence and would feel that instead of trees, his audience would one day be people.

That story showed me the importance of just doing something. I thought, if Billy Graham of all people can go out back and speak to the trees, then I can speak to ten elderly people at a little retirement community and find a level of contentment in that. And that's exactly what I started to do. I started to go to a retirement area and lead a little service there for people. It was a catalyst for my preaching.

During these early years I was trying to figure out how to help people who wanted to become Christians. Different churches do things differently, as do different traditions, and I don't believe there's a right way and a wrong way for a communicator to invite somebody to place their faith and trust in Jesus.

I remember giving a message, and at the end of it, I said, "Well, if anybody wants to be a Christian, why don't you stand up?" Nobody stood up. I waited and waited and still nobody stood up.

I walked out thinking, *Well, that didn't work.* It was horribly embarrassing. And so I thought about Billy Graham's approach—every head bowed, every eye closed. I've seen numerous pastors take that sort of approach at the end of a message, like Billy Graham would do at the end of a crusade.

So the next week I used that approach, and everything went so much better. People who wanted to take that step of faith in their life felt they could do it in a way that wasn't quite so intense for them. After that, I never looked back.

Those early years were really formative for me. I can still see even today the influence Billy Graham had on me. I pretty much took Billy Graham's playbook, and I still use it for the way that he invites people to come to faith and to accept Christ into their lives.

Whether I am preaching at one of our five churches or giving a talk on our online ministry, I still carry the inspiration that I received when hearing that story about a young Billy Graham speaking to the trees when he thought no one else would listen to him. It was really foundational for me. It inspired in me the realization that when you have something in you that you believe God has put there, you simply have to get it out. Even if you're not sure that others will accept it. Like Billy Graham, you just think, "This is what I'm called to do," and you have to do it.

·95·

DON WILTON

Billy Graham's personal pastor
and President of The Encouraging Word television ministry

With most people in the world who have great influence, the closer you get to them, the more you understand they have clay feet. However, my long and very close personal relationship with Dr. Billy Graham has had the exact opposite effect on me. The more I am with him, and the closer I get to him, the more I find myself deeply moved by the incredibly beautiful feet God has given him. I am referring to the passage in the Book of Romans: "And how can they preach unless they are sent? How beautiful are the feet of those who bring good news."

How much I love to think the Lord Jesus had Mr. Graham in mind when the Holy Spirit inspired those words. My friendship and association with God's servant bears testimony to this fact. I am his pastor and spend days on end with him. It is a very humbling thing for me, especially over the last ten years or so, to have the privilege of sitting at his feet. We talk together, laugh together, share endless stories together and spend many hours studying the Bible and praying together. I just love Dr. Graham so very much. Whether in his bedroom or around the kitchen table eating hot dogs and yogurt or playing with the cat who crept in demanding attention or sitting outside looking across the beautiful mountains he loves so well, Mr. Graham bleeds out his God-given passion to see people have peace with God through Jesus Christ. It's as though God in His divine goodness, and only in His grace, has allowed me to link arms with His choicest of all servants and to accompany him on his journey of life after death.

And it's in that journey that I've come to understand that for this man, Billy Graham, as it was for St. Paul, "to live is Christ and to die is gain." The greatest privilege that God has given to me in my life, other than that of being able to tell people about Jesus Christ, is that I have been allowed to see this truth through the lens of a man whose legacy will never go away. I believe that what God has done through Billy Graham will be spoken about and read about long after he goes to heaven. He is going to become part of the historic fabric of the world that is and the world that is to come. And because of the message he preaches about the Savior of the world, I think Billy Graham is already firmly etched in tomorrow's world.

The hand of God rests on his shoulders. I think God reached down from the portals of heaven and placed His hand of grace upon this man by the name of Billy Graham and appointed him for this hour and set him apart in a unique and striking way. And in my conversations with him over the years, I have been amazed at the number of events that have taken place that can only be attributed to the hand of God. The life and testimony of this man can only be explained and understood through the eyes of God's loving grace.

Let me provide an example. On one occasion many years ago, when he was a fairly young man but had already become easily recognized in evangelical circles, he was playing golf. While he was playing, a lady came running onto the golf course wanting to speak to him. His playing partners very politely asked her if she would mind waiting until they got back to the clubhouse where they would certainly accommodate her. When Billy had finished his round of golf and was in the clubhouse, this lady said to him, "I do want to talk to you about spiritual matters but I also want you to meet my son." Sometime later Billy was in Hollywood and met the son, whose name was Ronald Reagan. Amazing when one realizes Mr. Reagan had not yet been elected governor of California. I think this shows that God, only by His grace, had His hand upon Billy Graham. God knew there would come a time when President Reagan would sit in the White House and that he and Mr. Graham would have such a meaningful and lasting friendship.

There is another story about Mr. Graham and Mr. Reagan after the latter had become president. Mr. Graham and his wife Ruth were at a meeting in Washington, D.C., and at about ten o'clock at night, the telephone rang in their hotel room. Mr. Graham picked it up and heard the voice of President Reagan. The president said something to the effect of "Billy, what are you doing in Washington staying at that hotel? This is preposterous. Your bedroom is right here, the Lincoln Bedroom at the White House. I'm sending a car to come and get you immediately." So late at night the President's entourage arrived, packed up Dr. and Mrs. Graham, and drove them to the White House, where they were greeted on the portico by President and Mrs. Reagan in their pajamas! The four of them ended up having late-night tea as they sat on the balcony at the White House overlooking the Lincoln Memorial.

Needless to say, President Reagan was not the only U.S. President with whom Mr. Graham had a strong association. He was a close friend to many presidents. These men who had such awesome responsibilities found in him not only a friend but a spiritual counselor who was a tower of strength. It was the hand of God at work again.

As I continue to hear incredible stories about Mr. Graham's wonderful ministry, the impact he has had on so many, I must confess there have been times I have tried to remind him of "just how special" he is! But it seems he always deflects any and all accolades away from himself. Billy Graham's life is about God, not about Billy Graham. If you are with him, and you happen to mention his greatness, without making you uncomfortable he is quick to remind you that it is only about Jesus. It's almost like he looks at me and says, "Now Don, do you think we could just stop talking about me?"

Every time I am with him, there is something incongruous about it, because I always feel—and this is entirely due to his humility—as though I'm the important one. Now, is this not the most ridiculous thing you have ever heard? Here is a man with all his accolades and accomplishments and achievements. He is a man consulted and sought after by presidents, prime ministers, kings and queens, famous athletes, and so on. Just recently a Gallup survey found that he was in its annual top ten list of "most admired" people for the fify-fifth time since 1955! And yet there you are—you stand with him, sit with him, talk with him, and eat with him and feel constantly and continually that you are the important person.

The hand of God is seen also in the content of the message Mr. Graham has preached for generations. Mr. Graham's ministry has spanned six decades. Times have changed since those early crusades in the late 1940s, and Mr. Graham recognizes and understands shifts in time and culture in a very beautiful way. He sees the relevancy of growth and change and he knows how to relate that growth to the human heart. He has a deep, God-given spiritual understanding of the intricacies of the human heart as created by God.

Despite all the changes in society and culture, however, his message has always been the same in its simplicity and power. It is grounded in his God-given understanding of the human heart in relation to God and the unique individuality with which God has made each one of us. Mr. Graham celebrates individuality and has an incredibly warm embrace for every single person in his or her uniqueness: men, women, boys, and girls, and every race and creed under the sun. All are precious in God's sight, and Mr. Graham's message is the same: God loves you. And because God loves you, He sent His Son, the Lord Jesus Christ to die for you.

Wherever Dr. Graham was in the world—from Soviet Russia to Cairo, Egypt; from Jerusalem, Israel to apartheid-era Johannesburg, South Africa; from England to South America, or anywhere in the United States—you would see the same response. Thousands upon thousands of people came to hear him. And when they did, they heard the message about Jesus. Only God knows the extraordinary numbers of people who became reconciled to a holy God as a result. His message to such diverse people and societies was always the same. Mr. Graham did not need to adapt or change. His ministry was not a chameleon ministry, and he himself always remained the same person. He was very true to his God, to himself, to his family, and his calling. From my perspective, if I have ever been around someone who I can say is genuinely genuine, I'm talking about Dr. Billy Graham.

His profound love for his family is an example. Many years ago he was preaching in a crusade in Argentina. In crusades like that, he would be gone from his home for up to six months at a time. On this occasion he was in the Amazon Basin, doing a wonderful ministry reaching some of the most remote tribes in the world. Word came to him that Mrs. Graham, who was building a swing for her children, had fallen from a tree and had broken her back. So he was stuck in the jungle thousands of miles from home and she was in the hospital with a broken back. They managed to get a shortwave radio and Mr. Graham requested that plans be made for their immediate departure so he could be at his wife's side. He loved her always, so much. Gigi, the Grahams' eldest daughter, was standing at Mrs. Graham's side when Mr. Graham called, and she reported back to her daddy, "Mommy says that 'under no circumstances whatsoever are you to leave what God has given you to do, in South America, to come back to my bedside. After all, I have only broken my back, but there are millions of people down there who don't know Jesus.'"

The story illustrates Mr. Graham's passion to be the husband and father that he knew he needed to be even though the call of God and the demands of his ministry made that so extremely difficult. He knew this at a very deep level. He understood the sacrifices and the cost of being appointed by God for this purpose. When Miss Ruth passed away and went to be with the Lord Jesus, Mr. Graham said, "The music has left my house." There is hardly a time I am with him when we don't talk about Ruth in some way or another.

Just as his family life is animated by love, so was his ministry. He was never motivated by rancor, anger, or condemnation but only by the love of God in Christ Jesus, without compromise. He didn't present another Gospel. He never betrayed the truth of God's Word. He never lowered the bar of expectation. He embraced human individuality while recognizing that Jesus Christ died for all people. This was a message of hope for all people. There were times when he was roundly criticized by various factions for associating with people whom they regarded as unacceptable. He went to the Soviet Union at the height of the Cold War, for example. Many warned that his visit would be misinterpreted as fraternizing with the enemy, but he went nonetheless. At a conference in Moscow, a member of the politburo got up and roundly castigated him. When Mr. Graham's turn came to speak, he didn't even respond to the criticism. Instead, he shared the message of Christ. He spoke with a heart of love and tenderness and warmth. His message had a warm embrace from the heart of God. For many years after that, he preached in the Soviet satellite states and even there, behind the Iron Curtain, scores and scores of "communist" people would come to his crusades and hear the message of the Gospel.

Mr. Graham has a very deep theology. His knowledge and understanding of God is profound, and in everything he does he gives the honor to God. Many years ago, for example, he had just completed a crusade in London, and there had been an incredible response, with hundreds of people stepping forward. Two of his close associates, Cliff Barrows and George Beverly Shea, were celebrating with the team in the hotel room after one of the major outpourings. Cliff Barrows tells the story of how they suddenly realized that Mr. Graham was sitting rather quietly and wasn't participating in the celebration. They said something like, "Billy, wasn't that fantastic, wasn't that incredible?" And he looked up, and said, "Only God gets the glory, boys, only God gets the glory." It was entirely typical of him.

To God goes the glory indeed, and we can only be thankful that we have all been blessed by the long, Christ-centered life of Dr. Billy Graham.

·96·

DANNY WUERFFEL

NFL/NCAA champion football quarterback,
Heisman Trophy winner and director of Desire Street Ministries

My first exposure to Billy Graham and his preaching style came when I was in fifth grade and I went with my youth group to a Billy Graham Crusade in Denver, Colorado. I was growing up in a Christian home and my father was a chaplain. But this was the first massive public Christian event I had attended. It was unapologetically Christian, yet it was very public and in a football stadium that was filled to the upper deck. That made it clear to me that faith is who you are and doesn't have to be something that's expressed only in private. Billy Graham's example of living out his faith was very sincere, unapologetic, and bold but it was also very respectful and tasteful.

That approach to Christian life and preaching has been a model for me, as I too have been blessed to have a public platform. I try to model Billy Graham by being true and authentic to who I am and what I believe in a way that brings glory and honor to the Lord without creating unnecessary conflict and tension.

Billy Graham is world renowned as an individual, but he never let it go to his head. He was always very humble. That's a lesson I've had to learn on several occasions. A couple of years ago, for example, I was in New York City for the Heisman Trophy ceremony and there were a bunch of people wanting autographs from many of us former winners. One young boy chased me into the bathroom. As I left he handed me an orange Florida Gator helmet, so I grabbed it and pulled out my pen. I said to the young boy, "Who do you want me to make this out to?" He replied, "I don't know who you are but I was hoping you could take this into the other room and have Tim Tebow sign it for me." That's a funny reminder we are never who we think we are.

Not that long ago, I received another lesson in humility. I was going through the Atlanta airport and stopped to get my shoes shined. I wondered if the man shining my shoes was a football fan, and if he would think it was cool to be working on the shoes of a Heisman Trophy winner. Part of this was just curiosity, but I'm sure it was also tied into my own ego. I broached the subject casually, asking him, "In all your time have you gotten to meet any celebrities?" The guy stopped, very slowly looked up at me and said, "In my world, son, there are no celebrities. Anyone that's up on a pedestal is only there because they put themselves there, and it don't make no never mind to me." He put his head down and resumed shining my shoes.

That incident was another reminder to me of what Billy Graham has modeled very well: a humble servant's heart along with a world-renowned platform. Time and time again you see Billy Graham using his platform to bring honor and glory to the Lord. You don't see him trying to build a personal empire, or leveraging his status for his own gain. There are some leaders who are popular and know it, and almost feed off their celebrity status. Billy Graham, however, pays attention to everyone, whether he's talking to presidents or to the person cleaning the plates off the banquet table.

I think these qualities of modesty and humility have played a large part in enabling Billy Graham to live a life full of consistent and faithful ministry. Few people manage to achieve this. There are a lot of people in ministry who for all sorts of reasons become ineffectual, or burn out and experience different kinds of failure. At Desire Street a big part of our mission is learning how to avoid this. We see so many young inner-city ministry leaders who have vision and passion and then burn out. There are very few inner-city leaders who finish well. Billy Graham's example is a resource to help other inner-city leaders finish well. Not just in ministry, but personally and with family. There are so many detours and traps in life. It's a lot easier to ruin a life than to build one. To see somebody who finished well is very encouraging and inspiring to me.

It seems the people who can be humble and teachable do a whole lot better over the long haul than those who think they have all the answers. A lot of people try to do too many things. Being focused and having a simple organizational mission is key. When I think of Billy Graham, I think of someone who invested his life in sharing the good news of the love of Christ and our need for Jesus. That is the profound yet simple part of his DNA that drove his life. He isn't trying to do twenty things at once. That's a huge part of why he is finishing well.

As we work with leaders, the concept of self-care is just so important. What does appropriate, healthy, self-care look like over the course of one's life? It looks like Billy Graham.

·97·

FU XIANWEI

Chair of the National Committee of the
Three-Self Patriotic Movement of the Protestant Churches of China

In September 1988, when I was still a young volunteer at the Mu'en Church in China, Reverend Billy Graham came to visit Shanghai for the first time, at the invitation of the China Christian Council. On Sunday, Rev. Graham preached at two churches in Shanghai—one in the morning, the other in the evening. I helped with both. The first was in Mu'en Church and over 3,000 attended. The second gathering was in the evening, in Qingxin Church, and about 1,400 church members attended. He preached at an evangelistic gathering at Mu'en Church, and it was the first time I ever met him. I also met his wife Ruth at that time along with their son, Franklin.

Although Billy Graham was a well-known evangelist from America, I saw how very humble he was, and how he loved to communicate with people. When he finished the service at our Shanghai church and was about to leave, many parishioners came up to him, eager to greet the famous preacher. Reverend Graham took the time to shake hands with all of them, no matter if they were young or old, and no matter what their walk of life. He was so at ease, spending time with our Chinese community as if he was with any other group of Christians in the United States.

Recently, I was invited by the Billy Graham Evangelistic Association to visit their center in Charlotte, North Carolina. I paid a personal visit to Billy Graham, meeting him in his office, where he received me with great hospitality. Although he was in a wheelchair, he was in good spirits and he told me his impressions of his visit to China. I was very moved by his kindness. Our talk was so natural and friendly, and I could tell how much he loved China and the Chinese Church. He told me that Ruth was born in Qingjiang City and grew up there. Her father and mother were Christian missionaries in China who had opened a clinic in Qingjiang to help give medical treatment to poor people in that region. Even today, people in Qingjiang still remember their work, and they even set up an exhibit a couple of years ago in remembrance of Ruth, her parents, and Billy Graham.

Mr. Graham told me that his family would always continue to try and facilitate the relationship between the churches in the United States and those in China. Chinese Christians are still quite moved by the Graham family's great love for China. I could see that the presence of China is in their blood.

Billy Graham's lifetime commitment to worldwide evangelization is impressive. His organization has indeed made a difference in China. Since his visit in 1988, many evangelical church leaders have come to visit China, including Reverend John Stott, Reverend Luis Palau, Pastor Rick Warren, Pastor Bill Hybels, and Dr. Geoff Tunnicliffe, the Secretary General of the World Evangelical Alliance, etc. It has widely broadened the communication between the Church in China and evangelical leaders.

In September 2011, we held a China-U.S. Christian leadership forum in Washington, D.C. The event was jointly held by the

China Christian Council, the China Religious Culture Communication Association and the Billy Graham Evangelistic Association, and through that event Chinese Christians and church leaders got to know a lot of American Christians and evangelical leaders in the United States, which deepened mutual understanding and friendship.

Billy Graham is a good friend to the Church in China and one who I respect deeply. And he has personally influenced me as well, allowing me to witness firsthand the great passion he has for his work, inspiring me to continue my work for the ministry here in China.

·98·

PHILIP YANCEY

Bestselling author, twice-awarded
Evangelical Christian Publishers Association Book of the Year

During my writing career I had two personal meetings with Billy Graham. The first was in 1986, in connection with an article I wrote about Cameron Townsend, who founded a mission called Wycliffe, which translates the Bible into different languages. Townsend was quite a remarkable man. I sent the article to *Reader's Digest*, and they said, "Well, it's a good story, but nobody's ever heard of him. Is there any way you could get Billy Graham to work with you on this article?"

I contacted the Graham people, and they said, "Sure, we'd be glad to cooperate." I flew down and spent a good, long afternoon in Billy Graham's home recollecting stories about Cameron Townsend. One story he got a kick out of telling was about when he and Cameron Townsend had ended up in a taxi together, and Townsend spent the whole time trying to get Billy to stop being an Evangelist and become a translator of the Bible in a different country!

About twelve years later, I got called in to help gather some research when Billy Graham was writing his autobiography, *Just As I Am*. I spent weeks researching his life, reading everything I could, and then I went down to North Carolina and studied some of the papers that had been stored near his home. Some work had already been done on the book, and we met to go over it.

The Grahams lived on top of a mountain, and there was a long driveway on the way up. His wife Ruth had put together a series of old cabins, like log cabins, and it was very classic North Carolina, with the rocking chair on the porch. There was nothing pretentious about it.

When I was there Ruth served a bowl of tomato soup and grilled cheese sandwiches, with the everyday dinnerware. I was sitting there thinking, he's dined with kings and in the White House and the Kremlin, but this is who he is. This is his identity. This is where he feels the most comfort. He's just an ordinary guy.

We talked about the book. I said, "Mr. Graham, you can go one of two ways. You can either do a 1,000-page autobiography where you mention all the details of your life and give credit to the people that affected you and that you interacted with over the years, and that's fine. That probably should be done. But I am much more interested in your doing something where you take certain highlights of your life and build a book around them—let's say twelve to fifteen stories."

As we discussed it, I soon discovered that indeed, he had many incredible stories to tell. I remember him speaking about one of the times he was in India. There is a large pocket of Christians in northeast India dating back a couple of centuries. In 1977, he was visiting the country, holding a series of crusades in several cities. During his trip, a terrible cyclone struck Southeast India, killing tens of thousands of people. Neelam Reddy was the President of India at the time and he provided him with a helicopter to survey the damage. He described very vividly what it was like. As the helicopter came along the shore, he could see brightly colored saris caught in the thorn bushes and the trees. He said the tattered traditional Indian dresses looked like Tibetan prayer flags. It was a scene of utter devastation. Each one of those saris represented the remains of a woman who had died.

There was also the time that he had gone to Moscow in the early 1980s, at the height of the Cold War. This was quite controversial because of course Russia was our enemy, and conservatives who were largely of his faith were saying, "Billy Graham needs to confront them and critique them because they're persecuting Christians, and they're doing all these terrible things." But he did not do that and instead said in his very gracious way that when he met the leaders, all he insisted on was that they not censor what he said—and they didn't.

The press was critical of him for not taking a more confrontational stance, and there was one story from the crusade in New York in which a Christian leader said to him, "You have set the Christian cause back fifty years." Reverend Graham hung his head and said, "Oh, that's too bad. I was hoping to set it back 2,000 years."

He wasn't a confrontational person. Jesus taught "Love your enemies." Billy Graham took that seriously, and I think that's probably what he had in mind when he made that remark. His attitude was that he was not a politician but a representative of God, and just as God loves everyone, we are taught to do the same. He was genuinely humble in that way.

There is a book by David Aikman, who was a bureau chief at *TIME* magazine, called *Great Souls*, in which he writes of six great souls of the twentieth century. Billy Graham is one of them. The others are Nelson Mandela, Aleksandr Solzhenitsyn, Mother Teresa, Pope John Paul II, and Elie Wiesel. Part of that greatness was that Billy Graham stayed so true to his mission, to his vision, and was able to conduct himself with such integrity that while one person after another in the public eye fell prey to scandal, he did not. He built in protection to keep him from having any taint of that whatsoever.

I once asked Billy Graham, "Of all the presidents, which one did you spend the most time with?" To my surprise he said Lyndon Johnson. "Really?" I said. "Why is that?" Johnson was a rather coarse character and I never thought of him as particularly religious. Billy smiled and said, "Well, I think with the life he lived he kind of always wanted to have a preacher around him."

But it was more than that. Johnson, like other presidents, was surrounded by Washington people, and while everybody else was lobbying and manipulating, Billy Graham was someone he could trust when he bared his soul. Billy Graham wasn't going to betray him, and it was that solid American trustworthy, good heartland persona that I think even the most sophisticated people in the world responded to.

Those were the values that kept him grounded over the years. He learned to negotiate his way through the realities of the world out there, but he never let it get to him. He was always the North Carolina farm boy, with a kind of gee-whiz attitude toward life. He was impressed by other people, not by himself, and he had that sense of almost childlike wonder. He was always astonished that all this had happened to him.

One thing I really appreciate about him is that he learned from his mistakes, and he talks and writes quite openly about them. That is part of his humility. He doesn't feel the need to defend himself. Early in his ministry he unintentionally offended President Harry Truman. Billy Graham wore a white suit in those days, and after meeting with the President he posed, Tim Tebow-like, in a praying stance at the gate of the White House. Truman felt that was grandstanding. Reverend Graham learned from that, and he never did a grandstanding thing again. And he said that what he learned from his close association with President Richard Nixon was that it's best for him not to become too involved with partisan politics.

Billy Graham's humility showed up in other ways, too. I remember saying during our meeting that he had had an impact on a whole country, on whole cities. He immediately interrupted me. "Oh, no, no, I haven't," he said. "Some people have been changed because of my message, but not because of me; it was a result of my message." He always went through life feeling that he hadn't done enough.

His thrust of course was always toward individual salvation—the soul, the change, the transformation. I don't think he was particularly looking at cultural or political change. What made him come alive was standing in front of that pulpit and holding out the hope of a spiritual transformation that so many people desire. We all do some things that we regret and we want life to be a little different than it is for us, and I think Billy Graham's secret is that he genuinely believes in the message he proclaims: *It can be different. God can change you. God accepts you just as you are but doesn't want to leave you just as you are. He wants to remake you.*

That's a powerful message. We've all seen clips of thousands of people making their way down the aisle during a Billy Graham Crusade saying, "Yeah, I want that change."

As a journalist, I have often asked people, "How did you come to be a born-again Christian?" So many times the reply is, "Oh, it was when I heard Billy Graham preach," and they'll tell me their personal stories of transformation.

So what happened regarding my involvement with Billy Graham's autobiography? I went to a literary agency in New York and made a presentation explaining what I thought the book should be. "This is a book for the ages," I told them. "There's only one person who can tell these stories. You've got something really unique here."

I think it says something about Billy Graham that he decided against that idea for his autobiography. Rather than to do the "book for the ages" that I had envisioned, which would have focused on his own personal experiences, he felt it was more important to honor the people who had helped him, to tell the story of how those crusades happened, and to credit everybody along the way. And when his autobiography was eventually published, one of the striking things about Billy Graham that readers discovered is that the key people who started with him were still with him more than forty years later, and they are with him today. There aren't many people you can say that about, but when you understand who Billy Graham is, the character of the man, it is not in the least surprising.

·99·

RAVI ZACHARIAS

Indian-born Evangelist, award-winning author
and host of Let My People Think *global radio broadcast*

I first met Billy Graham in 1983, when he invited me to speak at the Billy Graham Evangelistic Association's International Conference for Evangelists in Amsterdam. At that time I was only in my thirties, and I didn't know that Billy Graham even knew I existed. But he wrote me a beautiful letter asking me to come and speak at the conference to the world's leading evangelists.

Before we gave our talks, Billy Graham walked over to the table where I sat with my wife, and we shook hands. This was the first interaction I ever had with him. Then he said, "I've read your sermon. It's the most powerful sermon I've read on the subject. Do you mind if I use it sometime?"

I was overwhelmed. That simple comment showed me the man Billy Graham is. He is very humble in everything he does. I replied, "Not at all! You will do a better job with it than I will." And I knew that he would, because he had long ago mastered the greatest challenge a speaker faces, which is to combine simplicity with sublimity. He was a great model for that.

A little later at the conference, I gave my talk on "The

Lostness of Man," and then Dr. Graham stepped up to give his talk. He began by saying that he didn't really need to preach after what had just been said and felt in the hall! But that's Dr. Graham: one who inspires and encourages everyone in making them feel singularly gifted for the task.

You can imagine how that comment made me feel, to have the world's most admired and revered speaker respond so positively to what I had said. The enthusiastic response, not only of Dr. Graham but of others, too, actually changed my life, because following that conference I made a number of big decisions, as a result of which I ended up where I am right now.

What struck me at the Amsterdam conference was that, wonderful as all the speakers were, we were basically speaking to people whose lives had already fallen apart. I sat there thinking: *Who is going to reach the person who does not feel life is falling apart but who has genuine intellectual barriers to belief in God? There are a large number of people like that.* I pondered these questions. I flew home and talked to my wife, and then went to India and saw the need there. I spoke with pastors who had no books and hardly a change of clothes.

As my wife and I discussed the matter, I told her that two things were needed: we must reach the thinker, certainly, but we ought never to lose our compassion. The neediest of the world must also feel our touch. So when we started this work it was on the twin feet of proclamation and compassion. My wife and I laid it before the Lord that if we had a $50,000 gift from somewhere we would start this work, but until that happened we weren't going to tell anyone about it, not even our family.

Shortly after this, in August 1983, I decided to resign from my position as chairman of the Department of Evangelism and Contemporary Thought at Alliance Theological Seminary in Nyack, New York. I gave them one year's notice.

· CHICKEN SOUP FOR THE SOUL ·

A few months later, in November 1983, I was speaking to a conference of lay businessmen and women in Cleveland, Ohio. Interestingly enough, they had started that conference on the heels of some meetings Billy Graham had held in Cleveland. There were several hundred people at the conference, and on the last day I asked people in the audience to pray for my wife and me that God would give us wisdom in a matter we had placed before Him.

I went back to my hotel, and a while later, as I was leaving, I saw a man waiting near the exit door. He looked at me and said, "I went back to my room, I got on my knees and I prayed for you. I said, 'God, what is that young couple looking for? What wisdom are they looking for?' And as I got to my feet I felt God prompting me to give you a check for $50,000."

This man was a total stranger to me. I replied, "Sir, you don't even know me."

"I'm going to trust you," he said.

"I can't take it like this," I replied, "because you are a stranger, but if you tell me where you live I'll fly to you sometime. I'll tell you what's in my heart and we can take it from there."

He replied, "Mr. Zacharias, you are a busy man. Tell me where you live. I'll fly in to see you."

It turned out that he lived in Youngstown, Ohio, and soon after our conversation he flew to New York and spent the day with me. At the end of the day, he said, with tears running down his face, "Ravi, I'm not an educated man. I've never been to college. But I know how to make money. If this is what God has laid on your heart, I'll take care of you. You do what needs to be done in reaching the skeptic. I'll get behind you."

This promise of support was the final link in the starting of my ministry. It all came about as a result of being at Amsterdam in 1983, at the invitation of Billy Graham, and sensing God's

· 388 ·

lead. I think God prompted my heart to help me see the need and how I could fill it.

With financial support now guaranteed, we pulled together some friends and in August 1984 launched Ravi Zacharias International Ministries. Today we are headquartered in Atlanta, Georgia, and have operations in ten countries. Our motto is "Helping the thinker to believe and the believer to think." We reach the skeptics, the people who are hostile to religion. Our message goes to four arenas: academic, business, political, and the arts, because these are the arenas that shape our culture. I have a global 120-person team, and we have about twenty frontline Christian apologists. We also have a radio program on two thousand stations called "Let My People Think" and a publication called *Just Thinking*. We are in some of the toughest universities on the globe, drawing packed audiences.

Throughout our endeavor, God has guided us, and I think the Lord used the conferences Billy Graham sponsored, such as the one in Amsterdam in 1983, in many ways to accomplish many ends.

At these conferences, it is not so much what you hear from the platform, important though that is, but the people you meet, the networking that happens, the inspiration that comes from the men and women from all parts of the world who sit around the tables. Scores of countries are represented. I think that was the actual catalyst for me, interacting with all those wonderful people that Billy Graham brought together.

That was, after all, his vision, to encourage and inspire the evangelists who were out preaching to people but often of necessity leading a very lonely lifestyle. I served on the program committee for the Amsterdam event, and I remember Dr. Graham sending the message that some of these evangelists felt very much alone. They spent hundreds of hours away from home, and in those days, before the Internet and cell phones, it wasn't so easy for them to keep in touch with their families. Dr. Graham wanted us to plan a program that would inspire all the evangelists, wherever they were.

This kind of networking and inspiration is one of the ways that Billy Graham has had a huge impact globally. He enabled people to forge links with one another and so multiply their ability to change people's lives through Christ. The impact of these links and connections is exponential, as is the impact of a single life changed through Christ: it connects and reconnects and like a hub spreads out in spokes. This is part of the legacy that Billy Graham will leave, the inspiration that came through a life that touched so many thousands of people.

This web of connection that Billy Graham has created had an impact on me very early in my life. I came to know Christ after I attempted suicide at the age of seventeen in Delhi, India. It was through the work of the Youth for Christ movement that I was reached. When I gave my life to Christ, he changed everything for me. Since then evangelism has been in my blood and bones. And who was the man who played a vital part in the forming of Youth for Christ in its earliest days? It was, of course, Dr. Billy Graham. He was, indeed, the first full-time evangelist employed by Youth for Christ International in the mid-1940s.

That dramatic incident from my youth is just another example of how Billy Graham's work has reached out through so many connections and touched so many people worldwide in vital ways over many decades. In that respect I certainly owe him a large debt, as do all of us evangelists. He devoted himself to a cause infinitely larger than himself, and he has never wavered.

·100·

LOUIS ZAMPERINI

WWII hero, Olympic athlete, inspirational speaker;
subject of the bestselling biography Unbroken

In 1949, I was married with a family, but I was also an alcoholic suffering from post-traumatic stress disorder (PTSD), following my experiences in a Japanese prisoner-of-war camp. A couple of young people tried to get me to go down and listen to this new evangelist by the name of Billy Graham, who was preaching in Los Angeles, but I wouldn't go. They took my wife to the crusade, and she made a confession of her faith in Christ. In the meantime she was in the process of filing for a divorce because I couldn't quit drinking due to PTSD.

After she accepted Christ, she came home and tried to get me down to the next meeting. I again refused, but then she said, "Because of my conversion, I'm not going to get a divorce." And that made me happy, so then, based on her experience and the fact that she was not going to seek a divorce, I decided to go to the crusade with her. But when Billy got to the invitation part, where Billy Graham calls people to come down and declare themselves for Christ, I got mad and grabbed my wife. I wanted out of there, so we left.

Later she reminded me again that she was not going to get a

divorce because of her conversion, and she talked me into going back a second time. That second time Billy Graham was preaching about how, when people come to the end of their rope and there's nowhere else to turn, they turn to God.

He was right. That's what had happened on the life raft, where one of my companions and I survived for forty-seven days after being shot down in the Pacific. We had no place else to turn. The same thing happened in prison camp, for thousands and thousands of prisoners. I talked to them. They talked to me. They were all praying the same prayer. "Get me home alive, God, and I'll seek You and serve You." Naturally, that's what they wanted to do—get home to their families.

I realized that God had kept His promise—I got home alive—but I didn't keep my promise, and that made me feel awful cheap. I knew I was still getting drunk, turning my back on God. So that night at the crusade, I went back to the prayer room and made a confession of my faith in Christ—and boom! While I was still on my knees my whole life changed. It was just a real miracle.

That night was the first in two and a half years I didn't have a nightmare. I had been waking up every night strangling Sergeant Watanabe, the brutal Japanese prison guard. One night I had woken up and I had my hands around my wife's throat. Boy, that scared us. It was one of the reasons I decided to go to the crusade. But since I accepted Christ on that day in 1949, I haven't had a single nightmare. Not one.

It was a miracle from God. The Army couldn't help me. The psychiatrist couldn't help me. But simply by receiving Christ as my Savior I received the help I needed. "Therefore, if any man be in Christ, he is a new creation," says the Scripture, and that's exactly what happened.

That also happened to be a big week for the Billy Graham

Evangelistic Association. I was a former Olympic athlete and in addition to my conversion, two other people who were famous at the time also got saved. The first was the radio personality Stuart Hamblen; the second was Jim Voss, who was the wire-tapper for the gangster, Mickey Cohen, helping members of his crime syndicate avoid capture by the police. This was big news, and it caught the attention of William Randolph Hearst, the newspaper magnate.

Up to that point, the newspapers had ignored Billy Graham's Los Angeles Crusade. They wouldn't put his name in the paper. It was just a big "no" against Christianity. But when three famous people were saved in the same week, all that changed. Hearst immediately called Joe Pine, his editor, and said, "Puff Graham." That meant give him front-page and good news. After that Billy became famous. Before that, nobody knew who he was.

After Jim Voss and Stuart Hamblen got saved, the three of us became buddies. And then Mickey Cohen started to invite my wife and me over to his home because he loved athletes. We'd have lunch together and we finally got enough Scripture into Cohen to whet his appetite, but he didn't want anybody to lead him to Christ other than Billy Graham. I said, "Well, that's wrong. When we accept Christ, we're all servants. We all have the ability to lead another person to Christ."

Nevertheless, Stuart and Jim called a man in Modesto, California, who had a plane. "Mickey Cohen wants to fly back east to have Billy Graham lead him to Christ," they said. I said again, "That's wrong."

Some while later, the three of us were in a big church in Bakersfield, California, and we had to leave early to meet Mickey Cohen at the Santa Monica Airport in Los Angeles. The guy from Modesto was going to fly down, pick him up, and fly him back to Billy Graham. I said once again that it was wrong, but no one seemed to be listening.

We drove to the Santa Monica Airport, where the night watchman would not turn the lights on. I kept telling these guys, "This is wrong. God's going to stop it." I was a new Christian but had enough sense to realize that. I said, "If he wants to accept Christ, I can lead him to Christ, and so can you."

Well, the plane landed without lights. Fine. Great. Then the pilot saw a line of airplanes, pulled to the left, and decided to park alongside them. Between him and the airplanes was a culvert about six feet wide and four feet deep for drainage. The plane nose-dived into that. I walked over to another airplane and sat on the wing. I didn't say a word. Even as a new Christian, I just knew that you didn't have to fly to someone special to lead you to Christ. Anybody could do that for you.

And so Mickey Cohen didn't get to fly back east because the plane was almost demolished. It was a big thing at the time, and I just kept my mouth shut, but I think they did learn a lesson.

Some of the journalists who covered Billy Graham at the time had a thing or two to learn as well. During the 1950s some people were picking on Billy, questioning whether the conversions that took place at the crusades lasted very long. Some big-name writers were saying, "Okay, I know you had 5,000 come forward here and 2,000 there, and you had 150,000 in the Coliseum and thousands came forward, but how many of them are still sticking to it after ten years? Are they still believers?" So in 1959, ten years after my conversion in 1949, Billy Graham came to the Hollywood Bowl and invited the three of us—Jim Voss, Stuart Hamblen and me—and he had me get up and speak. It was a big thrill to be on the platform with Billy Graham. After that he would invite the three of us to various meetings like the one in Oakland, California.

It was a thrill for us to be with Billy Graham. Everybody knew that he only had one purpose on his mind, and that was a God-led purpose. He was so convincing, and that's why so many people came forward in these meetings all over the world. God prepared him because of his background, his personality, and his humility. The humility of Billy Graham, that was all people talked about. He never takes credit for anything.

I was recently fortunate to be invited to speak at the Billy Graham Library. While I was there, I met people who were buying *Unbroken*, the bestselling book that Laura Hillenbrand had written about me. I autographed 734 books! The line was a quarter-mile long. Then I got to spend a couple of hours with Billy at his home with his family, and that was a great thrill. Billy's younger than me. I was ninety-four at the time; he was ninety-three. I have pictures of us together. The family told me that he rarely smiles now but he was smiling a lot with me, and we had a great time together. More than six decades had passed since that memorable night in Los Angeles in 1949 when Billy had helped changed my life so dramatically.

·101·

EFREM ZIMBALIST, JR.

Actor, appearing in the classic hit television shows 77 Sunset Strip,
The F.B.I., Maverick, Remington Steele *and others*

In 1979, Reverend Pat Robertson asked me to be master of
ceremonies for the inauguration of his sizeable new Christian
Broadcast Network complex in Virginia Beach, which even
included a modern broadcast studio. I had recently accepted Jesus
formally, and I was giving my testimony whenever it was required
of me. He had hired the Virginia Symphony Orchestra and
distinguished soloists for the occasion, and invited Billy Graham
to deliver the keynote address.

By that time I was quite well known for having starred in two
hit television shows, *77 Sunset Strip*, which ran for six years, and
then later, *The F.B.I.*, which ran for nine years. I figured I had two
things going for me—voice and hair. Two things the Lord gave
me. A lot of hair and a lot of voice, and not much
else—particularly not a lot of brains, but I didn't need too many
brains because I was an actor, and if anything brains hurt you if
you're an actor. Better not to have them.

I flew to Virginia from Los Angeles and on the morning of
the inauguration of the new CBN facilities we started rehearsals
that continued throughout the day and into the evening. The

broadcast was set for 8:00 p.m. and by 5:00 p.m. I was a little tired from the full day of rehearsals, so I asked the organizers if they had a place where I could rest for half an hour.

They took me into this beautiful, newly constructed building that was part of the facility. It was stunning, decorated and furnished with wonderful taste in the spirit of colonial Virginia. The organizers ushered me into a gorgeous room and after thanking them, I dropped down onto a plush sofa. The moment I lay down, I heard a key in the door. I got up, and in came this party of a few people, including Billy Graham. The group was obviously composed of people he knew and with whom he could relax.

Somehow the staff had gotten their signals crossed and put me in the room meant for Billy Graham. I stood up immediately and began to apologize: "I'm so sorry. I didn't know this room was for you. I'll get out of your way." He responded, "You get back there." I said, "I'm fine, really." Yet he insisted, "You get back on that sofa." So I did.

Dr. Graham pulled up a chair and sat down next to me, and we joked and chatted about this and that for half an hour. He told me how he loved California when he was living there, that he enjoyed playing golf and just the kind of things I needed to hear right then. Although I had appeared on stage, on TV, and in movies, I'm not an emcee and I was in unfamiliar territory doing this program. Although I was raised in a Christian home, I had never been a proclaiming Christian. I was nervous about the program. Having this kind of quiet fellowship with Billy Graham and his reassurance strengthened me. Then it was time to leave and go to the run-through and performance with the orchestra.

I'm enormously, endlessly grateful for the support Dr. Graham gave me that day, and also because my precious daughter Stephanie, who is also an actress, found the Lord at a Billy

Graham Crusade, through no prompting of mine. Even more, I admire him deeply because he is not only the greatest Evangelist of our time, but he is also a great human being. I cannot feel respect or reverence for anybody who preaches and doesn't have a true sense of normalcy about him and a sense of humor, particularly about himself. I simply don't care about blasting televangelists that scream at you. They don't belong in my world. Billy Graham on the other hand is an incredible person, a normal, fun-loving, self-belittling hero.

Our Virginia meeting was enough to make me a huge follower. He was an electric speaker, with the dynamics of every great orator and conveyor of truth. He's been extraordinary in that regard. However, underneath it all, he has always considered himself to be just a guy in service to his Lord, and I love him for that. I am so appreciative of his amazing ministry.

To me, Billy Graham has been a powerful conduit for the Lord's love and caring in my life, as he has been for so many others. He is such a unique person. How do you define him? You can't define God, and you can't define a servant like Billy Graham either, because he comes at you from all directions. You want a sterling orator, you've got it. You want a genuine friend, you've got it. You want a convincing witness for Christ, you've got it. Whatever it is, Billy Graham has it all in excess and always has his entire life, more than any Evangelist or proclaimer of the Gospel. He has been the greatest of our time.

I believe that more than anybody else who has ever entered heaven, Billy Graham is going to hear those famous words from Matthew 25:23, "Well done, good and faithful servant!"

BILLY GRAHAM

I am humbled by the gracious comments the contributors to this book have made about our ministry — although only God deserves the credit for any impact it has had. I am not a great man — but I do serve a great God, and I give Him all the glory for whatever my associates and I have been able to accomplish over the years.

Knowing that some readers of this book may not have had the opportunity to attend one of our crusades or view one of our telecasts, Chicken Soup for the Soul kindly asked me to write something they could include here that would give the essence of the message I have preached. Unfortunately, poor eyesight prevents me from writing anything new now — I recently turned 94 and have age-related macular degeneration.

In response the publishers asked if they might include instead a message I delivered to more than 250,000 people in New York City's Central Park on September 22, 1991. It is based on one of the most familiar verses in the Bible — a passage I've probably preached on more than any other.

I trust you will take time to read these words and reflect on them in your soul—and perhaps share them with a friend. May God richly bless you and give you His peace.

Billy Graham
December 2012
Montreat, N.C.

∿

GOD'S GREATEST GIFT

Today I want to speak to you on one of the most familiar verses in the Bible. It is John 3:16: "For God so loved the world that He gave His only begotten Son, that whosoever believeth in Him should not perish, but have everlasting life." That is the Gospel in a nutshell—because everything we need to know about our salvation is found in this one verse of Scripture.

Many people ask me, "If God loves the world, then why is there so much suffering? Why is there so much disease, war, poverty, hate, loneliness, boredom, emptiness, unemployment, violence? Why doesn't God just stop it all?" Some of you may be thinking, "I can't take it any more—the pressures of life are too great." Perhaps you're saying, "Why has God abandoned us?" But God hasn't abandoned us—we have abandoned Him.

Or you may even be asking, does God even exist? Yes, He does. I can't take you to a laboratory and prove to you that God exists—but the evidence for God's existence is all around us, if we'll but see it. But what is God like? What does the Bible say about Him?

The Bible tells us first of all that God is the Creator. "In the beginning God created the heavens and the earth" (Genesis 1:1). All the stars you see at night—God created them. And He created you.

Then the Bible also tells us that God is a Spirit. He doesn't have a body like you and I do; if He did, He could only be in one place at a time. But God is a Spirit—and because of that, He can be everywhere at once.

The Bible tells us something else very important about God. It tells us that God is absolutely holy and pure. He cannot even look on sin—and because He is holy and pure, He is also a God of judgment. The Bible says, "God shall bring every work into judgment, with every secret thing" (Ecclesiastes 12:14). Think of it: Some day all your secret thoughts, and all those things you thought nobody knew about, will be brought into the open. God has appointed a day when He will judge the world—and you are going to be there.

But the verse I just read from John 3:16 says something else about God. It says, "For God so loved the world...." God is a God of love! And if there is one thing I want you to take with you when you leave here today, it is this: God loves you. God loves *you!* He knows all about you; he knows all the sins you've committed—and yet He still loves you! *God is a God of love!* The Bible says, "I have loved thee with an everlasting love" (Jeremiah 31:3).

This is why God created the human race. Have you ever wondered why you are here? God is love—and He created us because He wanted someone who would love Him in return. He created Adam and Eve, the first man and woman, and He put them in a perfect paradise without sin or death. And He gave them a choice: to obey Him and be His friends—or to turn against Him and go their own way. God gave them a free will to choose which way they would go—and they chose to rebel against God. As a result they were cut off from God, and death entered the world.

What is wrong with human nature? Have you ever asked yourself that question? Why is there so much hate, and racial prejudice, and jealousy, and greed? Why are there so many wars and conflicts? It's because the human race has a spiritual disease—and that disease is called sin. Jesus said, "For out of the heart proceed evil thoughts, murders, adulteries, fornications, thefts, false witness, blasphemies" (Matthew 15:19). We are all guilty; the Bible says, "For all have sinned and come short of the glory of God" (Romans 3:23).

Sin not only comes between you and God. It comes between you and peace, between you and happiness, between you and the assurance that if you were to die tonight, you would go to Heaven. We can have Hell in this life—but we also can have Hell in the life to come. And we will, if we refuse God's way of salvation.

But God saw us, lost and stumbling in darkness, and He decided to do something about it—because of His love. What did He do? He sent His only Son, Jesus Christ, into the world to pay the penalty for our sins. God became a man—and that man was the Lord Jesus Christ. He came into the world for one reason: to die for our sins. One day the Romans took Him outside the walls of Jerusalem and nailed Him to a cross—and in that terrible moment all our sins were laid on Him. He was without sin—but all our sins were transferred to Him. Think of it: He became guilty of every sin you ever committed. The Bible says, "The Lord hath laid on Him the iniquity of us all" (Isaiah 53:6).

But Jesus didn't stay on the cross! God raised Him from the dead. I'm not speaking to you about a dead Christ—I'm speaking to you about a living Christ! And this living Christ can come into your heart and life today by His Holy Spirit. He can forgive you and cleanse you of all your sins, and He can make you a new person. Now when God looks at you, He doesn't see your sins; they have all been wiped away.

What does God require of you? First, you have to repent of your sins. The first sermon Jesus ever preached was "Repent" (Matthew 4:17). What does the word "repentance" mean? It means you confess to God that you know you are a sinner, and you want to turn from your sins. It means you are willing to let God have His way in your life, and that you want to follow Him and serve Him from now on.

Then you have to come by faith to Jesus Christ, believing He died for you and trusting Him alone for your salvation. You can never work your way to Heaven. No matter how good we are, we still fall short of God's standard—which is perfection. The Bible says, "For by grace are ye saved, through faith… not of works, lest any man should boast" (Ephesians 2:8-9). You deserve God's judgment for your sins—but on the cross Jesus took your place. He took that judgment for you. He gave His life for you. "For God so loved the world that he gave his only begotten Son, that whosoever believeth in Him shall not perish, but have everlasting life." That is God's promise to you. That is God's greatest gift!

Have you asked Jesus Christ to come into your life? Are you trusting Him alone for your salvation? Come to Him today, and by a simple act of faith commit your life to Him. I invite you today to pray the same prayer countless others like you have prayed:

> *Oh God, I know I am a sinner. I am sorry for my sins, and I want to turn from them. I trust Jesus Christ as my Savior, I confess Him as my Lord, and I invite Him to*

come into my life today. From this moment on, I want to make Him the foundation of my life, and to serve Him and follow Him in the fellowship of His church. In Christ's name I pray. Amen.

May God richly bless you.

Chicken Soup for the Soul.